TELEPEN

60 0326091 5

D1610653

ROYAL HISTORICAL SOCIETY

STUDIES IN HISTORY 54

JAMES BRYCE'S
American Commonwealth

James Bryce in 1880
Courtesy of the Bodleian Library

JAMES BRYCE'S
American Commonwealth

THE ANGLO-AMERICAN BACKGROUND

Hugh Tulloch

NOTTINGHAM UNIVERSITY LIBRARY

THE ROYAL HISTORICAL SOCIETY
THE BOYDELL PRESS

© Hugh Tulloch 1988

First published 1988

A Royal Historical Society publication
Published by The Boydell Press
an imprint of Boydell & Brewer Ltd
PO Box 9 Woodbridge Suffolk IP12 3DF
and of Boydell & Brewer Inc.
Wolfeboro New Hampshire 03894-2069 USA

ISBN 0 86193 211 0

ISSN 0269-2244

British Library Cataloguing in Publication Data

Tulloch, Hugh
  James Bryce's American commonwealth: the Anglo-American
  background. — (Royal Historical Society studies in history
  series, ISSN 0269-2244; 54).
  1. Bryce, James
  I. Title II. Royal Historical Society
  III. Series
  320'.092'4 JC223.B9/   326091
  ISBN 0-86193-211-0

Library of Congress Cataloging-in-Publication Data

Tulloch, Hugh.
  James Bryce's American commonwealth: the Anglo-
  American background/Hugh Tulloch.
      p. cm. — (Royal Historical Society studies in history,
  ISSN 0269-2244; 54)
      Bibliography: p.
      Includes index.
      ISBN 0-86193-211-0
      1. Bryce, James Bryce, Viscount, 1838-1922. American
  commonwealth. 2. United States — Politics and government. 3.
  United States — Social conditions. I. Title. II. Series: Royal
  Historical Society studies in history: no. 54.
  JK246.B957T86 1988
  320.4'73 — dc19   87-32544
                                                       CIP

Ⓘ Printed on long life paper
made to the full American Standard

Printed in Great Britain by
St Edmundsbury Press, Bury St Edmunds, Suffolk

Contents

The Society records its gratitude to the following whose generosity made possible the initiation of this series: The British Academy; The Pilgrim Trust; The Twenty-Seven Foundation; The United States Embassy's Bicentennial funds; The Wolfson Trust; several private donors.

Acknowledgements

My thanks for support and advice go, above all, to D. S. Porter, custodian of the Bryce Papers in the Bodleian library, and to Hugh Brogan my supervisor. I am also indebted to Bruce Collins of Glasgow University and to Janet Foster, Tony Halpin, Gordon Blair and the late Rick Murphy. I have been exceptionally fortunate in the editorial assistance I have received from Janet Godden and Christine Linehan and from my typist Ann Merriman. Lastly I would like to record my gratitude to the British Academy who generously provided financial assistance for two research trips to the United States some one hundred years after Bryce's own first journey.

Hugh Tulloch
Bristol, 1987

Abbreviations

There are only three abbreviations used in the footnotes; *NYN* for *The New York Nation*, *LC* for Dicey's *Law of the Constitution*, and *AC* for *The American Commonwealth*. The edition used for the *AC*, unless otherwise stated, is the 2nd edition of 1889. This is a two volume edition, incorporating authoritative revisions and corrections supplied by English and American friends of the three volume 1st edition of 1888.

In time, however, a democratic republic came to occupy a large portion of the earth's surface, and made itself felt as one of the most powerful members of the community of nations; and elective and responsible government became subject to the observations and criticisms which wait upon a great existing fact.

— J. S. Mill, *On Liberty*

Introduction

Three foreigners, one a Norman aristocrat and two liberal Glaswegians, stand apart as major foreign commentators on the American republic. At roughly fifty year intervals Alexis de Tocqueville, James Bryce and Denis Brogan have each surveyed the development of the United States and left, in turn, vivid impressions and influential interpretations of the Jacksonian, Gilded and Rooseveltian ages. Each contributor is quite unlike the others, not only because each witnessed a very different America — Bryce concentrated almost obsessively on the workings of a party system barely mentioned by Tocqueville, and Brogan analysed a New Deal whose vast extension of federal powers would have appalled the *laissez faire* beliefs of Bryce — but also because each to some degree reacted against his predecessor: Bryce against the abstract generalisations of Tocqueville, and Brogan against his fellow Scotsman's late Victorian patrician tone. Of the three the Frenchman has been best served, and the work of Pierson, Mayer and Schleifer, for example, reflects the contemporary renaissance in Tocquevillian studies. Brogan's protean output, his journalism as well as his academic writing, has yet to be assimilated.

Bryce received his obligatory two volume biography from a fellow liberal academic, H. A. L. Fisher, in 1927; a collection of essays written to celebrate the fiftieth anniversary of *The American Commonwealth* in 1938 threw more light on the concerns of the period than on its subject. More recently there has been Edmund Ions's highly competent biography. My own study differs from Fisher and Ions in being far more limited in range. Focusing primarily on Bryce as author of *The American Commonwealth* and advocate of Anglo-American unity, it touches on the multifarious life of politician, jurist and traveller only insofar as it contributes to this central theme. But while narrower in scope it does embrace a variety of larger issues,

1

various formative strands that went into the making of the book, ranging from topics as various as Tractarianism at Oxford to First World War atrocity commissions, from the influence of T. H. Green's social concerns to Bryce's involvement in the creation of the League of Nations. Though essentially the biography of one book by one man, an extensive range of eminent contemporaries, friends and associates such as Dicey, Lord Acton and Gladstone, E. L. Godkin of *The New York Nation*, President Charles Eliot of Harvard and Theodore Roosevelt appear, because each contributed variously to the book in its final form.

The American Commonwealth is now, I suspect, a book more frequently alluded to than read; the suspicious recurrence of one or two classic quotations — Bryce on the similarities of the two parties, Bryce on municipal government as the one conspicuous failure in American politics — and the perpetuation of quite fundamental errors such as Richard Hofstadter's misreading of Bryce on the west, a misreading of an over-quoted sentence wrenched entirely out of context, are the result of a ritual deference which tends to mummify and veil respectful neglect. The tendency of the biographer, of course, is to move his subject excessively to the fore and overstate his importance. But I hope I bear this in mind when I venture to suggest that *The American Commonwealth* along with Dicey's *Law of the Constitution* helped effect a quite new understanding of the United States which was to have incalculable practical consequences for the twentieth century. Before the 1880s, the emergence of a democratic America was feared and misunderstood in Great Britain, seeming in some vague way to threaten by its very existence, various traditions that Britain and her empire stood for. Bryce's singular intellectual and practical achievement was to help to bring about a realignment of understanding, a new perception of the United States as ally and friend, whose growing world influence could only add to and in no substantial way diminish those traditions. He did this by deftly asserting the historical continuity of Britain and America and by revealing the new world to be not a threatening subversive republic born out of revolution but, because essentially English, essentially cautious and conservative too. He was not the first to speak in broad terms of Anglo-American unity; prophets and precursors can be found in Tocqueville himself, in Bagehot and Mill, among the imperial schools of Froude, Seeley and Dilke, and in the radical tradition of Cobden and Bright. But it was Bryce and

Bryce alone who gave the definitive stamp of authority to this new appreciation and made it entirely acceptable by writing a book in which, in Harold Laski's words, 'the greatness of America was acknowledged in its due proportions' by the British public for the first time.[1] If this assessment of Bryce's role is even partly correct it is a striking instance of Acton's conviction that ideas, and the acts born of those new ideas, are the single most potent shaping force in history; that, in this instance, a short, red-bearded, pipe-smoking professor decisively reshaped Anglo-American understanding with consequences of immense practical import years later in Flanders, at the Paris peace conference, in the Mediterranean, the Atlantic, the Far East and on the Normandy beaches; at the Nuremberg war trials — that powerful legal reassertion of an international rule of law — and at the UN headquarters in New York. The Rotary Club rhetoric of 'hands across the sea' is seldom heard today and professional historians can find nothing 'special' in the 'special relationship' beyond a more civilised discourse than is usual among independent nation states in their international dealings. But seen in the wider post-1945 context of a 'free world' identity the common rhetoric, subsumed, takes on an overwhelming relevance in determining present global alignments. However vague in its historical grasp and haphazard in its understanding, the resonance of such phrases as Dicey's 'rule of law' continue to distinguish and affirm certain ways of life considered worthy of protection to such an extent that vast nuclear arsenals are built in its defence.

But these are tenuous and profound consequences far beyond the scope of this study. Instead its first two chapters attempt to investigate Bryce's formative intellectual background before his first journey to America with Dicey in 1870. Bryce was a nineteenth century liberal, the archetypal product of what Dicey termed 'the moralisation of English public life, and the triumph of English humanitarianism'. One source of that tradition, evangelicalism, was the first to exert its influence on the young Ulster-Scot bred in the stern school of conformity to nonconformist religious beliefs. It was a creed which affirmed the pre-eminence of the individual's search for salvation and which was easily assimilated at Oxford to that second source of liberalism, Benthamite reformism. This transmuted spiritual salvation and self-improvement into a secular mission for

---

[1]   *The American Democracy*, p. 16.

material improvement and general spiritual regeneration in this world. These two impulses together generated a political activism aimed against established authority both secular and religious for, as Dicey suggested, 'the appeal of the evangelicals to personal religion corresponds with the appeal of Benthamite Liberals to individual energy. Indifference to the authority of the church is the counterpart of indifference to the authoritative teaching and guidance of the State and of society'.[2] The struggle for secularisation and liberal values at Oxford, support for the Northern cause of the American civil war and the push for parliamentary reform at home reflect Bryce's early political engagement, and in each case the imagined and unvisited United States served as an approximate model for the ideal commonwealth of which he wrote so movingly in his contribution to *Essays on Reform*. America exemplified a disestablished state which entrenched principles of religious toleration within its fundamental laws; a commonwealth locked in battle powerfully symbolised the eternal struggle of good against evil, of aristocracy against democracy, and became entangled in the personal domestic preoccupation of extending further political privileges to the able middle class dissenter. The North with its republican principles and its politics of equality beckoned, offering a British future free of unjust privileges in which society would be linked together in one classless harmony. It was because mid-century English liberalism invested so heavily, intellectually and emotionally, in the war and interpreted it as democracy's greatest trial that Bryce could feel with Mill that its outcome 'was destined to be a turning point, for good or evil, of the course of human affairs for an indefinite duration'.[3]

Chapter Two turns its attention to the influence the historical method exerted on Bryce as a student at Oxford and particularly the historical writings of Goldwin Smith and E. A. Freeman. Both Bryce's teachers were liberals, both looked to the United States as somehow preserving the finest Anglo-Saxon traditions and whose duty it was to carry on the mission of the English race as civilising world agent. Both used racial theories to reforge Anglo-American links broken in 1776 and assert the primacy of genetic over environmental factors. Their contribution to Bryce's own understanding of the United States can be gauged most clearly in his treatment of the West. Bryce has

---

[2]   *Law and Public Opinion in England*, p. 402, and *The New York Nation*, 7 September 1905, p. 197.

[3]   *Autobiography*, p. 226.

been generally regarded as a precursor of Frederick Jackson Turner. I hope to show instead that he was a loyal disciple of the Teutonic school of historians, believing that English stock, in extending the Western frontier, were enlarging the capacities and potentialities of the English race rather than succumbing to the transforming Western environment; becoming greater Englishmen rather than new Americans. Similarly I briefly examine Lord Acton's review of *The American Commonwealth* because it is the most sustained critique of Bryce's over-dependence on the historical method, his assumption of Anglo-American continuity and therefore a measure of his reliance on Goldwin Smith and E. A. Freeman. In fact, however, Bryce's historical appreciation of the American experience was less simplistic and dogmatic, more complex and conflicting. The contrary pull of historical presuppositions and empirical experience and Bryce's keen awareness of American innovativeness encouraged a dialectic in his exercise in comparative politics. His approach was, as Acton correctly judged, whig, but he wrote as a 'bewildered Whig', for while his temperament and teachers stressed Anglo-American similarities he was too rigorous an observer to project England into a wholly American future, or reduce America to the status of English colony once again. America was England, but it was England with a difference; American grew from English traditions, but grew to become something altogether unique and distinct.[4]

Chapter Three, looks at the period 1870 to 1888 from Bryce's first visit to the United States to the publication of *The American Commonwealth*. It is a study of observation and information gathering, of creative gestation and writing. Assumption and expectations gathered up to 1870 were questioned; the actualities of 'the great existing fact' of America clashed with the previously idealised image and initiated a process of modification and reassessment, a subtle two way engagement between observer and observed:

When I first visited America . . . I brought home a swarm of bold generalisations. Half of them were thrown overboard after a second visit in 1881. Of the half that remained, some were dropped into the Atlantic when I returned across it after a third visit in 1883 – 1884; and, although the two later

---

[4]   *History of Freedom*, p. 580.

journeys gave birth to some new ideas, these views are fewer and more discreetly cautious than their departed sisters of 1870.[5]

The subject was approached with all the thoroughness and earnestness its Presbyterian author could muster. In aim and scale he deliberately and ambitiously set out to write a book which would bear direct comparison with Tocqueville's *Democracy in America*. Indeed insofar as he corrected Tocqueville's faulty *a priori* assumptions and intended to approach the matter in a purely objective and inductive spirit, he had reason to hope that his book's value would be more permanent both in its exact portrait of the United States in 1888 and in its explicit vindication of the scientific method. In this he was not entirely successful. Nevertheless *The American Commonwealth* remains vivid in its detail and massively concrete in its particulars, and a book so 'resolutely actual', to use Acton's phrase, constituted a prodigious achievement in the collection of data.[6] Sections of Chapter Three illustrate the moulding of the book by examining the various printed sources he used, the personal observations he remembered and which found their way into its pages, and the vital contributions made by his American friends. It concludes that while his network of contacts was wide it was generally limited to members of the 'outer circle' of 'mugwumps' and almost entirely excluded that professional political class which dominates the informal chapters of the book. It looks in particular at E. L. Godkin and Theodore Roosevelt, who in their distinct ways — the one advocating reform through independence from party, the other reform from within the party system — especially helped Bryce's understanding and interpretation of American political life.

Because the underlying purpose of the chapter is to suggest the various limitations which hampered an entirely value-free study of the United States, it is essential to place the author in his other role as party politician in the Britain of the 1880s, and discuss the tensions between the detached observer judiciously weighing advantages and disadvantages in the political laboratory of comparative politics and the MP for Aberdeen South employing his learning for party ends on the floor of the House. As the 'professor' in parliament Bryce's specific duty was,

[5] John Stuart Mill's 'On Liberty' reprinted in *Three Essays*, p. 8. *AC*, I, p. 4.
[6] Acton to Bryce, 25 March 1889, Ms. Bryce 1.

firstly, to further support for Gladstone's appeal for greater co-operation between the English-speaking world and, secondly, to publicise the practical example of America as successful federation in the intense intellectual debate against unionism over Irish home rule. Bryce was profoundly involved in this struggle and at the highest level. It was impossible for anyone, author or reader, to look at the United States and not think of Ireland. It was impossible for Bryce to keep the constitutional commentator and liberal parliamentarian apart. In this sense *The American Commonwealth* is a ringing vindication of achieved federalisation and a sustained three-volumed refutation of Diceyan unionism.

Chapters Four and Five turn their attention to the actual text of *The American Commonwealth*. Bryce's formal analysis of the American Constitution was not only a masterpiece of scholarly codification but also exemplifies the rich yield of the comparative method. While comparative historical research confirmed the essential continuity of the Anglo-American race, comparative jurisprudence initially claimed two distinct traditions which Bryce termed 'flexible' in the case of Britain and 'rigid' in the case of America. The immediate effect of this distinction was revelatory both in terms of Britain's perception of the United States and of Britain's self-perception. While on the one hand it brought home to Bryce an acute awareness of Britain's constitutional vulnerability — an awareness intensified within parliament where he witnessed the stark consequences of revolution by act of parliament — on the other it served to reveal the extraordinary conservatism and stability of American constitutionalism and temper. In the light of this discovery commentators plunged into a bout of 'Americomania' which lasted throughout the critical decade of the 1880s when parliamentary sovereignty and British unity seemed challenged as never before.

Conservatives such as Maine seized upon an American form of fundamental written constitution to halt democracy's progress; Dicey turned to the American device of the referendum as a means of evoking a groundswell of conservative public opinion to abridge parliament's revolutionary potentials; even Bryce hoped to strengthen a weakened House of Lords along senatorial lines to obstruct the omnipotent will of the Commons. In their turn liberal opponents like Gladstone, Morley, Acton and Bryce clutched at America's federal solution as a preferable alternative to Irish nationalist destruction of the union. More

7

generally America continued to suggest the republican alternative of self-determination over authoritarian dominion, of the rule of consent in place of continued coercion. As Acton put it with both senses in mind: 'To admit the American principle was to revolutionise Ireland.'[7] Concessions to Ireland were linked finally to the principle of absolute legal equality. Bryce, who had initially split the two nations asunder, ended by joining Britain and the United States together again, for English common law traditions were perfected in America where legal equality was enshrined in a fundamental and unchanging constitution above the whims of political man-made laws.

Chapter Five deals with Bryce's treatment of America's informal parties, those extra-legal associations unknown to the constitution but which breathed life into its political system. The result is as brilliant and innovative as Bagehot's discovery of 'dignified' and 'efficient' elements in the British Constitution and as original, for no one before him, not even Americans, had made a comprehensive study of America's all-important party system. In penetrating the unknown and shadowy world of lobbies, Lower East Side ward bosses and presidential nominating conventions, Bryce had to adopt an informal political language of 'strikes' and 'logrolling', 'stalwarts' and 'halfbreeds', and the whole vocabulary of the professional insider. Since he first witnessed the Tweed Ring's machinations at Rochester in 1870 he had grappled with the matter and tried to resolve various puzzling contradictions. Why, when the moral standards of the general public were high, were political standards so low, and why were the 'best men', the educated and respectable observers of the political 'outer circle', so decisively excluded from public life? If the average citizen were to be exonerated then the party system as it existed must be an unscrupulous imposition and the main source of political debasement. Like many intellectuals of his time Bryce shared a distrust of parties. If politics were a science then truth must be one and indivisible, and if conflicting opinions over ends and means remained after thorough scientific investigation then this must be the result of artificial party combat and mindless obstructionism. Bryce's contribution to *Essays on Reform* reflected the early ideals of America's founding fathers who envisaged a republican consensus based on the popular will united in the pursuit of a common political good. This ideal

---

7   Quoted in George Watson, *Politics and Literature in Modern Britain*, p. 165.

precluded the practical function of party as broker and resolver of conflicting interests in the open political market. Yet at the same time Bryce was the most loyal of party men, serving the interests of the liberal party for over forty years in its heydays from the Midlothian campaign to 1922 and the last year of liberal government in Britain. He believed that parties were justified only insofar as they pursued high ideals against low sectional interests and struggled on behalf of progress and enlightenment against inertia and reaction. This distinction was muddy to say the least; why, for example, did Irish home rule constitute a legitimate ideal while trade union protection merely reflected narrow class interests? In practice, like most party men, ideals were what one fought for and sinister interests were what one opposed. But at least in Britain parties appeared to split decisively along real and significant lines; Gladstone would galvanise the House with a striking peroration on Ireland's past injuries and urge a crusade for their redress, while congressmen cobbled together private bills in secret committee rooms to secure the petty interests of their district and ensure their re-election. Bryce exaggerated the real differences between the two systems and never understood why the American public should countenance a Republican and Democratic party he disapproved of. Certainly the two parties succeeded far more in serving the American electorate than in fulfilling the theoretical role Bryce expected of them. Be that as it may, *The American Commonwealth* in its criticism of party exerted as powerful an influence as its chapters on the constitution. Put simply, the American constitution was a good thing, its party system a disgrace, and any sign of emulating it, such as the Birmingham caucus, was to be strongly opposed. Instead, in the field of Anglo-American exchange, reformers in both countries approved the grafting of parliamentary characteristics on to the American stem; representative and responsible government, a strong but accountable executive, a permanent disinterested civil service, a preponderance of statecraft over manipulation and of selfless principles overriding selfish interests. Bryce's most damning condemnation was reserved for American city government, and once again corrupt Tweedism could be purged by copying the model municipal example of Great Britain.

In some respects Bryce's sole solution for all America's political ills — rule by Eliot's Harvard graduates — seems inadequate and naïve, his panaceas reflecting the last irrelevant years of the Gilded Age. But in other respects he might be regarded as one of America's first progressives, and *The American Commonwealth* as a seminal progressive tract. For the book served two causes: to inform Englishmen about the United States and bring both to a better understanding of the other, and as a call to reform in the United States itself. Progressivism was in part precisely the re-entry of Bryce's 'best men' back into the mainstream of political activity, of the application of political science by university graduates like Frederic Howe, Herbert Croly, Walter Lippmann and Felix Frankfurter: and not in the world of thought alone, for in time Bryce's readers and disciples came to inherit and transform America's political machinery, to modernise and purify and rationalise, all the way from Seth Low in Brooklyn and New York City up to Theodore Roosevelt and Woodrow Wilson in the White House. Most were personal friends of Bryce, others were encouraged by the persuasive common sense, the sympathetic tone and temperament of his style. Henry Sidgwick summed this up perfectly: 'The Americans believe in him: and I think he will manage to produce a favourable impression of them in the English mind without an air of *parti pris* — since he by no means thinks democracy has broken down — and also to tell them plain truth without losing their goodwill.'[8] The result was that, while *The American Commonwealth* continued to be read and admired in England, its separate life in America was, if anything, more vital and long-lived. One testimony — Frederic Howe's — will suffice:

> Mr. Bryce's *American Commonwealth* was at that time a work of Bibilical authority. When he visited our seminar on politics, professors and students accepted his opinions as above and beyond question. He talked about the spoils system, about the corruption of cities, and the decay of a sense of responsibility among the kind of people whom I knew. That was what impressed me most: the kind of people I knew had neglected their duties.[9]

This study might have concluded there but, although *The American Commonwealth* underwent only minor revisions after 1888, the underlying purpose of the book, the fostering of Anglo-American unity, continued to evolve and to dominate

---

[8] A. and E. M. Sidgwick, *Henry Sidgwick: A Memoir*, p. 404.
[9] *Confessions of a Reformer*, p. 3.

Bryce's thought and activity, so that an epilogue seemed in order. Extensive travel throughout the empire shed fresh light on the question of America's unique racial problem, and the coincidence of the Spanish-American and Boer Wars prompted a comparative analysis of imperialism's sources and its probable consequences. Lastly the First World War provided the great testing ground for the future of Anglo-American co-operation. For Bryce it was a trying episode fraught with tragic ironies; he could hardly have foreseen that friendship between the two democracies would be forged in war rather than in an extended era of peace and arbitration; that his pupil, Woodrow Wilson, would at first hold his country firmly to an impartial neutrality, or that, having entered the European conflict decisively on the side of Britain, he would then, at the zenith of Anglo-American world power, seemingly allow that unity to flounder and miscarry. Nevertheless Bryce's prophesies ultimately proved to be correct, and his life's work fulfilled; thereafter the United States was to remain inexorably embroiled in the affairs and defence of Britain.

1

The Formative Period 1838 – 1870

> Jowett also was in good form. I talked of the 'idea of
> development' as characteristic of the present age, and he
> said: 'Don't you think it is the word rather than the idea?'.
> — Henry Sidgwick, *Journal*

Oxford

James Bryce was born in 1838 into a family of Lanarkshire
Covenanters. His grandfather, a Presbyterian minister, had
been suspended from his parish of Wick in Caithness because of
his failure to conform to the local synod, and having crossed to
Northern Ireland and established himself at Killaig in County
Antrim again encountered official opposition when he refused
the *Regium Donum* (a grant to the dissenting clergy to encourage
conformity to the crown), with the cry 'Christ is my King'.[1] His
grandson and namesake was to display a similar though more
moderate dissent when, after gaining a first degree at Glasgow
University, he applied to Trinity College, Oxford, in 1857 the
year of his grandfather's death. For James had inherited a firm
religious independence as well as a belief in self-improvement
through education from his family. His grandmother, for
example, had taught herself Greek and Latin and tutored her
five sons in turn. But when the question of careers arose all five,
including James's father, entered the medical or teaching
professions rather than the church. In 1846 James Bryce senior
left the Belfast Academy to take up a teaching post at the
Glasgow High School in which his son was duly enrolled. In
1854, at the age of sixteen, James entered Glasgow University
and graduated in 1857.

---

[1] Fisher, *James Bryce*, I, pp. 2 – 4. James Bryce, *Irish Regium Donum Inconsistent
with the Kingly Rights of Christ and the Freedom of his Church* (1843).

In applying for Oxford Bryce, as Presbyterian and Scot, entered a wholly alien world, for the differences that existed between Glasgow and Oxford were indicative of much wider distinctions separating English and Scottish life and education in the mid-nineteenth century. Scottish universities 'were the creation and the minister of the whole people'. Bryce recalled that the best man in his Logic class had been a blacksmith who worked all summer to pay his fees: 'Needless to say, this was no social disparagement. Indeed, the men who supported themselves in this way were all the more respected.'[2] In contrast, Oxford in the 1850s served essentially as 'a training school of literary rhetoric for the upper class' and as an Anglican seminary. Surrounded by clerics, 'poll men' and fox hunting nobles, he was made uncomfortably aware of his being an outsider and of the injustices of English traditionalism.[3]

The University Bill of 1854 had officially abolished compulsory adherence to the Thirty-Nine Articles, but conservative colleges such as Trinity continued informally to insist upon them. Letters to his parents illustrate how Bryce coped with this dilemma:

> I think it likely that, if asked to sign at Trinity, I shall be told it is merely a form, but for me that would not make it less wrong to do it. From the moment I heard of it, I determined not for a thousand times the honour and the money to do it.

Bryce was then approached by Haddan, the Vice-President, who attempted to exact a promise of general conformity:

> But this I entirely refused, though greatly tempted, for he said the communion would be accepted, but I prayed for strength, and was enabled to refuse. He then went away, and I thought I had lost all my chance.[4]

Half an hour later, however, a messenger arrived with news that Trinity had conceded; Bryce was to be the first of the five scholars elected. While unshaken on the essential point of discriminatory tests, he had compromised over chapel attendance and grace in hall because he deemed these essentially institutional rather than religious requirements. He was conciliatory too because he appreciated that reform from within the

2 Fisher, I, p. 23. Bryce in *NYN*, 8 May 1884, p. 403.
3 Bryce, *Fortnightly Review*, March 1883, pp. 388, 399.
4 Fisher, I, pp. 38 – 43.

university for the cause of dissent and conscience would be more effective than ineffectual opposition from without, and on his election to a fellowship at Oriel in 1862 he rededicated himself afresh to the task of 'using aright so important a means of earthy advancement . . . remembering that it is good only as it is used'.[5] His earthly advancement thereafter, even by Glaswegian standards, was remarkably swift. Only nineteen when he came up, he had procured a fellowship at one of Oxford's most prestigious colleges at the age of twenty-two, published his prize essay, *The Holy Roman Empire*, at twenty-six which, as his tutor E. A. Freeman noted, 'by a single youthful effort placed himself on a level with men who had given their lives to historical study', and gained the Regius Chair in Civil Law when only thirty-two.[6]

Bryce's success at Trinity had been a notable victory for the liberal faction within the university and indicated a growing reaction against what he called Oxford's 'state of morbid theological excitement'. The influence of Newman was waning and Tractarianism with its religious sentiment, its respect for antiquity and tradition, its inclination towards casuistry (as Bryce put it), and its taste for symbolism was becoming no more than 'a matter for curious enquiry'. He records a long student discussion about Charles the Martyr in his diary, after which he returned to his rooms and hung up a portrait of Cromwell, 'England's greatest hero', as an act of defiance.[7] For Bryce had entered a university once again alive with intellectual ferment. But an entire intellectual system, a theology based on individual revelation and divine authority, had to be overturned before the forces of secular progress could regroup and advance. Mark Pattison, the Rector of Lincoln College, wrote of Newman's having broken not only with the religion of Anglicanism but politically, too, with the principles of 1688: 'He threw off not only the scum of democratic lawlessness, but the allegiance which the individual understanding owes to the universal reason, and too hastily concluded that authority could supply a basis for philosophical belief.' Newman's logic of faith was simple: 'We believe something first, and then we enquire why we believe it. The credendum is given, and we are all to find

5   Bryce to his father, 25 April 1862, Ms. Bryce 82.
6   Fisher, I, p. 65.
7   *North British Review*, March 1865, p. 118. Bryce to Dicey, 4 Nov 1913, Ms. Bryce 4. Bryce's 'Oxford Diary', 29 Jan 1858, Ms. Bryce Misc.

rational grounds on which to rest it.'[8] Faith had to be answered by reason and here John Stuart Mill's *System of Logic*, a sacred scripture for university liberals as Leslie Stephen termed it, became the textbook of counter-insurgence. In its opening pages the haunting influence of Tractarian dogma was boldly challenged and swept away. 'Logic', Mill insisted, 'is not the science of Belief, but the science of Proof, or Evidence. In so far as belief professes to be founded on proof, the office of logic is to supply a test for ascertaining whether or not the belief is well grounded.' Along with this destruction of *a priori* reasoning went intuitionalism, all ontological assertions and the entire tradition of metaphysical speculation. And in undercutting such false philosophies Mill also intended to undercut the dead institutions they sustained; he provided 'a logical armoury for all assailants of established dogmatism', and liberals with a potent weapon to combat Puseyism within Oxford.[9] But the lessons of Mill's *Logic* held more than short term significance for Bryce. Its call for rationalism and the methodology of empiricism, the submission of evidence to exacting scientific investigation and the emphasis placed upon careful observation and experience provided him with the means by which he later dissected the American commonwealth.

Faith as a valid emotion was not attacked as such, but revealed truth grasped by divine revelation had to yield to a new faith in the rigorous process of empirical observation and inductive method. Pusey, who fought a bitter rearguard action on behalf of the clerical establishment, defined the university's aim in terms of forming minds 'religiously, morally, intellectually, which shall discharge aright whatever duties God, in his Providence, shall appoint to them'. Bryce, in contrast, insisted that 'the university exists [for] education and learning, the training of the human mind, and the advancement of human knowledge: objects quite distinct from the enforcement of dogmatic truth, distinct even from the formation of a moral and religious character'.[10] To those for whom faith remained, and

8   *Mind*, I, 1876, pp. 85, 87.
9   Leslie Stephen, *NYN*, 12 Sept 1867, p. 214. Mill, *A System of Logic* (ed. by J. M. Robson), p. 9. Leslie Stephen, *The English Utilitarians*, III, p. 76. Mill confirmed in his *Autobiography* that 'The notion that truths external to the mind may be known by intuition or consciousness, independent of observation and experience, is . . . the great intellectual support of false doctrines and bad institutions' (p. 191).
10   Pusey quoted in V. H. H. Green, *Religion at Oxford and Cambridge*, p. 268. Bryce, *North British Review*, March 1865, pp. 112–13.

Bryce was one of them, Christianity was transformed into an active, positive creed; other-worldly disputations over revelation and ritual gave way to concern for the political and social rights of the individual. T. H. Green of Balliol in particular deflected Bryce from the field of theological controversy to that of secular duty. Gerard Manley Hopkins was contemptuous of Green's 'rather offensive style of infidelity', but then Hopkins was one of the last major Oxford figures to be received into the Catholic church by Newman in 1866, and Green's was very much the 'style' of the future. A very practical concern for the alleviation of poverty, an elevation of the masses along with their intellectual enlightenment, became a vocation worthy of the most devout believer, and after gaining a first in *Literae Humaniores* Bryce transferred to the relatively new school of History and Law with its greater relevance to contemporary concerns and political issues. Green's influence remained and in his contribution to *Essays on Reform* in 1867 Bryce was to fuse his political and religious beliefs and speak of democracy as the essence of Christianity, 'whose principle, asserted from the first and asserted until now, has been the spiritual equality of all men before God'.[11]

Within the university itself the Anglican tests were the most immediate obstacle to change for they arbitrarily discriminated against a large dissenting population, buttressed the role of Oxford as Anglican stronghold and encouraged an insidious nominal acquiescence ('scarcely one refused the test, and scarcely one believes it'), which Bryce found especially disturbing. But such requirements condemned the body which enforced them more than the individual who outwardly conformed to them. In fighting a long and hard battle against discrimination he insisted again and again that 'it is not the [university's] business to force opinions upon her pupils, which would have no real value to them if so forced, but to enable them to form true and just opinions for themselves'.[12] Throughout his distinguished Oxford career Bryce never held an MA because it required assent to the 36th Canon to which a conscientious dissenter such as himself could not subscribe.

As the struggle over tests continued he came increasingly to appreciate that Anglicanism's spiritual monopoly reflected, and was supported by, the political alliance of established church

[11] Bryce, *Studies in Contemporary Biography*, pp. 86, 87, 95. *Essays on Reform*, p. 273.
[12] *North British Review*, March 1865, pp. 114, 113.

and state; that to break this formidable opposition it was necessary to appeal to a wider constituency of non-conformists outside the ancient universities and bring their numerical pressure to bear on parliament. He was encouraged in this direction by the foremost university liberal of his day, Goldwin Smith, who wrote to Bryce that 'the hope of the Oxford Liberals lay not in any contest in Oxford itself — a narrow arena, where the enemy has long been and still is entrenched in overwhelming strength — but in victory in an ampler field. Liberalise the national legislature and the national legislature will liberalise Oxford at one stroke'.[13] Although Bryce had his doubts about the 'roughness and dirt' of Lancashire politicians working closely with refined academics, he took the opportunity when working on the Taunton Educational Commission in Lancashire in 1865 to link up with Manchester politicos like R. D. Darbishire in urging direct parliamentary pressure to abolish all remaining vestiges of religious discrimination. This campaign finally resulted in the Acts of 1871 and 1877 and liberalised and secularised Oxford. 'The clubs were pitted against the chapels', Smith concluded, 'and the chapels won.'[14]

Thus, starting with his initial conflict with Trinity's Toryism, Bryce's personal struggle had grown to embrace first convocation, then parliament and eventually mass party politics. This increasing political activity widened his narrow academic horizons and cloistered existence, and extended his range of friendships. He met London supporters of university reform such as George Brodrick, Lord Bowen, Frederic Harrison the Positivist, and liberal clerics like Frederick Temple, Lyulph Stanley and Dean Church. Similar battles fought at Cambridge led to the founding in 1864 of the joint university *Ad Eundem* club where he met such luminaries as Henry Sidgwick, Vernon Harcourt, G. O. Trevelyan, Leslie Stephen and the classicist Henry Jackson. But he was supported and sustained most of all by members of an Oxford coterie, the 'Old Mortality', which had been founded in 1856 by two Glaswegians, G. R. Luke and John Nichol, who had preceded him to Oxford. The society consisted of like-minded radicals like Swinburne, T. H. Green and Albert Venn Dicey, his closest life-long friend, who left an impression of Bryce as graduate student:

[13]   Goldwin Smith to Bryce, 7 July 1869, Ms. Bryce 16.
[14]   W. R. Ward, *Victorian Oxford*, p. 311. J. W. Burgon, *The Disestablishment of Religion in Oxford*, p. 45. *NYN*, 3 June 1880, p. 415.

The real strength of his character lies . . . in the happy combination of various qualities, each of which may be found separately as fully developed in other persons. Most successful at the university, he does not seem to possess extraordinary, so much as admirably balanced, talents. His papers, of which I have seen many, were not perhaps strikingly original, but they were always good and clear, and what was required for the occasion. He has, I fancy, great capacity for development. His most agreeable and, I truly believe, his most valuable quality is his childlike 'life' and go.[15]

The club's style was radical and romantic; Swinburne composed odes to Mazzini and burnt incense in front of a picture of Orsini, for Napoleonic imperialism was the enemy abroad as Palmerstonian torpor was the adversary at home. The club hoped to release England from the sterile grip of the *status quo* and made no excuses for its excessive enthusiam for, as Dicey wrote: 'There are seasons when enthusiam is the highest prudence.' It revered the 'odd and dangerous' writings of Carlyle, and listened to Goldwin Smith — Disraeli's 'wild man of the cloister' — holding forth on the inestimable benefits of an American republic freed from a clerical establishment and dedicated to religious toleration. But its greatest ardour was reserved for the heroes of European nationalism, for Bryce woke to political consciousness in 1848. He recalled his father taking him as a young boy to hear Kossuth speak, was only stopped from enlisting in Garibaldi's red shirts by a stern reprimand from the President of Trinity, and was among the jubilant crowds in 1864 when Garibaldi visited London.[16]

In 1865 Bryce began to read for the bar at Lincoln's Inn and his horizons were further enlarged when he was introduced into the wider sphere of London's liberal intelligentsia and met Grote, Mill and Thomas Hughes. To supplement his income and gain an audience for his advanced views he turned to journalism and found an outlet in *The Saturday Review* along with other young writers like Henry Sumner Maine, John Morley, James Fitzjames Stephen and Lord Robert Cecil. Although the most brilliant journal of its day, it was in many ways an unlikely outlet for Bryce. Its editor, Edward Venables,

---

[15] Fisher, I, p. 59.
[16] Edmund Gosse, *Life of A. C. Swinburne*, pp. 42, 54. Robert S. Rait, *Memorials of A. V. Dicey*, p. 50. *NYN*, 24 March 1881, p. 201. John Sparrow, *Mark Pattison and the Idea of a University*, p. 81. Fisher, I, p. 51.

was, he recalled, 'that type of Londoner who called itself Liberal, and was Conservative, disliked sentiment, and detested Gladstone', and had the habit of consigning Bryce's heterodox opinions to the back pages. Later, with the aid of Stephen and Freeman, he began contributing to the *Cornhill*, the *Pall Mall Gazette*, the *Nineteenth Century* and *The Fortnightly*. *The Fortnightly* was founded in the year of the second Reform Bill and dedicated to advancing further the cause of Millian liberalism, and when its editor, John Morley, came to review the *Essays on Reform*, he drew attention to the fact that eleven out of its twelve contributors were either dons, six of them from Oxford, or young men fresh from university, and concluded that 'the extreme advanced party is likely to have for the future on its side a great portion of the most highly cultivated intellect in the nation, and the contest will lie between brains and numbers on the one side and wealth, vested interest, rank and possession on the other'.[17] This crucial alliance of brains and number of which Morley spoke seemed then to hold the key by which the fortress of privilege could be assailed. Its joint forces had contributed towards making Oxford a truly national university open to all talents. Could not a similar response be called for in order to advance the more fundamental cause of parliamentary reform? Guided by a new middle class elect emerging from a liberalised Oxford, the forces of progress seemed irresistible, the possibilities intoxicating. Meanwhile the outbreak of the civil war in America come to the aid of domestic reformers. The conflict served to dramatise and universalise the local struggle for change and pitch it at a level of cosmic providence; its importance became almost entirely symbolic. The American Legation in London became the social centre for young radicals who mixed with an older generation which included W. E. Forster, Monckton Milnes, Bright and Cobden; all of them believed that the drama being enacted in the United States would have a decisive impact on the future direction of British politics. The American ambassador's son and secretary, Henry Adams, breathed in this heady rhetoric and prophesied a decisive and distinguished future for the cultivated liberals who possessed 'all the elements of a great reforming liberal party at work here. Then you will see the new generation . . . take up the march again and press the country into shape'.[18]

---

[17]   Fisher, I, p. 15. *The Fortnightly Review*, 1 April 1867, pp. 491 – 2.
[18]   Harold D. Cater (ed.), *Henry Adams and his Friends*, p. 97.

The American civil war

The civil war focused British attention on the United States as never before, for, although the government pursued a line of official neutrality, public opinion in the country was divided and the issues aroused became embroiled in the debate on domestic reform. Bryce, like other young liberals, experienced a sense of intense personal involvement, following military developments with great interest, joining the Union and Emancipation Society and going to hear Bright's great set speeches at the Manchester Free Trade Hall and the St James' Hall in London. Even more important was the intellectual debate which followed the outbreak of war. The future of the United States in particular and of republican government in general, and the relation of both to Britain's own future, profoundly influenced him and first turned his attention decisively towards the United States.

In so far as the American republic seemed gravely imperilled, the future of democratic experimentation seemed threatened. There was a frightening possibility that the union might disintegrate; that is, the future threatened to disappear — an unpleasant and disagreeable sensation to contemplate. As Bryce later recalled: 'There was no place in England where the various fortunes of that tremendous struggle were followed with a more intense interest than in Oxford and Cambridge, and none in which so large a proportion of the educated class sympathised with the cause of the North. Mr. Goldwin Smith led the section which took that view, and which included three-quarters of the best talent in Oxford.' The excessive emotional identification generated was the result of each observer projecting his own very personal and political preoccupations directly on to the distant American battlefield, the vicarious nature of the involvement serving only to intensify feelings further. T. H. Green's response was not untypical of liberals: 'He followed and watched every move in the military game. No Massachusetts Abolitionist welcomed the fall of Vicksburg with a keener joy. He used to say that the whole future of humanity was involved in the triumph of the Federal arms.'[19] The young conservative's response similarly proceeded from the personal to the specifically American on to the plane of universal application. During the war Lord Robert Cecil's wife woke to find her husband sleep-walking and deeply agitated, preparing to resist

---

[19]   *Studies in Contemporary Biography*, p. 90n.

forcibly the intrusion of federal soldiers in his bedroom.[20]

Edward Dicey, A.V.'s brother, had visited America and was one of the few at the time to expose the liberal myth that the English upper class was predominantly pro-Southern and the working class predominantly pro-Northern. Similarly, he questioned the lax American corollary that depicted the Unionist struggle as a middle class struggle against a confederate aristocracy. But, knowing little of workers or of aristocrats in England and even less about Americans, the intelligentsia were capable of far greater enthusiasm than their fellow citizens, and of analysing the conflict in terms of class. Mill explicitly identified the Unionist cause with that of England's progressive middle class, while the secessionists displayed 'the fanaticism of a class for its class privileges'. Goldwin Smith concluded that 'classes will be classes. The success of American democracy has always been a threat to aristocracy in England', and A. V. Dicey even defined Southern states' rights' doctrines as 'nothing but a theory of class rights carried out on a larger scale'.[21] Conservatives responded with similar class projections, interpreting the Union's attack on the confederacy as an indirect assault on aristocratic privilege in Britain. One curious result of this collective distortion was that for the duration of the war both sides were compelled to trim and change sides ideologically, the conservatives becoming bold upholders of the sacred right of insurrection, and the liberals, previously enthusiasts of nationalist minorities, now opposing one such minority.

Lord Robert Cecil had first-hand experience of popular politics in Australia and New Zealand, and Lord Acton in America; for both it served as a 'homeopathic cure for democracy'. Fitzjames Stephen and Maine had been taught the efficacious lessons of authoritarianism in India. All four identified utopian egalitarianism as the source of the American republic's inevitable self-destruction. 'Political equality is not merely a folly', Cecil insisted, 'it is a chimera. It is idle to discuss whether it ought to exist; for, as a matter of fact, it never does. Whatever may be the written text of a Constitution, the multitude always will have leaders among them, and those leaders not selected by themselves.' From out of this radically false abstractionalism had emerged the even greater unrealism of the abolitionist

---

[20] *Lord Salisbury on Politics* (ed. by Paul Smith), p. 11.
[21] Edward Dicey, *NYN*, 14 Sept 1865, pp. 336 – 7. Mill's *Autobiography*, p. 226. Smith in *The Atlantic Monthly*, Dec 1864, p. 754, and A. V. Dicey in *Essays on Reform*, pp. 80 – 1.

movement which combined 'an intolerant optimism claiming to be based on transcendental truths . . . and conscientiously believing itself to have a divine commission to remedy all the wrongs of the world and convert society into a Garden of Eden'. Inheriting such pernicious first principles nothing good or wholesome could come from republicanism; democratic institutions degraded everything they touched, even literature, which, Maine noted, was either rosily futuristic (he observed 'a melancholy preponderance of the future tense') or simply obscene: 'If the *Leaves of Grass* should come into anybody's possession, our advice is to throw them instantly behind the fire.'[22]

Cecil rejoiced at the commencement of hostilities for he hoped it would serve to destroy American democracy and its English supporters at one stroke. 'For a great number of years a certain party among us, great admirers of America, who even in their last extremity still worshipped faithfully at the old shrine, have chosen to fight their English battles upon American soil.' 'Clearly, the panacea has broken down. The philosophers stone of our political alchemy has turned nothing but cinders out of the crucible.' Acton too, from his singular stance as Catholic, Burkean and aristocrat, was aware of the 'power of attraction' America exercised over Europe. Deploying Tocqueville's concept of majoritarian tyranny with great skill and force he interpreted 1861 as the final struggle between the supremacy of law and the moral association of duty against the absolute will of the people and the physical association of force: 'It is bad to be oppressed by a minority, but it is worse to be oppressed by a majority . . . [for] from the absolute will of an entire people there is no appeal, no redemption, no refuge but treason.': 'in claiming absolute freedom, [the Union] has created absolute powers . . .. The North has used the doctrines of Democracy to destroy self government. The South applied the principle of conditional federation to cure the evils and correct the errors of a false interpretation of Democracy.'[23] It was the pluralistic principle inherent in states' rights and the fear of absolute and centralised power that led Acton to admire the political

---

[22] Cecil, *Quarterly Review*, Oct 1862, p. 547. Fitzjames Stephen, *Saturday Review*, 9 Jan 1864, p. 51. Maine in *Saturday Review*, 28 Feb 1857, p. 204, and 15 March 1856, p. 394.

[23] Cecil, *Quarterly Review*, July 1861, pp. 250 – 1, and Oct 1862, p. 538. *Saturday Review*, 14 Sept 1861, p. 267. Acton, *Historical Essays and Studies*, pp. 127, 142, and *The History of Freedom*, p. 11.

philosophy of Calhoun and the military leadership of Lee.

Unfortunately, however, support for the confederacy entailed implicit support for slavery in a country which unanimously condemned the 'peculiar institution'. Cecil did not condone slavery — he recognised it for the evil it was — but in his identification of threatened privilege in Britain with the threatened South he considered slave property as the American equivalent of landed property in Britain, both sustaining a privileged caste and therefore a balanced constitutional government. Again the Blacks, like the 'residuum' in Britain, were disfranchised; the poor and middling whites of the South had consequently to look to the slaveowner and not to the slave for political ally. By such means the Southern leaders could defy the levelling spirit of the North, unlike Britain where the combined forces of the lower and middle class — Oxford and Lancashire, for example — united to threaten the privileged order.[24] Acton was far more explicit in defending slavery on moral and not merely political grounds. The Catholic church, following the teachings of St Paul, distinguished between inward and outward slavery, between spiritual and material freedom, from which it followed that the slave could never be entirely enslaved if his soul were free and untrammelled by external forces. Good as well as evil could flow from the institution, evoking a spirit of charity in the master and of purifying sacrifice in that of the slave. Even in 1866 he considered it as wicked to remove slavery as to defend it, for the evils of democratic despotism were far greater: 'Slavery is the condition in which certain definite rights are lost by the slave. Absolutism is the state in which no rights are assured to the subject . . .. The decomposition of Democracy was arrested in the South by the indirect influence of slavery', because the South opposed equality, and because it upheld the rights of certain minorities — in this particular case the rights of a minority of White men to enslave Black.[25]

As rarefied justification this was impressive but it was unlikely to convince the Bridgnorth audience that Lord Acton addressed, for by 1866 abolitionism had given the North an overwhelming moral advantage. In the early days of the war, however,

[24] *Saturday Review*, 19 Oct 1861, p. 392, 7 Nov 1865, p. 599, 14 Dec 1861, p. 597, 14 March 1857, p. 459. *Quarterly Review*, July 1861, p. 224, and Oct 1862, pp. 554 – 5.

[25] *Essays on Church and State* (ed. by Douglas Woodruff), pp. 439 – 40. Acton's *Historical Essays*, p. 137. Acton stated explicitly in 1861 that 'slavery is essential to democracy' (*Essays on Freedom and Power*, ed. by Gertrude Himmelfarb, p. 223).

American war aims were unclear and the liberals were unable to play their trump card. Goldwin Smith's initial stance, for example, was precisely the same as Gladstone's, which was in turn close to Acton's; that separation was wholesome for the North and that it would be excessively bloody and impractical to attempt to force a recalcitrant South back into the union. On his return from America in 1863 Leslie Stephen disillusioned his liberal friends by reporting that, initially, Lincoln and the Republican party had invariably put preservation of the union before their hatred of slavery, and that the North was not destroying slavery because they were abolitionists but because the South depended upon slavery. But following the Emancipation Proclamation liberals could emphasise the propaganda advantage of abolitionism to the exclusion of everything else. To suggest that protectionism might have been a contributory cause of the war was dismissed by Smith as reflecting merely the materialism of Britain's commercial ethos. Mill hammered the point home: 'The South are in rebellion not for simple slavery; they are in rebellion for the right of burning human creatures alive.' Mill's immense prestige was thrown wholeheartedly behind the moral imperative of abolition not least because it by-passed the liberal's weakest point — the rights of minorities and the right of insurrection — and hit his pro-Southern opponents at their most vulnerable as slavery apologists:

> Secession may be laudable, and so may any other kind of insurrection; but it may also be an enormous crime. It is the one or the other, according to the object and the provocation . . . war, in a good cause, is not the greater evil which a nation can suffer. War is an ugly thing, but not the ugliest of things: the decayed and degraded state of moral and patriotic feeling which thinks nothing worth a war is worse . . .. As long as justice and injustice have not terminated their ever renewing fight for ascendancy in the affairs of mankind, human beings must be willing, when need is, to do battle for the one against the other.[26]

Mill continued to entertain an almost mystical faith in the

[26] F. W. Maitland, *Leslie Stephen*, p. 113. Goldwin Smith, *Letters to a Whig Member of the Southern Independence Association*, p. 40. Mill, *Dissertations and Discussions*, III, pp. 195, 204 – 5.

benefits of Northern victory. In the world of thought it served as a 'great concussion [which] must have loosened the foundations of all prejudice and secured a fair hearing for impartial reason on all subjects such as it might not otherwise have had for generations'.[27] In the most practical sense this is precisely what happened. The dire predictions of predestined American disintegration, which *The Times* continued to predict almost to the end, were unrealised; instead the republic survived and was strengthened. Such staple conservative predictions were never heard again. The 'great existing fact' of America and of American democracy could no longer be ignored. Instead the British intellectual was faced with the task, unpleasant for some, of having to come to terms with a flourishing post-war America which would continue, inevitably, to serve as an indispensible model. Moreover, the North's military triumph was interpreted as a moral vindication of democracy, and for Bryce the implications were obvious. Just as the image of America as a Christian commonwealth, freed of a clerical establishment and dedicated to religious non-discrimination, had sustained the Oxford dissenter, so the self-confident emergence of republicanism from its greatest crisis, free of the stain of slavery, encouraged him to apply the politics of equality and universal suffrage to domestic reform.

'Essays on Reform'

Because the Reform Bill of 1867 went much further than either party had initially intended, and because in retrospect 1867 was seen as a decisive turning point in Britian's transition to mass democracy, a myth grew up depicting the bill's passage as a great struggle between opposing principles. But the act was not forced through as a result of the breaking of the Hyde Park railings or because of the decisive contribution of philosophical thinkers. Instead there was a remarkable political consensus which recognised the need for a readjustment in the balance of power, and the 'synthetic conflict' fought out on the floor of the House concerned itself principally with less abstract but more vital matters, such as levels of enfranchisement and redistribu-

---

[27] *The Later Letters of John Stuart Mill* (ed. by F. E. Mineka and D. N. Lindley), XVI, p. 993. Also Hugh Elliot (ed.), *Letters of J. S. Mill* II, pp. 35 – 6. As A. V. Dicey wrote in retrospect: 'The surrender of Richmond was the victory of democracy in England' (*NYN*, 20 Jan 1898, p. 45).

tion of seats, which had far more to do with personal advancement and party advantage than with the future of democracy. All parties agreed upon a more representative redistribution of seats and a cautious extension of suffrage, but the liberals differed in that they felt they ought somehow to be seen to be doing more while, at the same time, fearing far more the abyss of unlimited extension which seemed to be fortuitously opening up before them. Bright, for example, that great champion of the people, vigorously denied the title of democrat, ('I never accepted that title, and believe those who know me and speak honestly of me never applied it to me') and, while having publicly to urge the opposition on to more generous measures, privately deplored the radical import of Disraeli's cynical exploitation. Edward Dicey observed that 'the whigs approve of reform in the abstract, but dislike it in the concrete'.[28] The ominous spectre of majoritarian tyranny and its levelling commonplace spirit, which so threatened the independence and integrity of the intellect, stalked their vocabulary, giving it an habitual tone of wariness and mistrust. More acutely aware of the threat to individual freedom in an era of mass politics, they suffered from nagging fears of which the 'stupid party', who rooted the individual more securely within the intricate tissue of social relations, were simply unaware.[29]

The party's intellectual wing was, if anything, even more cautious. Unlike the professional politician, Mill could not be sanguine about a glorious extension of voting stock. His experiences as member for Westminster made him scathing in his judgement of working class sense and intelligence ('no lover of improvement can desire that *predominant* power should be turned over to persons in the mental and moral condition of the English working classes'), and his reading of Tocqueville's second part of *Democracy in America* confirmed his worst fears concerning the latent tyranny of numbers and forced him to resort to any number of ingenious mechanisms — plural voting, proportional representation, Hare's scheme — that would neutralise this frightening portent. As he wrote to Fawcett: 'It is an uphill race and a race against time, for, if the American form of democracy overtakes us first, the majority will no more relax their despotism than a single despot would. But our only chance

---

[28]   The phrase 'synthetic conflict' is Maurice Cowling's (*1867; Disraeli, Gladstone and Evolution*, p. 5). Bright quoted in Asa Briggs, *Victorian People*, p. 211. Edward Dicey, NYN, 5 April 1866, p. 425.
[29]   Gertrude Himmelfarb, *Victorian Minds*, pp. 342 ff.

is to come forward as liberals, carrying out the democratic idea, not as conservatives, resisting.'[30] This is the authentic voice of intellectual liberalism; it was a question of Mill hoping to dish mass American democracy while Gladstone and Disraeli attempted to outdish each other politically in parliament.

The great defence against democratic despotism lay in representative government, and the election of Mill, Hughes and Fawcett in 1865, all in urban constituencies, appeared to confirm the encouraging trend towards an increasing working class electorate voting in members of the abler middle class to do battle against entrenched aristocracy. Mill believed that a public opinion incapable of ruling itself was nevertheless capable of electing representatives wise enough to mitigate the tyrannical tendencies of those who elected them. Mill's clarion call of 'government by members of the middle for the working class' was ultimately intended to admit the middle and not the lower classes to real political power and thus avoid the American form of democracy.[31]

Essays on Reform was remarkable in advocating American solutions, and in doing so its contributions were as far from Mill, Gladstone and Lowe as it was possible for liberals to be. The deprivations of the Lancashire cotton workers during the American civil war had confirmed that the working classes were capable of doing what the middle classes expected of them — suffering severe material hardship, selflessly and disinterestedly, for the right and higher cause. Lincoln, Gladstone and Disraeli were variously impressed. Their example encouraged John Morley to speak of an alliance of brains and numbers and J. R. Green to comment on 'the strength of a demand for reform which knits together two classes at first sight so unlike . . . as the artisan and intellectual classes and which springs out of the alienation of both from the present state of English politics'.[32] And it was because the new role of the masses was to assist the liberal intelligentsia into political power that the *Essays* aimed their attack at Robert Lowe and his 'pagan' doctrine of 'the necessary degradation of the many'.[33]

---

[30] *Ibid.*, pp. 386, 388.
[31] J. H. Burns, *Political Studies*, June 1957, p. 171. Mill added that 'The people ought to be the masters, but they are masters who must employ servants more skilful then themselves' (Burns, p. 167).
[32] Morley, *Fortnightly Review*, 1 April 1867, pp. 491–2. J. R. Green, *Saturday Review*, 6 April 1867, p. 438.
[33] T. H. Green to Bryce, 23 March 1868, Ms. Bryce 26.

For Robert Lowe was not only responsible for the second Reform Bill — the Adullamite revolt which he led destroyed Gladstone's hopes for a moderate bill and ushered in Disraeli's ministry — but also for the *Essays on Reform*. Like Robert Cecil and Lord Acton, Lowe as a young man had seen the democratic future in Botany Bay and decided he did not like it. His was the major theoretical contribution on the floor of the House opposed to reform, an opposition compounded, as Bryce said, of Plato, Tocqueville and New South Wales, and therefore called forth the only considered intellectual response: a response pitched at the highest possible level for, as Goldwin Smith argued in his anonymous preface to the collection, the demand for a more national parliament was not 'the expedient of the party anxious to attain power by the aid of popular agitation, but a conviction seriously entertained and capable of being supported by arguments worthy of the attention of those who wish to legislate deliberately in an impartial spirit and for the good of the whole people'.[34] Its contributors were precisely that class of young university radicals Mill had in mind as political leaders of the next generation, and, as such, they were most similar to Mill in their self-conscious élitism: 'The ancient idols whose worship had hitherto obstructed bold legislation', Leslie Stephen argued, must give way to 'the guidance of the cultivated intellect and talent of the country.'[35] They were similar too in wrapping their more radical proposals in cautious language. While they uniformly deplored Lowe's expedential arguments to oppose change, they were not above claiming expediency to urge it; Bryce spoke of 'genuine conservatism', of 'timely concessions and wise expansions of old forms', when he pointed out that the Adullamite attack on French democratic excess was really the consequence of a social and political imbalance, of a democratic society without democratic institutions. The same was now true of Britain, but change in such circumstances implied not revolution, but a return to a balanced constitution and a stable equilibrium. He accused the Adullamites of a partial reading of Tocqueville, of ignoring his underlying thesis of democratic inevitability, and thus of attempting to exclude the masses rather than educating and elevating them. It was with Tocqueville's assistance that he raised the argument from the level of expediency to that of

[34] *Studies in Contemporary Biography*, p. 308. Goldwin Smith's preface to *Essays on Reform*.
[35] *Essays*, p. 91, and *North American Review*, Oct 1868, p. 567.

inevitable historical progress and the coincidence of destiny with liberal party aims: 'The tendency of the last seven centuries of European history has been to an equalisation of the conditions of men — an equalisation not so much (in Europe at least) of wealth as of physical force, of manners, and of intelligence . . . political equality has become a passion in some countries, legal or civil equality is admitted to be necessary in all.'[36]

It was a greater faith in the future and trust in the masses that most clearly distinguished the younger contributors from anyone else writing at the time, and in this their mentor was not Mill, the political hypochondriac, but the idealist, T. H. Green. Bryce spoke of Green as 'loving social equality . . . [of being] filled with a sense of the dignity of simple human nature . . .. Everything was to converge on the free life of the individual in a Free State; rational faith and reason inspired by emotion were to have their perfect work in making the good citizen'. This assumption and belief underlay Bryce's specific task, which was to refute the arguments from history employed against moderate reform. The essay was more than an historical appendix; it was absolutely integral in undercutting the Adullamites, who had 'gathered together all the vices of democratic governments of all ages — the instability of Athens, the corruption of Rome, the ferocity of the French revolution, the lobbyists, caucuses, the wire-pullers of America' to condemn reform and obstruct change. It was, he continued, because 'the so-called argument from history has been very rife among us of late years, and has been unsparingly employed by public writers and speakers to discredit, not democracy alone, but in reality all free institutions' that it had to be decisively disposed of.[37] More especially the ever-present example of America had to be faced head on, and Goldwin Smith and Leslie Stephen dealt specifically with this issue, turning the Tory cliché of 'propitious circumstances' on its head. This stock in trade argued that any success in American democracy was attributable to entirely non-political

---

[36] *Essays*, pp. 252 – 98. Bryce went on to indicate that the 'stimulating power of democracy' would 'elevate the humbler classes by enlarging their scope of vision and their sense of responsibility' (*Essays*, p. 267).

[37] *Studies in Contemporary Biography*, p. 97. *Essays*, p. 242. Bryce reiterated in private that his essay was to prove 'that no valid argument against a (moderate) democratic reform in this country can be drawn from ancient and medieval communities or from recent history of continental states' (Bryce to E. A. Freeman, 29 Jan 1867, Ms. Bryce 5.)

factors such as limitless space, a small high wage labour force, isolation from European power politics. Both suggested instead that the singularly 'unpropitious circumstances' of decentralised government, fluid social structure and volatile frontier made America's stability in the face of such a lavish but disruptive endowment all the more remarkable. And this stability was overwhelmingly due to the politics of responsible democracy. Even the rich yields of the American prairies — far greater than that of the equally fertile soil of the Turkish and Austrian empires — reflected the greater efficiency of wise republican government. Neither attempted to deny the mediocrity and corruption of many American politicians, but again the unpropitious circumstances of a society in flux, freed of the 'unrecognised and secret bonds' which bound European society together, and still trapped in a 'colonial' stage of progress, helped explain these minor blemishes, while at the same time emphasising their essentially ephemeral nature.[38]

The contributors were at their most 'unflinchingly democratic' (the phrase is Morley's) when they went beyond correcting the conservative caricature of America and suggesting her as a model offering positive solutions to Britian's political ills. In the general welter of ingenious restrictions and qualifications suggested by philosophers and politicians alike, they were almost alone in advocating the primacy of numbers over interest and of the individual over class. The obvious objection to voting by head lay in the dismal fact that the working class constituted a numerical majority which would swamp all other classes. But Bryce would have nothing to do with the heaping up of property qualifications, which were a crude variant of the 'stake in society' concept in which the state became a trading company and a man's interest in it proportional to the capital he had invested. Similarly, Stephen mocked the 'dextrous trickery' of Mill and his friends, who hoped to load the dice in their own favour and thus 'retain a private fund, whilst professing to go into partnership; to handicap judiciously those who are already weighted in the race by poverty and ignorance'.[39] Dicey rejected representation by class because class interests were the most disruptive and divisive of all forces in society. The spectre of majoritarian despotism was a delusion — the farm labourer

---

[38] *Essays*, pp. 101, 102–3, 222, 87 ff., 95–6. Also Goldwin Smith in *Macmillan's*, June 1866, pp. 87–8.
[39] *Fortnightly Review*, 1 April 1867, p. 492. *Essays*, p. 270. *Macmillan's*, April 1867, pp. 534–5.

shared few interests with the urban artisan — employed by a privileged minority to perpetuate their own power. Acting themselves as a class and passing callous measures for the protection of corn, the ruling establishment was unable to conceive of a new electorate which would not act likewise and press for the legal protection of labour. The electorate could not be considered as constituting separate classes or representing distinct interests because an infinite variety of individuals and a multitude of opinions each pursued separate and diverse ends; unless voting were by head the state would fail to reflect and interpret faithfully the true wishes of the collective electorate. In substituting a classless for a class-ridden society, the problem of divisive interests seems to dissolve and harmony replace disharmony. Borrowing from classical economics, Bryce argued that 'the state is not an aggregate of classes, but a society of individual men, the good of each of whose members is the good of all'.[40] Class interest was retrograde as well as disruptive because the currents of progress were moving in the direction of equality. Drawing together the various threads of his co-contributors, Bryce conceived of the ideal state as Christian and democratic:

> The more that any man's mind in penetrated by the Christian spirit, so much the more hateful do class-distinctions and class-exclusions become to him; so much the more does he cherish the possibility of eventually raising the mass of mankind from their degradation, and making them the partakers of rational freedom. Hence the ideal of a Christian state is Democracy; a Commonwealth in which wealth is no honour, nor labour any degradation; all whose members are worthy of equal regard, although there be among them a diversity of gifts and government be assigned to the most gifted; wherein there is no strife of classes, because no divergence of interests, nor any need of coercion, because the law is the expression of their common will, and their will is to seek not their own good, but the good of all.[41]

Bryce went on to suggest that this ideal was a moral and a spiritual rather than political vision, but that any political progress had to be measured and judged by these standards,

[40]   *Essays*, pp. 67 ff., p. 278.
[41]   *Essays*, pp. 273 – 4.

and there is no doubt that it was the United States which most nearly approximated to this ideal. As Goldwin Smith made clear in his essay on 'The experience of the American Commonwealth': 'A step . . . has been made towards the realisation of that ideal community, ordered and bound together by affection instead of force, the desire of which is, in fact, the spring of human progress.'[42] Christopher Harvie has suggested in his study of the university liberals that the essayist's proposal to admit all within the pale of the constitution stemmed from a deep-seated desire to replace Anglican unity with political fraternity, and Bryce's essay most clearly illustrates this attempt to fill the spiritual void. A less conscious but perhaps more pertinent motive sprang from the intelligentsia's bid — an ostensibly radical bid — to gain the respect and devotion of the numerically superior disfranchised and inaugurate a reign of Platonic guardianship. In this they displayed a narrow arrogance and unreality nurtured by Oxford. Mill had his doubts; his young followers did not. Disraeli, too, knew otherwise and his sounder political instincts ultimately allowed his party to garner the fruits of 1867.[43]

Consequently the visionary radicalism yielded to disenchantment when reform failed to usher in the liberal millenium and the Bryce of 1884 was a far more cautious advocate of change. In retrospect, the bill was seen as forging an alliance between Tories and English wage earners based on dissent from liberal individualism, intended to 'swamp professional intelligence in a flood of ignorance and beer'.[44] But, ironically, it was one of the contributors, Bernard Cracroft, who most clearly questioned his co-contributors' image of leading the newly enfranchised into the classless state. The landed aristocracy, although they had long been swamped numerically, would, he argued, continue to exert a controlling influence based on indirect consent resting on social deference as well as direct parliamentary power.[45] The implications of this theory of indirect influence were so damaging to the main thrust of the *Essays* that Leslie Stephen

[42]   *Essays*, p. 218.
[43]   Christopher Harvie, *The Lights of Liberalism*, p. 23.
[44]   *Studies in Contemporary Biography*, pp. 298 – 9, 305. Goldwin Smith in *Contemporary Review*, March 1885, p. 322. Cracroft concluded his 'Analysis of the House of Commons, or Indirect Election' by questioning 'whether, under such a consitution as ours is, numbers as such as ever be heard there at all' against the landed aristocracy's 'tremendous consent of power' (*Essays*, pp. 162, 158).
[45]   *Macmillan's*, April 1867, pp. 532 – 3.

lost his temper. 'If Mr. Cracroft's arguments were sound they would almost amount to a refutation of any claims for the extension of the franchise, for they would prove that no such change could make a practical difference. He is so struck with admiration of the system which he describes, as almost to fall down and worship it.'[46] This was unfair; Cracroft was in favour of change, but was also acutely aware of how much more difficult real change was, and how little others might wish to follow the liberal blue-print. Bryce and Leslie Stephen hoped that the educative value of political responsibility would destroy the retarding structure of unthinking deference and that an extended suffrage would result in a greater reference to working class opinion: more attention, for example, would be paid to the lodgings of the poor and less to compensating landlords for cattle plague. This was undoubtedly correct, but it did not nullify Cracroft's contention. Instead it adopted the interest politics both affected to abhor. Stephen was ruffled because Cracroft undercut the collection's utopianism. It suggested that the representation of all classes would not dissolve class divisions but merely add to them. Bryce, however, continued to cling to the imagined ideal state as existing in America, although there too contact would bring with it a degreee of disillusionment. But the resonant word 'commonwealth' which evoked a free and harmonious community, and which he borrowed from Goldwin Smith's essay, became the title of his book of 1888 and many of its chapters echoed and confirmed the high optimism of 1867.

---

46   Bryce in *Essays*, p. 271 and Stephen, *Macmillan's*, April 1867, pp. 533 – 4.

2

Goldwin Smith, Freeman and Anglo-Saxon Unity

America would then be England, viewed through a solar microscope — Britain in a state of glorious magnification.
— Samuel Taylor Coleridge, *Table Talk*

Goldwin Smith

Before his death in 1910 Goldwin Smith received a new edition of *The Holy Roman Empire* from its author, dedicated 'in remembrance of all that I have been privileged to learn from you through your voice and your books, ever since I went to your lectures in the hall of University College'. It is significant that Bryce should recall the Oxford period when, ardent and impressionable, he was most under the dazzling spell of the Regius Professor of Modern History, who then exercised 'the most powerful pen in the English-speaking word'.[1] For he was then the incarnation of liberal Oxford, sitting on the Oxford Commission with Benjamin Jowett and Arthur Stanley, and receiving the Regius Chair, as a reward for his reform efforts, in 1858. But it was Smith, the vociferous champion of the unionist cause, drawing on a radical millenarian tradition which stretched back to Tom Paine and which imagined a utopian America whose example might yet rejuvenate Great Britain, who left the most lasting impression on Bryce. Smith's *US Notebook* of 1864 reflected the magnified hopes of the Manchester school at the stimulating prospect of a large and expansive continent opened up by pioneers freed of the feudal bonds existing in Europe. He admired the self-reliant localism of the Concord town meeting; he pictured America's immense economic resources 'an ocean of cornland . . . which seems to bid all that hunger in the world come there and be fed', and the

---

[1] Elizabeth Wallace, *Goldwin Smith: Victorian Liberal*, p. 9n. Bryce to Gamaliel Bradford, 19 June 1910, Bradford Papers.

consequent social mobility and personal advancement which could result: 'Mayor of Champaign — young lawyer of 25': 'Farm of 27,000 acres owned by a man who had risen from poverty and could scarcely write. He has given his sons a good education.' He admired a school system whose values reflected a democracy which encouraged and stimulated, raised expectations rather than narrowly inculcating submission as so often in Britain: 'The schools open to all — no compulsion — but their excellence produces a moral pressure.'[2] The polemical purpose behind the flood of pamphlets which issued from his pen on returning to England lay in these *Notes*. 'The attachment of this [Republican] party to American institutions and their country combined with their reverence for English institutions and character — indicating the real relation between the two countries. To bring this out and cultivate it.'[3]

He rewrote Anglo-American history as a preliminary to welding the two nations together as one. The schism in the Anglo-Saxon world, he argued, was not geographical and did not occur in the eighteenth century, but was spiritual and occurred in the seventeenth century, with the exodus of the Pilgrim Fathers to New England, where the struggle for liberty of conscience against Laudian persecution continued. Meanwhile the heritage of Puritan dissent lapsed in the homeland so that the political breach of 1776 merely reinforced the earlier spiritual separation of the race. That separation was salutary, possibly necessary, but unfortunate, for the breach came in war and revolution. Deprived of England's steadying influence the Americans lurched into a revolutionary bias and sought for their origins in 1776 rather than 1620. England, in turn, was deprived of the enlightened spirit of Milton and Cromwell and sank into the lethargy and reaction of a new Laudianism in the shape of Pusey. All that was progressive, all that was most politically advanced in the English-speaking community resided in its American branch. Just as the Lancashire chapels had come to the aid of liberal Oxford, so Goldwin Smith conceived of the United States as a vast new-world Lancashire capable of restoring the balance of the old. His analysis was both retrogressive and revolutionary; it was a classic appeal to the past to transform the present. England's golden age had survived substantially unchanged in America. His aim was to

[2] 'US Notes 1864' reprinted in *Goldwin Smith: His life and opinions* (ed. by Arnold Haultain), pp. 261–2, 268, 272, 276.
[3] *US Notes*, p. 253.

point to the superficiality of the schism and thus ease a reconciliation which would restore England's best lost traditions. 'Hampden and Washington in arms against each other' would give the world over to the powers of evil. With America, England 'may have a league of the heart. We are united by blood. We are united in a common allegiance to the cause of freedom'.[4]

Like his utopian predecessors, Smith fell foul of cynics like Bagehot and Lowe, and in *Lothair* Disraeli hinted at 'flunkeyism', knowing it would be especially painful to a radical professor who had tutored the Prince of Wales. 'The Professor', Disraeli continued, 'was not satisfied with his home career, and, like many men of his order of mind, had dreams of wild vanity which the New World, they think, can alone realise.' For Goldwin Smith had decided to accept a chair offered by Andrew Dickson White, President of Cornell, in up-state New York, in 1868. Being a thin-skinned pamphleteer as well as a hypochondriac, Disraeli's earlier squibs may have contributed to this decision to withdraw from English public life. But rather dramatic personal reasons — his father's suffering a severe railway accident swiftly followed by insanity and suicide by poisoning — also played their part in this most important decision of his life, for he was never to return permanently to England. But neither did he remain long in the country he had so extravagantly praised. Alas, he abhorred Ithaca's noisy profusion of waterfalls and, while in principle an enthusiast, objected to Ezra Cornell's literal insistence on self-help which involved faculty members working in shoe factories on the campus.[5] Once safely across the border in Canada he could indulge in long suppressed and venomous attacks on America and American politics. The seeds of disillusionment were already present in the 1864 *Notebooks* where nagging doubts impinged upon the rosy scene: 'General concurrence as to the corruption of Washington . . .. Abuse of the popular vote in New York . . . Cobden's view too ideal.' Rampant Anglophobia over the *Alabama* claims finally convinced him that he was in a foreign country after all.[6]

4   *The Atlantic Monthly*, Dec 1864, pp. 750 and 751. For a fuller discussion of Smith's Anglo-American thesis see his *Civil War in America* and *The Schism in the Anglo-Saxon Race*.
5   *Lothair* (London, 1927), p. 95. Wallace, pp. 41, 48, 49.
6   *US Notes*, pp. 261 and 287. Smith to Bryce, 7 July 1869 and 26 Jan 1871, Ms. Bryce 16.

In 1871 he settled for good in 'The Grange' in Toronto, marrying a wealthy widow and suffering, as Dicey put it, 'all the vices of an exile', recreating an English country house across the Atlantic and making frequent visits to England despite suffering appallingly from seasickness. Intellectually he atrophied. He had always given the historian J. R. Green the impression of closing rather than opening doors, and Bryce was saddened by his decline. 'No new light seemed to break on him. Everything was judged by the old doctrines and condemned by the old phrases.' There was nothing left for him to do except ceaselessly fight Disraeli's shadow and outlive as many of his successors in the Regius Chair as possible.[7]

Smith's influence on Bryce is most clearly discerned in *The American Commonwealth's* underlying idealism and in its assumption of Anglo-American unity. Bryce remained infected by Smith's early dazzling enthusiasm for the republican experiment. From his civil war pamphlets and his seminal contribution on the American example in *Essays on Reform* Bryce imbibed his vision of the United States with its promise of enhanced possibilities, of its answering to the highest human needs, of a classless and middle class republic destined in time to heal Britain's own divisive and distracting conflicts. But Goldwin Smith's history had a darker side to it, for it was a history of races; he speaks of the unity of blood as well as the league of the heart, and the obverse side of Anglo-Saxon inclusiveness and superiority was the inferiority and exclusion of the lesser breed. In isolation Smith succumbed to a racial paranoia played down by his most recent biographer.[8] An evil world conspiracy was held together by a fine thread; Puseyism was threatening republican government in America through the agency of Democratic priests who brought Irish and Black votes with Vatican money and perpetuated the Bourbon aristocracy of the South. The Irish in particular, who 'multiplied with animal recklessness', contributed 'a dark stream of barbarism' to history. An especially vicious attack in the *Spectator* aimed at the

---

[7] Dicey to E. L. Godkin, 29 Dec 1882, Godkin Papers. Dicey recalled Green's remark about Smith to Bryce in a letter of 14 June 1916, Ms. Bryce 3. Bryce to Dicey, 14 Nov 1913, Ms. Bryce 4.

[8] The subject is never fully raised by Elizabeth Wallace. In quoting from Dicey's meeting with Smith at The Grange in 1898, for example, she omits the last section of a discussion in which he deplored Smith's vicious anti-Semitism in the Dreyfus case. (Wallace, p. 64, and Robert Rait, *Memorials of Albert Venn Dicey*, p. 166).

Irish-American editor, E. L. Godkin, accusing him unjustly of antipathy to England and of support for Fenian outrages, forced Bryce and Dicey to come to the aid of Godkin, a close friend of both. Dicey's letter on this occasion helps to place and clarify Bryce's life-long friendship with Smith: 'The only difference between us is that I believe I have for years been accustomed to consider Goldwin Smith as one of the most unfair writers living, while you I think trusted him more than I have.' The late nineteenth century combination of historical method and racial theory constituted, in Dicey's opinion, a retreat from utilitarian assumptions of human equality, and contributed a new racial divisiveness which historians like Smith aided and abetted. And, while Bryce undoubtedly disapproved of Smith's explicit racial tone ('he was more prone to racial antagonisms than a historian ought to permit himself to be'), the two were closer in their emphasis on racial exclusion as a necessary corollary of the Anglo-Saxon commonwealth, and this too left its mark upon *The American Commonwealth*.[9]

E. A. Freeman

In his inaugural address as Regius Professor, E. A. Freeman gave an obligatory but highly personal estimate of his predecessor, Goldwin Smith: 'He went forth from us of his own will; but it was but to carry his light to another branch of our own folk . . . he has taught us to see, if not a "Greater Britain", yet a newer England [in] lands which have become more truly English colonies of the English folk because they have ceased to be provinces of the British Crown.'[10] The two professors were exact contempories, both born in 1823 and going up to Oxford in 1841. And like Smith, Freeman imposed a long period of self-exile on himself by marrying in 1844 and thereby forfeiting his Trinity fellowship. He retreated to his library at Somerleaze near Wells and did not return to Oxford till 1884, when Stubbs resigned his chair on being elevated to the bishopric of Chester. Nevertheless he kept his links with Oxford, examining for the School of History and Law and dining at Trinity, where Bryce

9   Smith, *My Memory of Gladstone*, p. 56. *The Civil War in America*, p. 19. Smith's article appeared in *The Spectator* on 21 Sept 1882 and Bryce came to Godkin's defence on 17 Oct 1882, Ms. Bryce USA 5. Dicey to Bryce, 1 Nov 1882, Ms. Bryce 2. Bryce in *The North American Review*, Vol. 199, 1914, p. 518.
10   *The Methods of Historical Study*, p. 9.

became a close friend and devoted pupil. The theme of Bryce's prize essay, *The Holy Roman Empire,* published in 1864, clearly demonstrates the seminal influence of his mentor in faithfully reflecting Freeman's central belief in the continuity of history. Bryce recorded the essentially uninterrupted growth of an ancient institution through 1,800 years held together by the single idea of Rome — 'her language, her theology, her laws, her architecture made their way where the eagles of war had never flown, and with the spread of civilisation have founded new homes on the Ganges and the Mississippi'.[11] His survey of Aryan development traced the Greek heritage in Roman civilisation and the rich classical inheritance bestowed, in turn, on the Teutonic branch of the race as it advanced in power and influence. Like Freeman, Bryce was an avid Germanophile, and in 1870, on the eve of his departure for the United States, he was loath to leave Europe at such a fateful juncture with a new Germanic enpire, its roots deep in the past, about to re-emerge and vindicate the theme of his book. Henry Adams recalled that 'the Germans were crowning their new Emperor at Versailles, and surrounding his head with a halo of Pepins and Merwigs, Othos and Barbarossas. James Bryce had discovered the Holy Roman Empire'.[12] But this discovery would have been impossible without Freeman's inspiration, which drew on the pervasive significance of the past to the present. His imaginative recreation of a medieval world peopled by heroic Teutonic warriors stirred Bryce emotionally and made him intellectually aware of the relevance of the historical dimension in his study of society. A common democratic stance, an admiration for nationalism — especially the oppressed minorities of the Turkish empire — the legends of Homer and the Icelandic sages, and long walks with Freeman magically recreating the past in the surrounding landscape; all helped to inspire Bryce and seal their friendship. Freeman's appeal was to the youthful, hearty and romantic side of Bryce. Their brand of liberalism was robust and open air, and had something to do with intimations of a primal democracy, and with ancient rites being enacted in pastoral settings under Alpine skies.[13]

11 *The Holy Roman Empire*, p. 370.
12 Freeman to Bryce, 20 June 1869, Ms. Bryce 5. Bryce held Napoleon III responsible for the Franco-Prussian war and hoped for a German victory. Henry Adams, *Education*, p. 304.
13 See Bryce's appreciation of Freeman, *English Historical Review*, Vol. VII, 1892, particularly p. 499.

Despite his kindness to chosen friends Freeman was truculent and boorish, happiest when harrying Froude and Kingsley through Victorian journals with an ugly perseverance. Opposed to fox hunting, he was not averse to hunting Anthony Trollope because he followed the chase. After three attempts to enter parliament ('I feel so keenly that, without a seat in Parliament, one is nowhere'), he found compensation in medieval history where the bullies tended to do rather well. He saw himself as an Anglo-Saxon thane, wrote execrable historical verse epics, named his two sons Edgar and Harold, and broke with Bishop Stubbs and Leslie Stephen and the *DNB* over the spelling of Athelstane. Deprived of an audience at the hustings, his prejudices resurfaced in his histories; his dicta that 'History is past Politics' could be rewritten as 'History is current controversy'.[14]

He claimed history as a science which recorded the data of racial progress just as natural science tracked the laws of natural evolution. The historical method had already yielded rich rewards in Maine's studies of ancient law, Max Muller's investigations into the origins of comparative religion and E. B. Tylor's research in sociology and anthropology. Freeman concentrated on the classification and labelling of constitutions and institutions, partly because they provided readily verifiable information and partly because they most clearly reflected the spirit and genius of race. He believed that Darwin's research into genetic evolution confirmed the unity of history and the continuity of races, or organic development over spontaneous generation and that this could be traced with scientific precision using the new tools of comparative philology, mythology and anthropology. Collectively races, like the genus, contained a seed, an inherent and inheritable genetic pattern, which controlled and dictated all future growth and response to adaptation. From its very beginnings the racial seed predetermined those peculiarly Teutonic characteristics — an innate capacity for orderly self-government — which identified the common origins of that race whatever its consequent diversity either in place or time. The Aryan, be he Greek, Roman or Teuton, could no more escape the burden of ineluctable progress than a sunflower seed could escape its destiny as a sunflower. Borrowing from Tylor's concept of 'survivals' in the

14 Freeman to Bryce, 3 April 1880, Ms. Bryce 6. Freeman and the Rev. George W. Cox, *Poems Legendary and Historical*. Leslie Stephen, *Some Early Impressions*, p. 121.

form of words, grammatical forms, legends, customs and beliefs
— Freeman hoped to compare racial diversities and distinguish
between direct racial transmission and indirect assimilation of
one race by another; to probe the origins and growth of the
Aryan race, and to rediscover through history 'a new world . . .
a world shut up within itself . . . where we have at last learnt to
look for our fathers'.[15]

He made large claims for this new historical method of
scientific measurement: 'On us a new light has come. I do not
for a moment hesitate to say that the discovery of the
comparative method in philology, in myth — let me add in
politics and history and the whole range of human thought —
marks a stage in the progress of the human mind at least as great
and memorable as the revival of Greek and Latin learning.'[16] As
historian he concentrated on the Teutonic branch of the Aryan
race and became a medievalist. Using the comparative method,
distinguishing between genuine transmission and spurious
imitation, searching for the racial likenesses which underlay
superficial dissimilarities, he was able to ferret out and discard
the fake replicas which might otherwise confuse the clear
delineation of racial continuity. Thus careful research revealed
the spontaneous reproduction of the Greek Achaian league by
their American descendants in their federal constitution, thereby confirming Washington's direct lineage from Arminius and
Hampden. But such direct replications, confirming direct racial
descent, were not to be confused with unworthy borrowings,
such as Switzerland's doomed imitation of America's federal
model in 1848. 'To master analogies of this kind,' he wrote, 'to
grasp the laws which regulate the essential likeness, is the true
philosophy of history.'[17] In 1881 – 2 Freeman visited the United
States and his researches bristled with the pursuit of etymologi-
cal origins which might conclusively prove Anglo-Saxon continuities. Many Americanisms revealed their Germanic roots:
'bairn' for child, and 'fall' for autumn were Old English.
Similarly, as a boy he recalled that railways had been called
'railroads', a word no longer current in England but a 'survival'
in America. Inherited customs offered another index of racial
continuity. The New England town meeting harked back to the

15 *Comparative Politics*, p. 303. More generally, *Comparative Politics*, pp. 1-36
    and W. R. W. Stephens, *The Life and Letters of Edward A. Freeman*.
16 *Comparative Politics*, pp. 195-6.
17 *Comparative Politics*, pp. 13-23, 1, pp. 32-3. *A History of Federal Government in
    Greece*, p. 251.

41

English vestry meeting and beyond that to the Teutonic gemôt. Unconsciously the Southerners had emulated their Saxon forebears by reproducing the 'bondsman' — 'assuredly not thinking that the followers of Hengest and Cedric had done the like'.[18]

Freeman was lucky to enter a congenial academic environment at American universities for the Teutonic cult was at its peak, and an extraordinary number of college presidents and historians — Daniel Coit Gilman and Herbert Baxter Adams at Johns Hopkins, C. W. Eliot and Henry Adams at Harvard, Andrew Dickson White at Cornell, for example — were German trained. Freeman and Bryce crossed paths at Johns Hopkins in December 1881 where its director of research in advanced institutional history, Herbert Baxter Adams, emphasised that 'the whole tenor of our researches . . . is to show the continuity of English institutions in America'.[19] Freeman frankly obliged: 'I have made it somewhat of my business to set forth the essential oneness of the two great branches of the English people . . . . I feel that it is a subject on which I am an enthusiast, and that my enthusiasm may possibly bias and colour any report that I may try to make.' These lectures entitled 'The English People in its Three Homes' traced the expansion of the Aryan race from the Teutonic forests *via* England through the second migration to New England. Alone on a desolate continent the race went back in search of its oldest institutions and reproduced the ancient 'folk moot' and flourished until Middle England, Great Britain, apparently forgetting the salutary example of their Hellenic forebears with regard to racial colonisation, neglected New England and caused the breach of 1776. But this colonial revolution, rather than breaking the thread of racial continuity, served to confirm it and constituted the race's greatest triumph: 'By that act the people of those true English colonies . . . did not cease to be Englishmen, but became Englishmen in a truer and higher sense. By independence . . . you, Englishmen in America, rose to the level of your fellow English in Britain.'[20]

This history as saga and myth, while acceptable within the Anglophile east coast universities, proved disastrous outside them. Theodore Roosevelt might be pleased to hear that his family, with typical strenuosity, had slipped Middle England

[18] *Some Impressions of the United States*, pp. 50 ff. Stephens, II, p. 254. *Lectures to American Audiences*, p. 182.
[19] H. Hale Bellot, *American History and American Historians*, p. 19.
[20] *Some Impressions*, pp. 33, 16 – 17. *Lectures*, p. 60.

and gone directly to the predestined home of his race, but such an interpretation was unlikely to appeal to a mass mixed audience. More especially Freeman's favourite epigram: 'This would be a great land if only every Irishman would kill a negro and be hanged for it', and his support of Californian race rioters who attacked their Chinese minorities, was unlikely to find favour with a larger public, and revealed, as in the case of Goldwin Smith, a dark racial phobia which underlay his advocacy of the Anglo-American kinfolk.[21] Few travellers could have been less temperamentally suited to confronting the real republic. He found Americans and the American landscape dull, was surprised to discover, rather ingenuously, less Teutonic past and more newness than he had expected; he went no further west than St Louis or south of Virginia, and showed no interest in America's economic or social progress. He was especially mortified to find his lecture halls emptied in New York by Oscar Wilde, who had similarly arrived to declare his genius. As an admirer of the typical American's wholesome manliness, and rejoicing in the 'youthful and healthy barbarism' of the Aryan tradition, he had hoped to avoid competition from such a quarter, and relieved his asperity by suggesting that it was 'unbecoming that a man, an Oxford man, and the son of a decent father should, like a ballet girl, be photographed [by Sorony] in all manner of odd postures'.[22]

Freeman's writing was an extraordinary inversion of Whig history. It conceived of progress, but of progress through retrogression, and considered the post-medieval world as a declension from purity and unity to racial mix and diversity. For him even more than for Goldwin Smith, America somehow preserved England's primal racial qualities undiminished, frozen as it were, in time. Less sullied by the modern world, American colonists in 1776 once again exercised their Teutonic instincts and revolted to further the cause of future racial freedom. Shorn of its more extreme overtones, Bryce in his *American Commonwealth* conceived of the American revolution in similar terms. His *Holy Roman Empire* was written as an act of

21 Freeman to Roosevelt, 11 Jan 1891, Roosevelt Papers. *Lectures*, p. 138. Freeman to Bryce, 4 Jan 1891, Ms. Bryce 8. In letters home Blacks were variously referred to as 'great black apes' and 'big monkeys dressed up for game' (Stephens, II, pp. 234, 236, 237).
22 *Impressions*, pp. 241–2. Freeman to Godkin, 19 Dec 1881, Godkin Papers. Freeman to Bryce, 22 March 1882, Ms. Bryce 7. *Studies in Contemporary Biography*, p. 268. *Lectures*, p. 117. Stephens, II, p. 249.

homage to illustrate Freeman's thesis of historical unity. Deeply embedded in *The American Commonwealth* lie two crucial assumptions inherited from his mentor: the first is the explicit concept of Anglo-American racial unity, and the second is the implicit understanding of the American as essentially an Englishman writ large on a new frontier. The imaginative limitations which Bryce failed to escape, despite his far wider experience of the United States and his more open mind, are ascribable in part to Freeman. This is the measure of his influence.

The Anglo-Saxon basis of 'The American Commonwealth'

The reassertion by British observers in the 1880s of British and American unity, and the reforging of the links broken in revolution and perpetuated by the civil war, was achieved at the cost of underplaying America's distinctiveness. The American eagle had not been dismembered by civil war, but her wings had been clipped and her claws blunted. The United States even began to look just like England; Freeman commented on the strangeness at the lack of strangeness, Matthew Arnold thought Staten Island just like Richmond on the Thames with 'not a single Mohican running about', and Dicey could ask rhetorically whether it wasn't a mistake to regard the United States as a new country at all.[23] If Bryce's experience gave him a more complex appreciation of the United States, it remained a greater understanding capable of fitting into a framework devised by Smith and Freeman.

Like Freeman, Bryce concentrated on constitutional and institutional history because he believed they were the finest expression of national character, which was in turn defined by race. Their study would also demonstrably forge the links connecting the Englishman in America with his European counterpart. Searching for evidence of New England 'survivals', Freeman replied to Bryce's enquiry at length:

'Would it do to say that the old thing, gemôt, what you please, got mixed up with other ideas in Middle England, and the old thing stood out again? . . . in the American settlements they had gone back to the circumstances of the fifth and sixth centuries, adding all the experience up to the

[23] Stephens, II, p. 234. *Letters of Matthew Arnold 1848 – 1888* (ed. by George W. E.Russell), II, p. 258. Dicey to Bryce, 13 Dec 1884, Ms. Bryce 2.

seventeenth. That is, a nation can do what a man can't, go back to its youth, keeping the knowledge acquired up to age'.[24]

This and similar information allowed Bryce to follow up the etymology of 'township' from the Anglo-Saxon 'tûn' which appeared in a cramped and learned footnote of *The American Commonwealth*. It was not in the least surprising that Bryce should turn up such evidence, but what is revealing is the length to which he would go to discover and confirm these inevitable links. The township in particular received his attention because it had survived unsullied in rural areas to confirm the Anglo-Americans' genius for orderly grass roots government, and because its origins could most clearly be linked with 'those Teutonic traditions of semi-independent local communities, owning common property and governing themselves by a primary assembly of all free inhabitants, which the English had brought with them from the Elbe and the Weser, and which had been perpetuated in the practice of many parts of England down till the days of the Stuart kings'. His description of the township is glowing and uncritical, and appears to escape all the darker features of American democracy: indebtedness, pauperism, police and parties are rare; the educational system, controlled and financed by the township, is excellent, and each member contributes to the well-being of the minature commonwealth; even the venerable Emerson takes his turn as field driver, which derives from the Anglo-Saxon 'hog reeve'. The town meeting, he concluded, 'has been not only the source but the school of democracy'.[25]

One of Bryce's most original achievements was to analyse carefully the important intermediate role of State Constitutions which had been ignored by Tocqueville and by most Americans. His detailed sifting, which took up a quarter of the book and over 200 pages, did not merely reflect the addiction of a constitutional lawyer, for these constitutions contained the vital missing link between English laws and the Federal Constitution for which Bryce was searching. Given the complex interplay of character and institutions, it followed that such self-governing

---

[24] Stephens, II, p. 354.
[25] *AC,* I, pp. 565 n. 2, 563, 591, 576 n. 1. 'All sorts of old English institutions have been transferred bodily, and sometimes look as odd in the midst of their new surroundings as the quaint gables of a seventeenth-century house among the terraces of a growing London suburb' (*AC,* I, p. 480).

traditions embodied in state laws could flourish in English hands but perish under alien influences. Under the unnatural conditions of a semi-feudal and slave-owning South the self-reliant 'township' was worthlessly modified into artificial rectangular 'counties' which would inevitably perish in time. Likewise, the infusion of Irish and French Canadians diluted New England's stock and led to a withering away of the town meeting — a prediction of 1888 which Bryce confirmed in 1910. Again and again he asserted the primacy of human over environmental factors, of race over geography. Sharing a common New England terrain, for example, the English stock had not lapsed into the ways of the Algonquin Indians; instead aboriginal life had been absorbed or destroyed. And this illustrated another characteristic of the Anglo-American race, for the saga of the westward moving frontier was a saga of domination and assimilation by a 'higher' race. And wherever the Englishman went he took with him his superior forms of political organisation. The rural townships of Illinois were more 'American' to Bryce than the polyglot urban concentration of Cook County in Chicago: superior and more successful too in that the New England settlers in the North formally established the township system in four-fifths of the States' counties under the Constitutions of 1848 and 1870, despite the intrusion of pioneers from Kentucky and Tennessee in the South with their separate traditions. Here as elsewhere the ultimate domination of English stock was predetermined and ineluctable. Woodrow Wilson grasped the implication of this and a multitude of other examples when he wrote that Bryce's 'conspicuous merit consists in seeing that our politics are no explanation of our character, but that our character, rather, is the explanation of our politics'.[26]

It has been a commonplace to present Bryce as a precursor of Turner and the frontier thesis.[27] In doing so historians tend to

[26] AC, I, pp. 561–2. AC, 1910, II, p. 605. AC, II, pp. 693–4, 725. AC, I, p. 572. Woodrow Wilson's review reprinted in Robert C. Brooks (ed.), *Bryce's American Commonwealth: Fiftieth Anniversary*. The initiation of money bills in the lower houses of nineteen States was given as an example by Bryce of the vital intermediate role of State constitutions linking parliamentary and federal traditions, and as yet another case of spontaneous Freemanesque transmission (AC, I, pp. 467–8).

[27] E.g. Richard Hofstadter, *The Progressive Historians*, p. 58, M. Kraus, *The Writing of American History*, p. 278, and Howard R. Lamar, 'Frederick Jackson Turner' in Marcus Cunliffe and Robin Winks (eds.), *Pastmasters*, p. 84.

exaggerate Turner's novelty — in many ways the graduate of Johns Hopkins replaced the Teutonic by the Mississippi forests. More importantly, these historians have read Bryce entirely out of context; they have alighted on his famous pronouncement of the west as 'the most distinctly American part of America . . . the part where those features which distinguish America from Europe come out in the strongest relief'. Bryce continues, however: 'But the character of its population differs in different regions, according to the parts of the country from which the early settlers came', thereby affirming a premise which is essentially contra-Turner, which emphasises racial as against environmental determinants, people rather than place, and which asserts that the line of westward democratisation is latitudinal and not longitudinal.[28] In fact Bryce defined two distinct types of westerner. The first was a crude, rudimentary American who injected elements of instability, violence and irrationalism into American life, and Bryce went out of his way specifically to refute Emerson's prophecy of a continental genius emerging from the transforming environment of the western frontier. The west, he insisted, 'has contributed less of a ''new and continental element'' than [Emerson] expected and . . . the majesty of nature has not yet filled Congress with its inspiration'. In conclusion:

> Western opinion is politically unenlightened, and not anxious to be enlightened. It dislikes theory, and holds the practical man to be the man who, while discerning clearly his own interest, discerns nothing else beyond the end of his nose. It goes heartily into a party fight, despising Independents, Mugwumps, and bolters of all sorts. It has boundless confidence in the future of the country, and of the West in particular, of its own State above all, caring not much for what the East thinks, and still less for the judgement of Europe.[29]

The second type of westerners were 'the stalwart sons of New England', those who had carried the true democratic spirit laterally across the continent; men such as Samuel Eliot, the son of the President of Harvard, who, along with other Harvard men, had protected the Chinese and Japanese minorities during

---

28 AC, II, pp. 301 – 2, 697.
29 AC, II, pp. 729, 301.

the Californian race riots against 'that scum which the westward moving wave of emigration carries on its crest and is here stopped, because it can go no further'. The west, Bryce implied, did not create a uniquely American spirit but rekindled an English one by providing a large, unexplored land and scope from which Anglo-Saxon stock could alone fully benefit. In the west the Englishman was enlarged rather than transformed, had space to realise his Englishness to the full. For, as Bryce reminded his British and American readers: 'A transplanted tree may bear fruit of a slightly different flavour, but the apple remains an apple and the pear a pear.'[30]

The historical method and the debate over the American revolution

Goldwin Smith and E. A. Freeman had suggested that the spirit of 1776 could be safely accommodated within the innocuous limits of a sudden but essentially organic enlargement of English freedoms. Superficial similarities between the America of 1776 and the France of 1789 had led to confusion and the assumption that republics were somehow synonymous with permanent revolution. 'Republicanism shook, or appeared to shake, the very foundation of society', Dicey wrote, 'and, because the attempt to establish Democratic institutions produced revolution, calm observers find it difficult even now to believe that a republic when established has not necessarily a close connection with what is called a revolutionary spirit.' The task was to disassociate the revolution of 1776 from Jacobinism and 'the theatrical tradition of the great French drama', and place it firmly instead in the bloodless English tradition of 1688.[31] Ancient and specific rights guaranteed under the ordered liberty of the Anglo-American world were too intoxicating for the Gallic temperament, which transformed them into fetishistic dogmas and abstract formulas which unleashed destructive forces and inaugurated radical change. Freeman observed that the declaration of the 'Rights of Man' had extinguished Swiss democracy at a stroke, while the cosmopolitan Acton held that 'the English

---

30 *AC*, II, p. 727. Samuel Eliot to Bryce, 3 Jan 1888, Ms. Bryce USA, 24. *AC*, II, pp. 388, 658.
31 *NYN*, 15 April 1880, p. 283, and 3 June 1880, p. 414. Henry Sumner Maine thought that there was 'no doubt that the credit of American Republican institutions, and of such institutions generally, did greatly deceive through the miserable issue of the French experiment' (*Popular Government*, p. 200).

Constitution was excellent until removed by foreign writers into the domain of theory'. On the other hand, 'no exorcism is so potent to lay the spirit of unreasoned fear [of the Jacobin terror] as a study of the United States as they actually exist'.[32] The colonists made limited claims against George III based on their rights as true born Englishmen and similar to those their forebears had exacted from the Stuarts. 'No men were less revolutionary in spirit than the heroes of the American Revolution' Bryce wrote. 'They made a revolution in the name of Magna Charta and the Bill of Rights: they were penetrated by a sense of the dangers incident to democracy.'[33]

Although Dicey was a major contributor to this intellectual realignment he became increasingly dissatisfied with Freeman's constitutional interpretation and, more generally, of the historical school to which Freeman belonged. It was not simply the all-inclusive concentration on political institutions or the over-formal approach which led Freeman to look to the 'forms' rather than to the 'essence' of constitutionalism, but the undercurrent of blatant anti-intellectualism which disturbed him, and the theory of retrogressive progress by which 'every step towards civilisation has been a step backwards towards the simple wisdom of our uncultured ancestors'.[34] The wedding of Darwinism to the historical method led disastrously to what Dicey termed 'the apotheosis of instinct'. Without faith in the equality of races, which interpreters of Darwin had done so much to shatter, abolitionism in America would not have succeeded, and this example, 'absolutely required by the principles of utility and by the conscience of mankind', suggested the most troubling feature of the historical method — its innate conservatism, its encouragement of legislative inertia, its intellectual atrophy and limiting determinism. Organic theorists not only tended to look backwards for seeds and origins, but also assumed that growth and longevity, mere survival, was good in itself. Thus, why should not a flourishing weed be nurtured rather than cut? In its appeal to the negative weight of tradition

---

[32] *Lectures to American Audiences*, p. 387. Acton quoted by N. Pilling in *Political Studies*, March 1970, p. 117. Dicey, NYN, 25 March 1880, p. 117.

[33] AC, II, p. 259. Gladstone echoed these sentiments in his 'Kin Beyond Sea': 'Their Revolution, as we call it, was like ours in the main, a vindication of liberties inherited and possessed. It was a conservative Revolution' (*North American Review*, Sept/Oct 1878, p. 185).

[34] NYN, 12 Sept 1872, p. 170 and Dicey, *Introduction to the Study of the Law of the Constitution*, p. 17.

the historical method tended to paralyse change and exposed positive progress as vain and self-defeating. Intellectually it diverted interest away from current reform to a consoling obsession with the certitudes of the past. Dicey's illustrations show that his criticisms were aimed specifically at Freeman: the discovery of the 'Witenagemot' would have been of no material aid to the authors of the *Federalist Papers*; an understanding of the 'landesgemeinden' of Uri 'throws as much light on the Constitution of the United States as upon the Constitution of England; that is, it throws from a legal point of view no light upon either the one or the other'. This was all mere pedantry and antiquarianism.[35] In essence Dicey, along with John Stuart Mill and Henry Sidgwick, identified historicism as the major adversary of progressive utilitarianism.

Yet ironically Mill's *Logic* had emphasised the historical dimension in charting his philosophical framework for a new science of man and only later came to appreciate the powerful weapon he had offered to backward-looking obscurantists like Freeman in what he considered their assault on reason.[36] In his *Representative Government* he attempted to undo any damage and remind his readers that 'political institutions . . . are the work of men; owe their origin and their whole existence to human will . . .. In every stage of their existence they are made what they are by human voluntary agency.' From his own position as Utilitarian philosopher Sidgwick deplored the intrusion of historical method into the field of political theory. It was not simply that the school's contribution was negative, limitative, confirmatory and sceptical which led him to object to 'the most widely and strongly entertained philosophical conviction of the present day' — the date is 1886. A far stronger objection was that any historical biology, derived from observations of organic life was entirely irrelevant to the abstract task of determining what ought to be. He denounced the discipline in his *Elements of Politics* as damaging to progressive thought. Likewise to Dicey it seemed no accident that Maine, who in his *Ancient Law* pioneered the historical method and undermined

---

[35] *Law and Public Opinion in England*, pp. 457–64. LC, pp. 11–19.
[36] 'The fundamental political institutions of a people are considered by this school as a sort of organic growth from the nature and life of that people: a product of their habits, instincts, and unconscious wants and desires, scarcely at all of their deliberate purposes' ('Representative Government' reprinted in *Three Essays*, p. 146). For a comprehensive treatment see Stephan Collini *et al.*, *That Noble Science of Politics*.

the authority of analytical jurisprudence, should have gone on to question the efficacy of democracy in his *Popular Government*.[37]

Now, above all, Bryce was a historian, and in so far as he was a legalist he drew on the historical jurisprudence of Maine rather than the Benthamite jurisprudence of the Utilitarians. He was by nature a profound empiricist, deeply distrustful of any grand abstract formulations or futuristic blue-prints. He was also a democrat, but a democrat of the Freeman school, which looked to secured inherited freedoms and the perpetuation of traditions, habits and customs. He had had a thorough scientific training — albeit organic and biological rather than pure and inorganic — and the historical method fitted his intellectual temperament perfectly. Like Freeman, he believed that history's scientific credentials rested on biological laws of transmission and adaptation, adjustment and survival. His *Holy Roman Empire* was pure historical method and a good third of *The American Commonwealth* is historical too. It is specifically a history of racial unity and continuity and of the adjustment and enlargement of English stock in time and place. Lord Acton was *par excellence* an intellectual and not an institutional historian. He had come to conceive of history in terms of permanent revolution born of revolutionary ideas, and not in terms of evolutionary adaptation, and when *The American Commonwealth* appeared he took the opportunity decisively to cut such links as Bryce had carefully joined together. He subjected the Freemanesque historical assumptions of the book to a sustained indictment of what he called Bryce's 'organic constitutionalism' and 'ethical materialism'. Reviewer and author could not have been further apart. Bryce's search for institutional links and the continuity of customs was interpreted by Acton as laying a false emphasis on the sluggish evolutionary pull of existing structures and the imposition of a misleading traditionalism on the American experience. 'I descry a bewildered Whig emerging from the third volume with a reverent appreciation of ancestral wisdom . . . and a growing belief in the function of ghosts to make laws for the quick.' Acton saw 1776 as the supreme example of the liberal act of revolution, a radical breach with the past, destroying Whig consensus and inaugurating the reign of abstract ideas and of acts born of those ideas: 'All through,

---

[37]   *Three Essays*, p. 147. Sidgwick in *Mind*, April 1886, pp. 203, 207 and *Elements of Politics*, pp. 6 – 8. Dicey's *Law and Public Opinion*, p. 461, n. 1.

American meant: escape from History. They started fresh, unencumbered with the political Past.' Or, as he expressed it in a letter to Bryce, the Americans 'went on from the written to the unwritten Law, from the law of England to the law of Nature'.[38]

This clash of interpretation over the character of the American revolution was highly relevant. Both took unnecessarily extreme positions on the issue because it reached to the heart of their distinct understanding of America. As Mill made clear in the opening pages of *Representative Government*, political man both inherits and recreates. Bryce chose to lay emphasis on the constitutional reaction of 1787 and Acton on the abstract ideas and Jeffersonian spirit of 1776, though he did concede the conservative influence of the *Federalist Papers* and the Constitution, and did distinguish between the American revolution that consolidated its gains as against the French that did not. But the stark difference of opinion was more than an historical disagreement or a differing philosophical approach — the one appreciating the potency of the past, the other stressing the abstract ideals which will always break irreparably with that past. For 1776 held direct relevance for 1888. If Acton was correct then the American example and Anglo-American unity were invalid, because America continued to reaffirm the legitimacy of revolution which Britain had traditionally rejected: 'European revolutions had been just, *a fortiori*, if the American revolution was just.' In other words, the American example offered the Whig historian a thorn and not a cushion. It was because America had created a radically new and un-English tradition that Acton could challenge Bryce's assumptions by quoting an American, Emerson: 'We may make a good; we may make better.' It was because he felt Bryce had failed to consider the full implications of this proposition that he found *The American Commonwealth* flawed:

If [Bryce] had guarded less against his own historic faculty . . . he would have had to expose the boundless innovation, the unfathomed gulf produced by American independence, and there would be no opening to back the Jeffersonian shears against the darning-needle of the great chief-justice.[39]

---

[38] *History of Freedom*, p. 580. Ms. Acton Add. 4897: 4898: 4896. Acton to Bryce, 25 March 1889, Ms. Bryce 1.

[39] Acton to Bryce, 25 March 1889, Ms. Bryce 1. Ms. Acton Add. 4897. *History of Freedom*, p. 585. The Chief Justice referred to is, of course, John Marshall who presided over the Supreme Court from 1801 to 1835.

It is unnecessary here to adopt either a Brycean or Actonian interpretation of the American historical experience, both elements being distinctly present. But Acton's severe critique does serve a useful purpose; that of throwing Bryce's own whig assumptions and his belief in Anglo-American continuities into sharp relief.

3

Methods and Motives 1870 – 1888

A curious fierce-faced little man with a dash of red in his pointed but straggly beard, and with a sharp nose in the air, exactly in the attitude of Captain Kettle . . . .. 'Greek culture', said his sister-in-law, 'Why do they want to revive that here and made us all go about in togas?' 'No, dear', [Bryce] interrupted, 'not togas, it was not Greeks who wore togas but the Romans.'
— Henry W. Law and I. Law, *The Book of the Beresford-Hopes*

Bryce as traveller

The American Commonwealth appeared approximately one hundred years after the founding of the union and some fifty after the publication of Tocqueville's *Democracy in America*, but it is far more than auspicious timing which distinguishes these two classic accounts from all those ephemeral impressions, travel journals and polemical pamphlets which flooded the European market in the nineteenth century. Nor was it simply, as Bryce reported to Sidgwick in 1883, that Tocqueville's work was hopelessly out of date and that there was an urgent need for a new study of 'the curious economic and political problems being worked out in a way which no books really convey'.[1] Bryce's task was infinitely more ambitious; it amounted to nothing less than a comprehensive survey of American life and institutions, a definitive re-evaluation that would, like Tocqueville's, be of lasting value in treating the topic with the full seriousness and engagement it deserved. In this task he was distancing himself from, and reacting against, an overwhelming prevalence of partisan opinions, undigested prejudices and

---

[1]   25 April 1883, Ms. Bryce 15.

sheer ignorance which passed for intelligent comment on the republic in his time. At Oxford, for example, Freeman found that his colleagues assumed that the constitution guaranteed universal suffrage and that it lacked provisions for amendment. He assumed after 1888 that 'those who perhaps have fancied that they know something about the matter will be the first to acknowledge how much less they know about it than Mr. Bryce'.[2] Bryce's first and primary task was educative: to get the facts right.

Growing interest in the democratic experiment and improved speed and comfort in steamship crossings made the United States an acceptable substitute for the European grand tour. Erratically kept diaries padded out for publication with random reflections sold well, but Bryce was scornful of such light-weight products — 'always sketchy, casual, hasty, personal' — whose wide-ranging assumptions and conclusions were invariably based on such flimsy and fleeting observations. The usual deduction that New York City was somehow typical of America was as absurd as assuming that Liverpool was equally 'typical' of England.[3] 'A European who makes a hasty visit of a few weeks, running from New York to Washington and out to Chicago and back again, has not had time to take in the real quality of American life . . . for these things time is needed.' The young Lord Rosebery's spilling a burst bottle of champagne on his unread copy of Tocqueville on setting forth for America in 1873 can be taken as heavily symbolic of this *genre*.[4]

Rosebery proceeded to fall into the clutches of a group of snobbish *roués*, scooped up and lionised because of his title and connections. Other English celebrities tended to be passed round a small group of friends, shown only the most obvious well-trodden 'institootions' and respectfully placed aboard the transatlantic steamer for home. Such, Bryce believed, was the fate suffered by Archbishop Randall Davidson. 'It is a sad pity that he is being run round in this way, for he will depart having seen only the outside of America. He ought to have put on a grey tweed suit, slipped from his keepers and gone to Niagara [and] the Democratic Convention at Saratoga: done what Dicey and I did in 1870.'[5]

---

2   *The Manchester Guardian*, 26 Feb 1889.
3   NYN, 16 Oct 1884, p. 329. *Macmillan's Magazine*, Jan 1872, p. 209.
4   *A Speech at the New York English-Speaking Union*, 29 Sept 1921. *Lord Rosebery's North American Journal: 1873*, p. 27.
5   Bryce to C. W. Eliot, 25 Sept 1904, Ms. Bryce USA, 2.

Having travelled all the way to America only to miss it was bad enough, but far graver was the charge levelled against most of his fellow-countrymen — that of lacking sympathy and an open mind. Too many went merely to confirm their worst suspicions about the vulgar republic. An inordinate sense of his own superiority united to an arrogant insularity made condescension the Englishman's cardinal sin. As an Ulster-Scot Bryce found the English 'too stiff, too dry, too unsympathetic, too much disposed to make their own notions and customs the universal standard of right. They are contemptuous or at best condescending'.[6] Descending upon Americans as though unearthing a horde of black beetles from under a stone, Goldwin Smith spoke of his fellow-countrymen as carrying their own bathtubs with them and dressing as though they were missionaries among hunter tribes. Two tourist clichés were repeated interminably: 'Americans are not gentlemen', and 'Englishmen are', along with the rider that any commendable American features must derive automatically from the English model. 'There is no place like England', Charles Kingsley confided in his diary, 'and all the superior Americans say so themselves . . . [my American trip] has taught me many things — especially to thank God that I am an Englishman, and not a — well, it is not the fault of the dear generous people, but of their ancestors and ours.'[7] Freeman's complaint that America was too 'new', and Matthew Arnold's that it was 'uninteresting', were merely aspects of the truism which lay at the root of all criticism: America was not England.[8]

Even that small band of enthusiastic visitors was usually worn down by the rigours of American travel; the unexpected extremes of climate, the over-heated hotel rooms, the ubiquitous tobacco spitting, the interminable train journeys without First Class apartments or corridors to escape the talkative natives, the 'salaried incivility' of servants, the endless numbing shaking of hands and the hoarse pitching of voices sufficient to

6 *England and Ireland: An Introductory Statement*, p. 29.
7 Goldwin Smith, *The Schism in the Anglo-Saxon Race*, p. 33. Robert B. Martin, *The Dust of Combat*, p. 290. Sir Lepel Griffin wrote in his *Great Republic* of 1884 that 'The good in American institutions is of English origin and descent; what is bad is indigenous, and this she now desires to teach us.' (p. 8.) For a brilliant critique of English insularity see Leslie Stephen, 'Some Remarks on Travelling in America' and 'Thoughts of an Outsider: International Prejudices' (*Cornhill*, March 1869 and July 1876).
8 Matthew Arnold, *Civilisation in the United States*. Freeman, *Some Impressions of the United States*.

be heard in large theatres and halls on the lecture circuit. All helped to erode the comforts of the enthusiast and generate a physical and nervous exhaustion which made him testy and ungenerous.[9] Even the robust and level-headed Anthony Trollope, determined to make good his mother's injury to American national pride, arrives in Cairo, Illinois 'of all towns in America the most desolate', admits to being depressed in spirit, finds a two-day sojourn sufficient, intends to leave early the following morning, oversleeps, is forced to wash and pack with great speed and dash to the station ('nobody who has not experienced [such moments] can understand the agony'), only to find on arrival all the seats taken and the bystanders derisive and unhelpful. 'To whatever period of life my days will be prolonged, I do not think I shall ever forget Cairo.'[10]

In an essay written on America in 1836, John Stuart Mill urged the value of travel and history in breaking down insularity and widening horizons through the enlarged perspective of cultural relativity. The study of history was a journey taken in time into the altogether different world of the past; travel was a journeying in space to societies quite distinct from one's own. Both were salutary. Just as Mill sought to enlarge the diversity, scope and tolerance of the individual in his *Essay on Liberty*, so, he believed, a greater awareness of the individuality of nations served a similar purpose in breaking the narrow bond of cultural absolutes. Bryce combined the role of historian and traveller to an unusual degree; indeed, as a recent writer has put it, 'as a political scientist [Bryce's] genius largely consisted of an infinite capacity for taking trains'.[11]

Frank Harris recollects outlining a daring Greek itinerary for Bryce, who is alleged to have replied that such a route was impossible without beds and servants. 'I saw at once', Harris smugly concludes, 'that his desire for comfort would prevent him learning anything valuable about Greece or the Greeks.' This invented conversation could not have been more wide of the mark, for the youthful climber who ascended Mt Ararat

9   The phrase about domestic servants comes from Griffin's *Great Republic*, where he goes on to insist that 'the absence of quiet and respectful service is to an Englishman an ever-renewing source of annoyance' (pp. 77, 82). The rigours of the American circuit doubtless hastened the deaths of Dickens, Arnold and Kingsley.
10   *North America*, pp. 201 – 4.
11   *The Collected Works of J. S. Mill*, XVIII, pp. 93 – 115. Collini et al., *That Noble Science of Politics*, p. 243.

alone when a mist descended and his porters fled, and the over-curious explorer who almost fell into the crater of Krakatoa, was the last man to be put off by bed bugs.[12] Instead travel suggested escape and stimulus. On the 'cars' he could catch up with his voluminous correspondence, study the passing scenery and encounter new people and new opinions.

> I am a good listener . . . and I wrote [*The American Commonwealth*] out of conversations to which I listened. I talked to everybody I could find in the United States, not only to statesmen in the halls of Congress, not only at dinner parties, but on the decks of steamers, in smoking cars, to drivers of waggons upon the Western prairies, to ward politicians and city bosses.[13]

President Eliot of Harvard recollected long afterwards the vivid appearance in Cambridge of two Oxford men 'one of them [Bryce] asking a most prodigious number of questions', and the venerable abolitionist, Colonel Higginson, recalled their being cordial, intelligent and radical but, most of all, eagerly interested in everything American. This curiosity, coupled with a relaxed approachability, an ability to elicit a response rather than impose an opinion, an avoidance of patronage and pontification, made Bryce the perfect observer, and out of these casual but fruitful encounters, he insisted, came five-sixths of the raw material for his book.[14]

Travel offered a welcome alternative to the mundane grind of daily duties and a recharging tonic to enervated nerves. As he explained to his mother:

> The sort of intellectual excitement it keeps one in all the time, new objects, characters, ideas, continually presenting themselves, and striking fire in your mind. You will say this is exhausting: I don't think so . . . . It is worry, anxiety, indecision, depression of spirits such as often comes over me

---

[12] *Pearson's Magazine*, Feb 1922, pp. 14 ff. Lady Bryce refers to the Krakatoa incident in typed notes on her husband (Ms. Bryce Misc.).

[13] *Speech at a Pilgrims' Dinner*, 23 March 1907.

[14] Eliot, *Address to the Harvard Club of Cincinnati*, 22 April 1908. Edmund Ions's *James Bryce and American Democracy, 1870 – 1922*, p. 44. Bryce wrote that the observer 'must have a magnetic quality which draws information, and yet a detachment of mind which enables him to receive statements from every quarter and every party with equal caution. He must be one who inspires more confidences than he gives' (*Quarterly Review*, July 1905, pp. 174 – 5).

that is bad for the health. You can't imagine how completely one forgets European affairs here.[15]

The American Commonwealth, and Dicey's *Law of the Constitution*, and *Law and Public Opinion*, which he called 'the tardy and inadequate result of my 1870 experience', were testimony to this creative confrontation with the New World and the intellectual ferment which it sparked off.[16]

Bryce and Dicey shared their first experience of America together in 1870, and both adapted naturally to American ways. In retrospect Dicey was to characterise this 1870 journey as the youthful pursuit of an ideal, but more evident at the time was their eager response to America's bristling energy and the relaxed informality of its social life, more especially, for two bachelors, the easy sociability of the young American lady. There is, Bryce wrote, 'a sort of spirit and freedom about the place and people which one doesn't get in England'.Dicey could barely be dragged away from Harvard ('O Eliot, we are *so* happy together'), and Leslie Stephen spoke of having to moderate their ardour on their return to England — 'they cannot speak too warmly of the United States'.[17]

Because of this generous predisposition they overcame at once the major obstacle to Anglo-American understanding — a proverbial English *hauteur* — without lapsing into indiscriminate apologetics. The relationship on the American side was more complex and ambivalent. Aggressively independent, many Americans nonetheless sought approval from their English cousins and were prickly and sensitive to every shade of criticism. Sidgwick was convinced that *The American Commonwealth* would be successful because Bryce remained a democrat and the Americans trusted him because of this. But it was James Russell Lowell, author of the famous essay 'On a Certain Condescension in Foreigners', who wrote of the two visitors: 'If all Englishmen could only take America so "naturally" as they did! I think, if it could be so, there would never be any risk of war.' Bryce's relish of the simple 'pleasantness' of American life

[15] Bryce to his mother, 6 Dec 1881, Ms. Bryce 82.
[16] Dicey to Eliot, 20 Jan 1912, Eliot Papers, 'It is curious', wrote Dicey to Bryce, 'to think how much in one way or another our journey in 1870 affected both of our lives and I should say on the whole affected them happily' (12 Feb 1907, Ms. Bryce 3).
[17] Dicey to Bryce, 23 Aug 1920, Ms. Bryce 4. James to Kate Bryce, 18 Oct 1870, Ms. Bryce 82. Eliot to Bryce, 21 April 1874, Ms. Bryce USA. 1. Stephen to Oliver Wendell Holmes, 4 Jan 1871, Holmes Papers.

disarmed the American reader and put him at his ease, and reviewers who tried to capture the unique tenor of the book frequently alighted upon the analogy of a friendly family doctor: they saw Bryce as the judicious consultant 'cheerful but not too cheerful: inspiring confidence in one's admirable constitution, but alarming one just enough to secure obedience to his régime'. Lord Acton wrote of a bed-side manner 'enough to sweeten and lubricate a medicine such as no traveller since Hippocrates has administered to contrite natives'.[18]

If anything, friends felt he had excessively sweetened the pill and muffled the message of 'quiet reproach'; even Dicey found Bryce's conclusions on American corruption 'more remarkable for the width of their worldly charity than for the severity of their moral tone'.[19] There is substance in this criticism. Too frequently Bryce's legal training led him to balance the accounts nicely, pursue a blank impartiality, neatly advocate the pros and cons and abstain from final judgement. Thus six pages devoted to 'The True Faults of American Democracy' are matched by another seven on 'The Supposed Faults of American Democracy'; the chapter headed 'Wherein Public Opinion Fails' is neutralised by the next, 'Wherein Public Opinion Succeeds'. 'Merits of the Federal System' follows on from 'Criticisms of the Federal System'. Often when troubled he reaches for the stale formula of time as the cure for all ills or, when all else fails, appeals, as he appeals in chapter 74 on 'Types of American Statesmen' to luck, when the hour brings forth the man, as in the case of Lincoln in 1860: 'If this was luck, it is just the kind of luck which makes a nation hopeful of its future.' A serious and informed chapter whose final appeal is to luck is limp and unsatisfactory and goes some way towards substantiating the criticisms of Dicey and Sidgwick, who urged Bryce to modify some of his more sanguine conclusions.[20]

But if Bryce erred in his too-buoyant optimism he erred in the right direction, balancing the excessive English criticism of decades, and he could further argue that if the pill were sugared

[18] *Henry Sidgwick: A Memoir*, p. 404. *Letters of James Russell Lowell* (ed. by C. E. Norton), II, p. 77. Sidwick to Bryce, 1 Oct 1888, Ms. Bryce 15. *History of Freedom*, p. 575.
[19] *The Edinburgh Review*, April 1889, p. 505.
[20] AC, II, pp. 213, 229. Henry James wrote to his brother William of *The American Commonwealth* being 'a perfect bag of reasonableness . . . one fairly longs for a *screech* of some kind' (Ralph Perry ed., *The Thought and Character of William James* II, p. 697).

the pill might at least be swallowed. Even more compelling was Bryce's wish to attain a new degree of detachment of approach. He was acutely aware that 'for many years every book of travels in America had been a party pamphlet, or had at least fallen among partisans, and been pressed into the service of one party or another'.[21] In striving to escape this restriction he intended to avoid such *parti pris* by writing as objective and unbiased a survey as possible, and this he intended to achieve by adhering to a strictly scientific methodology.

Tocqueville and the scientific method

Bryce had received a thoroughly scientific training as a boy. Each summer between 1853 and 1856 he made careful surveys of Arran's flora and fauna and contributed to his father's *Geology of Arran*. From his Uncle William he received instruction in botany and was encouraged to collect and classify plants and grow his own herbarium.[22] He was an excellent pupil for he possessed a scientific temperament, happiest when memorising chemical formulae, classifying data, and wary of metaphysical speculation and flights of imagination. Oxford confirmed the scientific method as the outstanding intellectual achievement of the century, enabling loose disciplines to pass 'from the chaos of conjecture into the cosmos of science'.[23] Like botany or geology politics would in time attain to the precision and status of a science, and political phenomena, scrutinised under a microscope, could be measured, compared and catalogued. The science of politics was also a progressive science: 'The interests of science and the interests of democracy are one', wrote Morley, and Mark Pattison insisted that science buttressed knowledge in its struggle against unthinking tradition. Science had already come to the aid of secularism at Oxford. Mill had dismissed the *a priori* principle as habitually sustaining the existing intellectual order. No scientist would end a book, as Newman ended his *Apologia*, by postulating the revealed truth of God and then building a metaphysical edifice which flowed from and confirmed this supernatural and unverifiable first principle.[24]

21 *NYN*, 16 Oct 1884, p. 329.
22 Fisher, I, p. 32.
23 *The Relations of the Advances and the Backward Nations of Mankind*, p. 6.
24 Morley, *Oracles on Man and Government*, p. 83. *Apologia Pro Vita Sua* (Everyman ed. 1921), pp. 215 – 17.

Bryce had been trained to study society in a scientific spirit. Like Jefferson, he looked upon the American states as a vast and fascinating laboratory for controlled experiments and when, for example, the people of Montana rose up and threatened to adopt the views of Henry George, Bryce hoped they would succeed, not because he was a supporter of George's socialist principles, but because he was eager to observe the consequent repercussions. 'A comparatively small commonwealth like an American State easily makes and unmakes its laws; mistakes are not serious, for they are soon corrected; the other States profit by the experience of a law or a method which has worked well or ill in the state that has tried it.'[25] The law reinforced his scientific bent. From the contrary evidence of advocacy, truth, he believed, would emerge, and the judge could pass a correct sentence.[26] As an academic he tended to eschew the principles of jurisprudence, preferring the humbler task of codification and planning throughout his lifetime a life of Justinian, the great codifier of Roman law.

Although he greatly admired Tocqueville, he believed that large sections of *Democracy in America* were essentially conjectural and therefore pre-scientific and necessarily flawed; indeed, *The American Commonwealth* can be read as a sustained critique of Tocquevillian assumptions. Tocqueville has committed three major errors. The first was clearly stated in the opening pages of *Democracy*: 'I confess that in America I saw more than America; I sought there the image of democracy itself.'[27] In assuming that 'democracy' was a single unchanging phenomenon Tocqueville had endowed the American experiment with direct relevance and applicability to Europe: the future lay with 'democracy'. Thus to travel to America was to travel into Europe's future. Bryce would have none of this. Like Mill, he believed that democracy could be studied in the United States, 'but *studied* it must be', within its singular context and sifting the essential from the inessential. As a Darwinian he insisted upon treating human institutions in terms of challenge and response to a specific and changing environment, and, just as all forms of life could be measured and judged by their powers of adaptation and survival, so 'the true value of a political contrivance resides

25 Bryce to his mother, 27 Sept 1890, Ms. Bryce 82. *AC*, I, p. 345.
26 'Advocacy is at the service of the just and the unjust equally . . . yet experience shows that the sifting of evidence and the arguing of points of law tend on the whole to make justice prevail' (*AC*, II, p. 294).
27 *Democracy in America* (ed. by Phillips Bradley), I, p. 15.

not in its ingenuity but in its adaptation to the temper and circumstances of the people for whom it is designed'. The chief value of his study lay in the flexible laws of 'political biology' it illustrated, and it was in this sense that Charles Eliot spoke of *The American Commonwealth* as Darwinian.[28] For Bryce intended to show in what ways American democracy was specifically and uniquely American and, as a corollary, that American demo-cracy would not — could not — have a direct application for Europe. In his chapter 'How Far American Experience is Available for Europe' he insisted that 'nothing can be more instructive than American experience if it is discreetly used, nothing will be more misleading to one who tries to apply it without allowing for the differences of economic and social environment'. He was willing to concede 'the incomparable significance of American experience', that Europe 'may proba-bly follow' paths already trodden by Americans, but concluded that she 'supplied few conclusions directly bearing on the present politics of any European country'.[29] Throughout the book he destroys again and again the simplistic and static 'America = Democracy' equation. In the chapter entitled 'Why Great Men are not Chosen President' he rejects the lax assumption that 'Democracy = America = Hayes, Garfield, Arthur and Harrison'. In a parallel chapter, 'Why the Best Men Do Not Enter Politics', he refutes the widely-held belief that democracies discouraged public-spirited citizenship. Such pat generalisations could be destroyed by reference to the specifi-cally American factors at play: politics was not the 'great social game' it was in England; America offered the far more challenging, lucrative and satisfying alternatives of business and finance, and the stranglehold of two corrupt monolithic parties suffused all political activity with an air of sordid jobbery which alienated the dedicated citizen and frustrated reformist zeal from the outset.[30]

The consequences of this approach were significant. In emphasising the particularity and distinctiveness of the United States he not only provided a more authentic picture of

---

[28] Mill, *Collected Works*, XVIII, p. 106. *AC*, I, pp. 349, 9. Eliot to Bryce, 2 April 1889, *Ms. Bryce USA. 1*. Elsewhere Bryce wrote that the 105 State constitutions he studied provided a 'science of comparative politics' and a 'natural history of democratic communities' (*AC*, I, p. 434).

[29] *AC*, II, pp. 493, 488. *AC*, I, pp. 3 – 4.

[30] 'The Predictions of Hamilton and Tocqueville' reprinted in *Studies in History and Jurisprudence*, I, pp. 385, 388, 389. *AC*, II, pp. 487 – 93, 627 – 36, 115, 65 – 71, 73 – 80, 66 – 8.

America, but also suggested that 'democratic' evils were neither inevitable nor ineradicable; specific American evils could be remedied by applying specifically American antidotes. Explicitly he laid to rest the Tocquevillian spectre that haunted Europe — the tyranny of the majority, the atrophy of intellectual life — and, once and for all, implicitly undercut the assumption, held by Lecky and others, that British reform would unleash the worst excesses of American democracy-demagoguery, wire-pulling and corruption. Bryce could reject the facile inference that the Birmingham caucus would emulate the American spoils sytem, or that Joseph Chamberlain must inevitably emerge as the English equivalent of Silas P. Ratcliffe, the 'giant from Peoria' of Henry Adams' cynical novel *Democracy*.[31] Instead the American example might encourage rather then deter reform; England's cautious traditions and hierarchical structure could provide a safe and suitable medium in which the turbulence of democracy could be safely channelled.

Bryce's second criticism, closely connected with his first, was of Tocqueville's deductive method, his use of vast abstract generalisations like 'liberty', 'equality' and 'democracy', which were used to confirm a 'democratic spirit' which supposedly imbued American institutions. Bryce knew nothing of the 'democratic spirit'. Instead, in reaction, he dismissed such empty evocations as Platonic or scholastic and therefore unverifiable, and employed an inductive method, meticulously accumulating data before attempting any model building or mooting universally applicable laws. Consequently his book is a huge and comprehensive compendium of detailed information, a book which, in Lord Acton's phrase, was 'resolutely actual', and which concentrated on the minute and the factual, on 'the Boss and the Boom, the Hoodlum and the Mugwump'.[32] When he did generalise it was usually to explode the generalisations of *a priori* assumption:

It is not Democracy that has paid off a giant debt and raised Chicago out of a swamp. Neither is it Democracy that has denied her philosophers like Burke and poets like Words-worth. Most writers who have dealt with these matters have

---

[31] W. E. H. Lecky, *Democracy and Liberty*, I, p. 83. Bryce in *The Fortnightly Review*, Oct 1882, pp. 634 – 55.
[32] *History and Jurisprudence*, I, pp. 364 – 423. *The History of Freedom*, p. 577. *The Spectator* referred to Bryce's 'harassing impartiality' (22 Dec 1888, p. 1814).

not only laid more upon the shoulders of democratic government than it ought to bear, but have preferred abstract speculations to the humbler task of ascertaining and weighing the facts. They have spun ingenious theories about democracy as the source of this or that, or whatever it pleased them to assume; they have not tried to determine by a wide induction what specific results appear in countries which, differing in other respects, agree in being democratically governed. If I do not follow these time-honoured precedents, it is not because the process is dificult, but because it is unprofitable.[33]

'Let us then', Bryce concluded, 'bid farewell to fancy.' It is worth noting that this method reached down to the smallest detail; the poor paving of American streets, so frequently commented on by foreigners, was due not to democratic inertia, but specifically to greater winter frosts and the endless laying and relaying of pipes in rapidly expanding cities.[34]

Bryce's third criticism was that Tocqueville had used America for purposeful polemic, 'to learn what we have to fear or to hope from [democracy's] progress', and to prepare France for the peaceful acceptance of its inevitable advent. Engaged in a didactic exercise, thinking always of France when he wrote of America, Tocqueville disqualified himself as an objective observer: 'Being already prepossessed by certain abstract principles, facts do not fall on his mind like seeds on virgin soil. He is struck by those who accord with, he is apt to ignore those who diverge from, his preconceptions. 'His *Democracy in America* was 'suffused with strong, though carefully repressed, emotion', and, as such, was much as a work of edification and art as a scientific study.[35] Bryce hoped, in contrast, to claim a scrupulous detachment and examine the United States in a neutral spirit. So much so that he refrained from dealing with such topics as the tariff, civil service reform, the Black question and the struggle between capital and labour as bearing too closely on burning current issues. Even Acton's critical review had to concede a marked degree of impartiality: 'The two American presidents who agreed in saying that Whig and Tory belong to natural

[33]   *AC*, II, p. 629.
[34]   *AC*, II, p. 630. *AC*, I, pp. 623 – 4.
[35]   *AC*, I, pp. 3 – 4. *History and Jurisprudence*, I, pp. 385, 388, 389.

history proposed a dilemma which Mr. Bryce wishes to elude.'[36]

How successful was he in avoiding the Tocquevillian pitfalls he detected or, put another way, how scientific a work was *The American Commonwealth*? Probably only partial. Undoubtedly he did largely succeed in placing American democracy resolutely within its own context, but throughout there was a strong countercurrent, for as a disciple of Darwin, Freeman and Smith, the dynamics of environmental adaptation interacted with and were hampered by the static predeterminations of race; instead of seeing an American, he tends to search for an Anglo-American. Tocqueville could probe the complex underlying 'moeurs' which largely determined 'les lois' without having recourse to race as an explanation. All too often Bryce, the child of science, receded from profounder psychological and sociological insights to narrower ground. He could never have brought himself to write, as Tocqueville wrote so unequivocally to Gobineau, that: 'I do not believe that there are races destined to freedom and others to servitude.'[37] Again, he never entirely escaped the hold of reductionism, not least of all because he thought he had. Once more the kudos of science was to have its drawbacks; along with this belief in the absolute objectivity of the author/judge was his faith in the neutrality of facts; if the data were sifted dispassionately, truth would emerge unforced. His aim, quite simply, was 'to paint the institutions and people of America, as they are . . . to present simply the facts of the case, arranging and connecting them as best I can, but letting them speak for themselves'.[38] But facts by themselves do not 'speak'; only through 'arranging' and 'connecting' can they be given a voice. The selection of a fact and the linking of one to another implies a significant ordering and a conceptual framework; that is, the fact itself is neutral till made significant by its selection and linkage to another. *The American Commonwealth* displays far more artistry and far less cold scientism than Bryce

---

[36] *AC*, II, p. 409. *History of Freedom*, pp. 579–80. Bryce's yearning for the objectivity of pure science may be gauged from the following wistful reflections: 'hydrogen has neither friends nor enemies. No passion can distort the fairness or disturb the calmness of a student of the hydrocarbons' (*Quarterly Review*, July 1905, p. 179).

[37] The Tocqueville-Gobineau correspondence on race and determinism is brilliantly analysed in James T. Schleifer, *The Making of Tocqueville's 'Democracy in America'*, pp. 68–72.

[38] *AC*, I, p. 4.

ever acknowledged, and this truth was implicitly grasped by two perceptive reviewers: 'The facts, not the principles derivable from them, are prominent' (Woodrow Wilson); 'Facts, not comments, convey the lesson' (Acton).[39]

Bryce did not, could not, approach the United States with entire detachment. Just as Tocqueville tended at times to underestimate America's English roots and thus overrate American innovation, so Bryce tended to replace Tocqueville's Franco-American insights by his own Anglo-American preconceptions. He refers frequently to 'transatlantic politics' and 'transatlantic phenomena', and at one stage halts momentarily to answer a question which may be puzzling his reader: 'As generalisations like this are necessarily comparative, I may be asked with whom I am comparing the Americans . . . . Primarily I am comparing them with the English, because they are the nearest relative of the Americans.'[40]

For all this he was uniquely qualified as a dispassionate observer, not least because of the element of Gradgrind in his temperament. He was meticulous to the point of neurosis and an obsessive collector; there are memos to put double locks on his travel bags, neat piles of transport tickets in paper bags; a small pad remains recording the careful adjustment of a new watch down to seconds day by day, perhaps the same watch with which he recorded that it took precisely twenty-three minutes to read the American Constitution aloud. 'To Bryce', William James commented, 'all facts are born free and equal.' James intended this as criticism; Bryce would have taken it as a compliment. But both would have been wrong. Bryce would in later life almost shrink to an interrogation point and Harold Laski would warn of the dangerous virtue of his appalling omniscience, but happily, despite himself, *The American Commonwealth* pursues a purpose no less than *Democracy in America*, even if that purpose is submerged under the subterfuge of amassed detail.[41] Deprived of a synthesising framework a book of such length and diversity would have disintegrated. Instead, tightly constructed and conceptually controlled, Bryce ended by achieving insight through involvement rather than detachment.

[39] Wilson reprinted in Brooks, p. 180. *History of Freedom*, p. 575.
[40] *AC*, I, p. 593. *AC*, II, pp. 5, 681.
[41] *AC*, I, p. 363. James quoted in H. H. Asquith's *Memoirs and Reflections 1852 – 1927*, p. 165. *The Holmes-Pollock Letters*, I, p. 119, and *The Holmes-Laski Letters*, I, p. 304, both edited by Mark de Wolfe Howe.

Gladstone, Liberalism and Ireland

What prompted Bryce to write *The American Commonwealth*, and why in the 1880s? Admittedly he was extremely busy and preoccupied in the 1870s — establishing his reputation at Oxford, travelling on legal business and leisure, attempting to enter parliament — but certainly less so than in the following decade, for after 1880, as MP for the constituency of Tower Hamlets, he had to combine both political and academic careers. Yet during this, the most intensely active period of his life, he paid a second and third trip to America, in 1881 and 1883, and wrote his *magnum opus* between 1884 and 1888, completing it in the period following the fall of Gladstone's administration over home rule, between August 1886 and December 1888. He felt by 1883 that the vast amount of material he had collected 'must get somehow into print' and confidence in his ability to tackle such a huge subject increased with each visit and further reading, but his involvement in Gladstone's government (he was appointed Under-Secretary for Foreign Afairs) was an equally important motivating force in the publication of the book. For, just as he pursued dual careers at this period, so the book reflected personal and political as well as strictly academic concerns. To probe these motives further it is necessary to turn to Bryce's political concerns — towards his party and his party chief — because, however seemingly distant, the genesis of *The American Commonwealth* leads back through Ireland and the Liberal Party directly to Gladstone's decisive influence.

By the 1880s Bryce had concluded that Gladstone was the Liberal Party, and had swung into the orbit of that powerful personality; without him he wrote, 'the arch would fall in forthwith, the keystone withdraw: and we should have chaos'. The Midlothian campaign and the Eastern Question had carried Bryce into active politics. In 1877 he considered dedicating his *Transcaucasia and Ararat* to Gladstone in gratitude 'for what you have done in awakening our callous national conscience', but recognised that this travel book with its virulent anti-Turkish fulminations would be interpreted as a party tract and withdrew the suggestion.[42] Bryce became one of Gladstone's *protégés*; it was Gladstone who appointed him to his Regius Chair, sent a letter to the constituents of Tower Hamlets supporting Bryce's

---

[42] Bryce to Godkin, 9 March 1886, Godkin Papers. Bryce to Gladstone, 22 Sept 1877, Ms Bryce 11. R. T. Shannon, *Gladstone and the Bulgarian Agitation*, pp. 225 – 6, 257 – 9.

candidature, and his son Herbert to assist on the hustings. In return Bryce served his chief long and loyally — and mainly uncritically — in Irish, American and East European affairs.

Lord Rendel's jottings of Gladstone's latter-day conversation has the GOM recalling how he urged Bryce to spend another year in America and how he considered himself the chief inspirer of *The American Commonwealth*. This is confirmed in a letter dated 30 October 1888 where Bryce reminded Gladstone that his chief had initially suggested the book to him in January 1884 after his return from his third American trip, and Bryce's *German Notebook* records that he began writing the first pages in June 1884 at Maria Laach.[43] Gladstone had some considerable knowledge of American politics himself and since October 1862, when he had delivered his fateful Newcastle speech proclaiming that Jefferson Davis had created a new nation, found himself heavily implicated in the 'American Question'. After 1865 the *Alabama* claims bedevilled Anglo-American relations and kept the civil war and Britain's attitude towards it very much alive. The matter, Gladstone admitted, 'bristled with difficulties'; it seemed to challenge the Tichborne case in its bickering interminability.[44] The Johnson-Clarendon Arbitration Convention of 1869 failed disastrously in the Senate and gave Charles Sumner, Chairman of the Senate Foreign Relations Committee, the opportunity to claim Britain's general moral culpability during the war. He demanded 'indirect claims' not only for 'the vaster damage to commerce driven from the ocean [but] that other damage, immense and infinite, caused by the prolongation of the war, all of which may be called national in contradistinction to individual'.[45]

Gladstone was appalled by these trumped-up claims, dismissing them as quite indefensible on legal grounds but typical of an American disposition to remember her wounded sentiments in financial matters. As past-master of the balanced budget he was particularly incensed by this duplicity, but in dismissing Sumner's 'irrelevant trash' he failed to take account of the true feelings underlying these claims, however much some Americans might disapprove of putting a price tag on injured national

---

[43] *The Personal Papers of Lord Rendel*, p. 131. Bryce to Gladstone, Ms. Bryce 12. Ms. Bryce Misc.

[44] John Morley, *Life of Gladstone*, II, p. 313. Leslie Stephen in *NYN*, 6 June 1872, p. 370, and 10 Oct 1872, p. 233.

[45] James Ford Rhodes, *History of the United States, 1850 – 1905*, II, p. 449.

pride.[46] For even New England, the Anglophile centre, had been offended by English indifference to the war. 'It is difficult', Godkin wrote, 'to give anyone who was not in personal contact with the American public between 1862 and 1870 an idea of how very much deeper than pecuniary "damages" the *Alabama* question went.' Goldwin Smith, resident in America during this period, observed beneath the Americans' habitual geniality 'something which is not good nature, and of which England is the standing and traditional object'. Bryce noted this undercurrent for himself and the reticence of Oliver Wendell Holmes Jr, Thomas Wentworth Higginson and James Russell Lowell when the topic was broached in 1870.[47] Clearly Anglo-American friendship was impossible so long as this issue remained unsettled.

Gladstone was, of course, fully attuned to the wider international ramifications of the *Alabama* question, but also for deeper, very personal, reasons the issue had to be faced and decisively dealt with. At Geneva in 1871 the American delegation brought forward the *Case of the United States* with chapter 1 headed 'Unfriendliness of Great Britain', which commenced: 'Her Majesty's Government was actuated at that time by a conscious unfriendly purpose towards the United States.' More specifically, pages 87 to 100 were devoted to proving 'the unfriendly feelings of members of the British cabinet and Parliament'; now Gladstone happened to be the sole remaining member of that cabinet in office and Prime Minister of a country charged with 'insincere neutrality' and of pursuing 'tortuous courses' against the United States.[48] In a letter to Schenck, the American minister in London, he collected a mass of contemporary evidence to rebut this embarrassing and damaging charge, arguing that passages in the *Case* were taken from debates in which he had argued against a motion favouring recognition of the South; that not only did he not wish the Union harm or predict its inevitable collapse, but, like many pro-Northern radicals of the time, argued against war only from motives of 'sheer humanity and hatred of the effusion of blood'. This letter helped to undercut

[46] Agatha Ramm (ed.), *The Political Correspondence of Mr. Gladstone and Lord Granville*, I, pp. 185, 299.
[47] Godkin in *NYN*, 29 Aug 1872, p. 133. Smith to Bryce, 29 Oct 1870, Ms. Bryce 16. *1870 Journal*, 2 Sept. Bryce noted on 21 Sept the passing of a motion by an Irishman, Richard O'Gorman, attacking Britain over the *Alabama* question at the State Democratic Convention at Rochester (Ms. Bryce Misc.).
[48] Rhodes, II, pp. 475–6. *The Gladstone Diaries*, VIII, pp. 183–4.

America's spurious justification for extending damages but was also published as a public expiation of a personal residue of guilt, atonement for the 'gross blunder' of his Newcastle speech when retrospectively the victory of the 'commanding moral influence of the North' and the destruction of the 'hideous solecism' of slavery appeared providentally ordained. 'It seemed clear', he wrote to Lord Granville, 'that I should send a letter . . . if it materially betters the position which I hold in the American *Case* for that position is a very bad one indeed'.[49]

Even under the pressure of intense historical research Gladstone's moral and political complexity has not yielded up all its secrets: the simplicities of J. L. Hammond's idealistic crusader have tended merely to evoke a counter-image of consummate party tactician. Yet the two images are not mutually exclusive for, as Dicey gnomically remarked, the trouble with Gladstone was that he refused to be Gladstonian. Even Bryce was baffled by his chief's 'singularly complex nature whose thread it was hard to unravel. His individuality was extremely strong . . . .. Yet it was an individuality so far from being self-consistent as sometimes to seem a bundle of opposite qualities capriciously united in a single person.' But if we concede this essential complexity and response at a multiplicity of levels it is possible to agree with H. C. G. Matthew, the editor of Gladstone's *Diaries*, that politics and principle, strategy and crusade, were to him inseparable. Recognising this, recent historians have attempted to integrate the disparate elements in Gladstone's character, to appreciate the uniting of political and moral motives — what Boyd Hilton has called his 'Theological Politics' — rather than to divide and dissect. In this light Gladstone's response to the United States can be seen as displaying elements of political 'game', the 'high art' of statesmanship, and aspects of his peculiar Christian vision.[50]

The effect of the Geneva settlement on Anglo-American relations was incalculable, and Gladstone judged the fine 'dust

---

[49] *North American Review*, Sept/Oct 1878, pp. 183 – 4. *Gladstone Diaries*, VIII, pp. 243 – 50. Ramm, I, pp. 193, 313. Gladstone's *Autobiography* (ed. by John Brooke and Mary Sorensen), pp. 134 – 5, 250.

[50] Dicey in NYN, 27 May 1886, p. 444. *Studies in Contemporary Biography*, pp. 400 – 1. *Gladstone Diaries*, VII, p. xxxv. 'Gladstone's theological politics' in *High and Low Politics in Modern Britain* (ed. by Michael Bentley and John Stevenson), pp. 28 – 57. More unguardedly, when a drunken Colonel he met in Nubia suggested that Gladstone was mad, Bryce added 'of course he's mad' (Fisher, I, p. 249).

in the balance compared with the moral value of the example set when these two great nations . . . went in peace and concord before a judicial tribunal rather than resort to the arbitrament of the sword'. Bryce, reporting home from America in 1881, confirmed a significant improvement in relations.[51] Seizing upon this advantage, Gladstone cast wide his net in an attempt to draw America into his all-embracing Midlothian constituency and enlist American reformers into the ranks of the Liberal Party. He evoked 'the European investment of transatlantic experience' and hoped to bridge the English-speaking world — a phrase he coined — because he considered the British parliament as 'a universal church in politics'. He summoned up American support for his home rule policy and posed as first American politician because he considered the Anglo-American liberal community as the political arm of a religious ecumenicalism which aimed to heal the schism in western Christianity. In foreign policy he pursued peaceful universalism through arbitration and here the Anglo-American community had set new standards. Admittedly this English-speaking church adhered to differing national dogmas — America was egalitarian and republican, British inegalitarian and monarchical — but the church was ultimately held together by a union of ethics rather than of blood, by the rational politics of persuasion and popular government rather than by force and absolutism.[52] This ethical bond, because advanced and non-coercive, allowed for a greater degree of diversity and spontaneity among its members. The ascendancy of the English-speaking race, though providential:

> ought to be a natural, orderly growth, requiring only that you should be reasonably true and loyal to your traditions: and we to ours . . .. The substance of the relationship lies, not in despatches from Downing Street, but in the mutual affection, and the moral and social sympathies, which can only flourish

---

51   Morley, II, p. 300. Bryce, 'United States Public Opinion on the Irish Question', 31 Oct 1881, Ms. Bryce 11.
52   *North American Review*, Sept/Oct 1878, pp. 180 – 212. Robert Kelley, *The Transatlantic Persuasion*, pp. 205 – 34. 'It sounds extravagant' Godkin wrote to Bryce, 'but I really believe that nothing has as much hold as Gladstone on the American nation today' (17 Oct 1887, Ms. Bryce USA 5).

between adult communities when they are on both sides free.[53]

Behind these generalised pronouncements lay more practical considerations. The late Chancellor of the Exchequer was deeply impressed by America's burgeoning economic strength, its resilient self-reliance and its rapid disposal of the National Debt. He looked to a vital partner in free trade and, having read Barham Zincke's *The Plough and the Dollar*, published in 1883, as a field for Britain's surplus population. Strategically he spoke of Britain's diminishing strength as she augmented her empire, the growing excess of imperial responsibility, and hinted at a future shared distribution of the international burden. Totting up the figures he reckoned that by the 1980s there would be 1,000 million English-speaking citizens inhabiting the globe, and wrote articles preparing America's youth for their providential future, and requiring them to brace themselves for their 'colossal' and 'superhuman' destiny.[54] Pre-eminently the United States remained relevant while Ireland dominated the Gladstonian agenda. At the very least an amelioration in Anglo-American relations would alleviate the Irish question by hampering the Democratic Party's traditional pulling of the lion's tail, and cut off vital supplies of men and money and moral support to the Fenian cause — nine-tenths of the Land League's financial support came from America. Past British oppression had dangerously combined emigration and resentment and established in the United States and elsewhere 'centres of adverse foreign opinion'. In his campaign to win over American public opinion he hoped to bring 'that paramount authority, the general judgement of civilised mankind' to bear on the vexed question and legitimise his Irish initiative. Hammond misplaces his emphasis when he suggests that home rule was a form of atonement and reparation for the wrongs Gladstone committed against the federal cause during the civil war, but Ireland and the Irish in America were linked together in a joint policy of pacification'[55]

---

[53] Francis H. Herrick, *The Journal of British Studies*, Nov 1972, p. 154. Gladstone in *The Nineteenth Century*, Sept 1878, p. 572.
[54] *North American Review*, Sept/Oct 1878, pp. 180 – 8, 190. *The Nineteenth Century*, Sept 1878, p. 558. *Youth's Companion*, November 1888.
[55] *Gladstone Diaries*, VII, p. xl. J. L. Hammond, *Gladstone and the Irish Nation*, p. 738.

The historians of high politics have traced the party priorities which conjured up the 'Irish Question' and enabled the party leaders, Salisbury and Gladstone, to quell a nascent centralist coalition, and Hamer has emphasised the unifying and con- servative aims underlying the Liberals' Irish obsession. All of this is true as far as it goes, but it does not go far enough, for it is difficult to study the home rule crisis and not appreciate that substantive principles, and not simply party and personal power, were at stake. If the 'moral entrepreneurs' (the phrase is Cooke's and Vincent's) had a field day it was because the Irish Question entered into the very fibre of English political self- definition.[56] The home rule debates marked the climax of a mandarin liberal ideology — the 'English ideology', as George Watson miscalls it — in which Lord Acton was high priest, Gladstone its prime implementer, Bryce an auxiliary, and Ireland the chosen testing ground, and in this debate it was essential to be right as well as expedient, even to the point of glorying in the achievement of failure as the measure of undeviating rectitude.[57] That ideology, put simply, was the subject of Acton's 'Madonna of the Future', the unwritten *History of Freedom*, the providential enlargment of the sphere of individual liberty, of the reign of conscience over power. In political terms this was translated into pluralism, as against the growing coercive omnipotence of the monolithic state. Acton first conceived of the dangers of centralised despotism during the American civil war, and his essays on that conflict and the contemporaneous 'Nationality' first brought him to Gladstone's attention. 'I have read your valuable and remarkable paper', Gladstone wrote. 'Its principles of politics I embrace: its research and wealth of knowledge I admire: and its whole atmosphere . . . is what I desire to breathe.'[58] Acton continued to insist that 'the process of civilisation depends on transcend- ing Nationality', that 'the nations aim at power, and the world at freedom', but, along with Gladstone, he now conceded that democracy was a prerequisite for personal liberty so that the republic came to offer the key to an outstanding political

---

[56] D. A. Hamer, *The Historical Journal*, 1969 No. 3, pp. 511–32. A. B. Cooke and J. R. Vincent, *The Governing Passion*, p. 52. For an analysis of intellectuals and the home rule crisis similar to my own see Tom Dunne in *Irish Historical Studies*, Nov 1982, pp. 135–73.

[57] George Watson, *The English Ideology*, pp. 10-67. Acton was the greatest advocate of measuring ideological success in Ireland in terms of political failure. See *Letters of Lord Acton to Mary Drew*, pp. lxiv, 181.

[58] *Selections from the Correspondence of Lord Acton*, p. 158.

dilemma. An America which in the 1860s illustrated the disease of democratic despotism might now, in the 1880s, supply its antidote. 'Liberty', Acton wrote in 1884, 'depends on the division of power. Democracy tends to unity of power. In the view of increasing democracy, a restricted federalism is the only possible check upon concentration and centralism.'[59] After the passing of the third Reform Bill, that 'advent to power of principle, the commencement of disinterested policy', the influx of Irish nationalist MPs into parliament and the growing demand for national self-determination pointed inevitably to home rule. As Acton put it: 'To admit the American principle was to revolutionise Ireland'; that is, the response to democratic self-determination was continued unity through federation.[60]

Thus as 'patentees of the modern world' America became implicated in the Irish struggle, and 'Americomania', as Dicey termed it, swept through and divided the ranks of Britain's intelligentsia in the 1880s. The Unionists, including Salisbury, Dicey, Maine, Fitzjames Stephen, Lecky and Froude, were eager to borrow certain aspects of America's rigid constitution, her theoretically powerful executive and a second chamber reinforced along senatorial lines in order to stem the tide of popular democracy, but unequivocally rejected her concomitant federalism. Dicey, an archetypal Unionist, argued for the indivisibility of sovereignty and the rule of law. Parliament and courts, as joint inheritors of a common law tradition, upheld the conjunction of power and law, of the rule of law sustained by the power of parliamentary sovereignty; sovereignty, union and empire were the indivisible power base on which Britain's mission of spreading the rule of law to Ireland and to the rest of the world depended, and federalism, 'as the dissolution of the United Kingdom is absolutely foreign to the historical and . . . instinctive policy of English constitutionalists'.[61] The Unionist

---

[59] Gertrude Himmelfarb, *Lord Acton*, p. 183. *Acton-Drew Letters*, p. 98.

[60] Himmelfarb, p. 175. George Watson, *Politics and Literature*, p. 65. Acton spelt this out in a letter to Gladstone in 1888: 'It is precisely because Democracy can put up with no effective checks on the concentration and abuse of power, excepting the local division of Federalism, that Home Rule became the normal consequence of the last Reform Act' (*Correspondence*, p. 90).

[61] Dicey, *Edinburgh Review*, Jan 1890, p. 120. Dicey entitled an *NYN* article 'Americomania in English Politics', 21 Jan 1886, pp. 52 – 3. *LC* (8th edn.), pp. xc, xci. For a fuller discussion of the Unionist case see Hugh Tulloch, *The Irish Jurist*, Summer 1980, pp. 137 – 65.

case was grounded on undivided power and drew strength from an authoritarian vision; it required the sterner rule of a 'new imperialism', an unquestioning belief in 'the total depravity of the discontented' Irish and a policy of sustained coercion towards them. If, as Salisbury insisted, the Irishman possessed the instincts of a Hottentot, then it followed that Ireland needed a Cromwellian approach.[62]

Acton, Bryce, Gladstone and Morley sought, in contrast, to test liberalism by partially divesting themselves of authority, by widening the sphere of independence and responsibility, and were thus drawn to federation, both of the United Kingdom and of the empire, as a means of reconciling localism and unity, diversity and power, as against an overpowering centralism. Because the principle of educative self-government was deemed to have worked in 1867 and again in 1885, the federalists hoped to dissolve the problem of Ireland by advocating, as Bryce put it, 'a policy of faith; not, indeed, of thoughtless optimism, but of faith, according to the definition which calls it "the substance of things hoped for, the evidence of things not seen" '.[63]

Bryce was himself a reluctant home ruler and his conversion slow and ambivalent. He was aware of the intricate constitutional complications and, given his Ulster connections, of the 'fiery language' of the Orange lodges. He was initially critical of Gladstone's strategy, of his rapid changes and secret disclosures, his lack of balance on all matters touching on Ireland and his failure to prepare English public opinion. Nevertheless he sensed in what direction Gladstone was leading the party and his reasons for doing so: 'I began to perceive a change in Mr. Gladstone's views', he wrote around 1883; 'he disliked coercion in principle. His love of liberty was repelled by it. It seemed to him to lead nowhere, and he was beginning to look out for some path that would led out of this interminable morass.' Herbert Gladstone reported Bryce perplexed but loyal in December 1885; on 7 April 1886 Sidgwick reported a conversation he had with Bryce at the Athenaeum, where Bryce insisted that: 'Democracy will not coerce, and therefore we must come to [Home Rule] in the end; so we had better take it at once quietly.' By 1887 Acton

---

[62] 'It is curious', wrote Lecky in 1883, 'how Irish affairs turn us all into tories' (*Irish Historical Studies*, Nov 1982, p. 151).

[63] Bryce's Introduction to *Two Centuries of Irish History*, p. xxii and *The Handbook of Home Rule*, p. 242.

was commending Bryce for his exemplary courage and support for the PM.[64]

The risks were great but loyalty to his chief and his hopes for a unified and moderate Liberal Party sustained him. British and American opinion had to be educated on the Irish Question and Bryce was to be its teacher. In a confidential memorandum of 11 December 1885 he touched on the value of a study of the United States' Constitution 'for giving effect to federal authority' and began collecting and analysing historical material. Acting as Gladstone's American arm he had assessed opinion there in memoranda of 1881 and 1883 which showed substantial public support for home rule and opposition to Fenian extremism. Gladstone drew up a plan for this 'great subject' of education and Bryce sounded out contributors, including Godkin, for American parallels: 'Gladstone is eager for a literary campaign to convince the people through books and newspapers . . . . I was deputed to ask you.'[65] In 1887 a *Handbook of Home Rule* appeared and in 1888 *Two Centuries of Irish History*, edited by and with contributions from Bryce.

But his greatest contribution to the cause was his *American Commonwealth*. In 'Kin Beyond the Sea' Gladstone admitted he had a 'faint and superficial understanding' of the United States and urged a more careful study to dispel 'the frivolous and offensive criticisms which were once in vogue among us':

For the political student all over the world it will be beyond anything curious as well as useful to examine with what diversities, as well as what resemblances, of apparatus the two great branches of a race born to command have been minded, or induced, or constrained, to work out, in their sea-

---

[64] Bryce was not unaware of 'Ulsteria' as John Wilson (*Campbell-Bannerman*, p. 107) and Cooke and Vincent (*The Governing Passion*, pp. 149 – 50, 156 – 7) have suggested. See Bryce's 'Alternative Policies in Ireland' (*The Nineteenth Century*, Feb 1886, pp. 16 – 17), and his 'Memo to Gladstone on the Irish Question', 11 Dec 1885. He visited Ulster in 1885 to put the home rule case and used what influence he had to bring Ulster to the notice of Gladstone and Spencer (Bryce to his uncle, William Bryce, 17 May 1886, Ms. Bryce 82. Herbert Gladstone, *After Twenty Years*, p. 311. *Correspondence of Lord Acton*, p. 266).

[65] Gladstone Add. Ms. 44770. Bryce to Godkin, 1 Aug 1886, Godkin Papers. Bryce's 'Memo of Oct 1881' emphasized that the majority of Americans supported some degree of home rule and were opposed to Fenian extremism (Ms. Bryce Misc.).

severed seats, their political destinies, according to their respective laws.[66]

By the 1880s the need for this study had taken on greater urgency and relevance. It is not an exaggeration to suggest that the writing of this decade was saturated in the Irish problem, theoretical speculation and current controversy becoming inextricably mixed. Lecky, for example, could launch a vituperative fifty-page attack on Gladstone's Irish revolution in a new edition of his *Democracy and Liberty* while at the same time undermining Froude's Cromwellian solution to Irish ills by advocating his own panacea of gentry paternalism — all of this through the medium of an ostensibly objective historical study of eighteenth century Ireland. Again, Maine might assume an air of academic detachment in his *Popular Government*, but anonymously in the pages of the *Pall Mall Gazette* his fierce anti-Gladstonian partisanship was all too clearly evident; even Dicey admitted a marked lack of intellectual disinterestedness in the matter.[67] *The American Commonwealth* has to be seen in this context and against a background of heightened controversy. Bryce was himself heavily engaged in rifling history for confirmatory material to back the federal cause, as can be gauged in a letter he wrote to Acton in April 1886: 'Croatia and Hungary don't get on at all — their case seems nearest to my scheme, so that is unlucky.' Regarded in this light the book can be interpreted as a definitive three-volume analysis of successful federalism and a decisive refutation of Diceyan unionism. Lord Courtney, reading a manuscript chapter on the relations of the federal government to the western territories, wrote in the margin: 'In reading this paragraph Ireland seems everywhere underwritten' — and Bryce in a private and unguarded note added in the margin: 'Why not? It is true. No need to modify.'[68] This single piece of marginalia is not intended to convict Bryce of enlisting America in an apologia for home rule, but merely to insist that he, no less than his reader, moved in a political atmosphere obsessed with the Irish Question, and that the

[66] *North American Review*, Sept/Oct 1878, pp. 186, 181–2.
[67] *Democracy and Liberty* (1898 ed.), pp. v–lvi. On Maine cf. George Feaver, *From Status to Contract*, pp. 211–50, and *Journal of Politics*, May 1965, pp. 290–317. Dicey, *NYN*, 18 Jan 1883, p. 54.
[68] Bryce to Acton, 30 April 1886, Acton Papers. Papers marked 'L. H. Courtney Suggestions, Criticisms', Ms. Bryce Misc.

example of the United States held peculiar relevance to this debate.

Glastone had suggested the subject of America to Bryce, and Bryce had agreed to write. Undoubtedly Gladstone exaggerated his initiating role; just such a book had been gestating in Bryce's mind for a long time. But the Prime Minister could justly claim to be the vital catalyst in that he not only encouraged its author to pay serious academic attention to the United States and to comparative studies, but also inspired a tribute to the greater cause of liberalism and the Anglo-American friendship which Gladstone had forged. Certainly Gladstone read the book in such terms when he received a copy. 'It is', he wrote to the author, 'an event in the history of the United States, and perhaps in the relations of the two countries.'[69]

Sources of material

Bryce justified a new study of the United States on three grounds: that an up-to-date account of contemporary developments was lacking, that previous writers had neglected the practical, informal workings of the political system and that, above all, what was urgently needed was a comprehensive and wide-ranging factual approach as a preliminary to fuller understanding. Despite making it clear that he intended to avoid matters of current controversy and strictly social observation, each of his aims required a fresh and acute probing behind the formal constitutional façade; that it was not sufficient to analyse the Federal Constitution or to sift through the one hundred and five largely neglected State constitutions, past and present, but go further and investigate motives and aspirations, those social, political and economic currents which underlay each article in order to grasp 'the natural history of democratic communities'.[70] More especially in his later chapters he was forced to rely on less conventional sources. 'Hitherto we have been on comparatively firm ground . . . But now we come to phenomena for a knowledge of which one must trust to a variety of flying and floating sources, to newspaper paragraphs, to the conversation of American acquaintances, to impressions formed on the spot from seeing incidents and hearing stories

[69] Gladstone to Bryce, 3 Oct 1889, Ms. Bryce 10.
[70] AC, I, pp. 434, 399.

and anecdotes.'[71] During three trips to the United States — in 1870, 1881 and 1883 — often hurriedly fitted in to parliamentary recesses and amounting to no more than nine months in all, he embarked on a formidable and concentrated information-gathering exercise which relied on printed materials, contacts with many friends and personal experience.

Bryce was an omnivorous reader of all things American: state constitutions, published government commissions, statistical compilations, party slip tickets, campaign literature, newspapers, advertisements, political memoirs such as Blaine's *Twenty Years in Congress*, reformist tracts, satirical descriptions of city politics such as *Solid For Mulhooly*, even mediocre studies by his fellow countrymen.[72] Along with this range of reading went a tenacity in hunting down useful, often esoteric, material. A careful perusal of cheap biblical literature and its advertisements was used in a chapter on 'The Influence of Religion' to show that Christian fundamentalism moulded the American imagination far more than the European. State constitutions were crucial to his work but they were difficult to get hold of and frequently out of date. Roosevelt helped out in New York but could find no state digest or analytical study. Theodore Dwight, librarian at the State Department, after a careful search admitted that there was a marked paucity of materials.[73] So Bryce was forced back on Stimson's *American Statute Law* and *The American Cyclopaedia of Political Science* — a very patchy compilation. McPherson's *Handbook* and Hitchcock's *Study of American States* appeared in 1884 and 1887 respectively and filled some gaps, but four new states (the Dakotas, Montana and Washington) had been admitted since their publication, along with thirty-eight amendments to existing State constitutions. He worked through Poore's *Federal and State Constitution*, cataloguing and codifying as he went, but even this standard work was perpetually

---

[71] *AC*, II, pp. 3 – 4. It was the dissection of the amorphous party system which constituted, in Woodrow Wilson's judgement, 'the crowning achievement of the author's method' and which, Ostrogorski wrote, was 'the first methodical description of the existing party system, which was a revelation, not only to readers in the Old World but to the Americans themselves' (Brooks, p. 176. Preface to *Democracy and the Organisation of Political Parties*, I, pp. liv – lv).

[72] Bryce reprinted a variety of 'slip tickets' at the end of ch. LXVI (*AC*, II, pp. 143 – 8). The use of similar phrases suggests that Bryce read Griffin's *Great Republic*. Compare, e.g., *AC*, II, p. 388, and Griffin, p. 9.

[73] Roosevelt to Bryce, 17 July 1887, Ms. Bryce Misc. Dwight to Bryce, 18 Oct 1889, Ms. Bryce USA 24.

superseded by events and he wrote urging annual or biennial supplements for 'at present it is very difficult, especially for a resident in Europe, to ascertain exactly how the constitution of each state stands'. His pleas were unsuccessful for he was writing to Roosevelt in 1891 to use his influence with Lodge on the matter of supplements and exerting what direct pressure he could on Speaker Henderson and Congressman William Wilson to the same end.[74]

He had similar problems when trying to procure vital statistical information, but again triumphed over the limitations of his sources, as his chapters on race and *laissez-faire* show. In both he pioneered statistical method, though in both cases he used the figures for an ulterior purpose. In the case of population trends he aimed to scotch the racial myth of Black fecundity and allay White fears. Aware of the Census underestimate of the Black population relative to White in 1870, he was at pains to keep the 1880 Black figure of 13.1 per cent in perspective by revising the distorted 1870 figures upwards and emphasising the first census return of 1790 which put the Black percentage at a high 19.3 per cent. This enabled him to conclude that the 1880 figure 'did not constitute a present source of danger'.[75] He was able to confirm this relative decline when he recorded the falling ratio of 11.6 per cent in 1900 and 10.7 per cent in 1910. He looked to Black education as the major solvent of racial prejudice and because of this bombarded A. F. Childs, Superintendent of the Census, and W. Harris, Commissioner of the Bureau of Education, with requests to break down literacy skills along colour lines.[76] But for his earlier editions he had only state returns to go on, and those of 1880 revealed appallingly high illiteracy figures in the South: South Carolina's for example, was 48.2 per cent, Louisiana's 45.8 per cent, as against the average over-ten figure of 13.4 per cent. The 1900 returns showed a welcome decline in the illiteracy figures of these two

---

74 *AC*, I, p. 420 n. 1. Bryce to Roosevelt, 12 Dec 1891, Roosevelt Papers. Henderson to Bryce, 12 Jan 1902, Ms. Bryce USA 14. Wilson to Bryce, 11 Jan 1892, Ms. Bryce USA 21. Bryce, in 1905, lamented the fact that the last, full collection of State constitutions had appeared twenty years ago (*Quarterly Review*, July 1905, p. 173).

75 *AC*, II, p. 724, and n. 1. *AC*, 1910, II, p. 933, n. 1. *The Statistical History of the United States* confirms the underestimation of the 1870 returns, which put the total Southern Black population at only 5.39 m. as against 34.35 m. White (p. 14).

76 Childs to Bryce, 19 May 1891, Ms. Bryce USA 4. Harris to Bryce, 23 Jan 1893. Ms. Bryce Misc.

states to 25.7 and 29 per cent respectively, but not until 1910, and partly at Bryce's instigation, were the disguised state figures broken down into White and Black to pinpoint racial discrimination in Southern education, when the figures laid bare a ratio of 6:1 (or 30.4:5 per cent) in the White's favour. Bryce firmly believed that, having elicited such irrefutable data, understanding and appreciation of the problem would begin to promote a remedy.[77]

His most daring and successful use of quantification appeared as a large appendix of seven tables and eleven pages attached to a general discussion of 'Laissez-Faire' where he effectively exploded another myth, held by most English thinkers and a good many Americans, that the United States, unlike Great Britain, was decisively non-interventionist. A detailed analysis of British, Federal and state laws with reference to public health, professional qualifications, regulation of alcohol, inspection of company accounts, railways, shipping and industry revealed little federal control beyond the Interstate Commerce Act of 1887, but considerable state regulation, in some cases far greater than in Britain, particularly in the field of voluntary arbitration (Massachusetts and New York State) and the restriction of working hours for men (Pennsylvania, Illinois, New York State and California).[78] He was helped in the preparation of these tables by Alfred Marshall, A. B. Houghton of Harvard and F. C. Montague, a fellow of his own Oxford college, but the use to which this marshalling of evidence was put was entirely his own.

As a visitor Bryce's credentials were impeccable; a colleague and friend of Gladstone and Bright and a sympathetic observer, he gained an immediate *entrée* to America's intellectual and professional classes. Leslie Stephen's introduction to the New York editor, E. L. Godkin, was invaluable, for he stood at the very centre of liberal America. Through him friends and assistance spread and fanned out through an intricate system of contacts across the union. Godkin's literary editor, Wendell Phillips Garrison, and his deputy editors, Edward Clark and Bucklin Bishop, placed their wide knowledge and experience at Bryce's disposal, reading large sections of the manuscript and

[77] *AC*, I, p. 589, n. 2, and *AC*, 1910, I, p. 624, n. 3.
[78] *AC*, II, p. 425. For tables, see *AC*, II, pp. 426–36. Cf. Appendix 2 for specimen copy of tables.

offering suggestions and amendments for the second edition.[79] When Bryce was looking for a competent contributor to write on female suffrage, it was Godkin who carried out the search, first sounding out James Thayer of Harvard (too busy), Colonel Higginson (too partisan), Bishop of the *New York Evening Post* (too much of a *Nation* man), and Woodrow Wilson (who could only imagine he was asked because he was then lecturing at a women's college, Bryn Mawr).[80] When Bryce finally decided to write the chapter himself President Eliot of Harvard, his closest American friend, placed a large number of strategically situated Harvard graduates at his disposal, while Andrew Dickson White, President of Cornell, was collared in Oxford in 1885 and likewise charged to assist in the enterprise.[81] When Bryce was stuck in a paragraph on the executive assumption of extra-legal powers in times of crisis it was to White he wrote asking for the provenance of Lincoln's civil war remark that he would willingly violate the Constitution to preserve the union. White wrote in turn to the eminent legalist Judge Thomas Cooley, whom he knew from his University of Michigan days, asking for clarification on Bryce's behalf, for 'he is one of the best men alive. Warmly American in sympathy, one of Gladstone's devoted supporters — and a "rising man" by virtue of his qualities of head and heart'.[82] While Bryce wrote directly to John Hay, Lincoln's biographer, Cooley consulted Robert Todd Lincoln, the president's eldest son in Chicago, and both independently threw doubt on the authenticity of the anecdote. While Bryce concluded in his text that Lincoln had assumed extra-legal powers based on his powers as Commander-in-Chief in time of war, two long footnotes suggest that he remained

---

[79] *1870 Journal*, p. 1. Bryce-Garrison Correspondence (Ms. Bryce USA 4); Bryce-Bishop Correspondence (Ms. Bryce USA 11); Bryce-Clark Correspondence (Ms. Bryce USA 12).

[80] Bryce to Godkin, 25 Feb 1886, Godkin Papers. Wilson to Bryce, 6 March 1888, Ms. Bryce USA 20. *Papers of Woodrow Wilson* (ed. by Arthur Link), V, pp. 707 – 8, VI, p. 31.

[81] Bryce to Eliot, 21 January 1892, Ms. Bryce USA 2. Albert Shaw to Bryce, 27 November 1885, Ms. Bryce USA 18. White to Bryce (n.d.), Ms. Bryce USA 25. Bryce thanked twenty-three Americans specifically in his Preface and by 1910 he had added twenty-three more. Cf. Appendix 1 which is not, admittedly, comprehensive.

[82] White quoted in Everett S. Brown, *Michigan Law Review*, January 1933, p. 347. Brown documents fifty minor modifications Bryce made in the light of Cooley's criticism. As Bryce wrote to Cooley: 'So far from disliking free criticism, I value it far more if it speaks without reserve' (pp. 350, 352).

uncertain about the issue.[83] What does emerge clearly, however, is his determined pursuit of elusive details and the invaluable assistance of friends in hunting the quarry. 'If I have . . . understood American better than most Englishmen', he wrote to Holmes, 'it is because I have friends who have admitted me to a knowledge of all that is best in America, and made me live it through them.'[84]

But he preferred field studies most of all; to see for himself and trust to his own impressions rather than gather it from books or from friends second-hand. When the historian Henry Lea suggested that he had exaggerated the corruption of the Gas Ring in his native Philadelphia, Bruce was able to reply that his chapter was grounded on personal observation in 1881 rather than gleaned from a book which Lea had recommended on the subject. Contingency played its part and contributed to his wide experience. On board the Atlantic steamer in 1870 he met McQuaid, the Catholic Bishop of Rochester, returning from the Vatican Council, who invited him to stay and observe the New York State Democratic Convention planned for September in his home town. Through conversations with John Brooks and John Murray Forbes in Boston and the writings of Arthur Sedgwick in the *New York Nation* and Henry and Charles Francis Adams Jr in the *North American Review*, he was already made aware of the Erie scandal and Tammany's complicity.[85] But in Rochester he was able to witness Boss Tweed in action — 'a fat, largish man, with an air of self-satisfied good humour and a great deal of shrewd knavery in eye and mouth'. He sat back while the

83 Hay to Bryce [1887?], Ms. Bryce USA 14. Bryce to Hay, 3 June 1887, Ms. Bryce 106. Brown, pp. 350 – 1. *AC*, I, pp. 289, n. 1, 373, n. 1 and n. 2, 388, n. 1.
84 Bryce to Holmes, 18 November 1912, Holmes Papers. On Bryce's fourth visit to America in 1890, Eliot prepared the way for an excursion to Chicago with introductory letters to four citizens. Two of these letters survive, indicating that Bryce was unable to avail himself of the introductions. One of them to a Mr Salter, helps to explain the readiness of Bryce's friends to co-operate. 'I thought you might show him', Eliot wrote, 'some aspects of the life of Chicago which without guidance even his acuteness might miss. There is no aspect of social life in America which does not interest him' (Eliot to Bryce, 23 September 1890, Ms. Bryce USA 1).
85 Bryce to Lea, 10 December 1887, Ms. Bryce USA 2. *1870 Journal*, pp. 74, 25, 26, 35. Arthur G. Sedgwick of the *NYN* drew Bryce's attention to the Adams' articles. Nothing was left unused. During a tour around McQuaid's cathedral the bishop admitted that only paid ticket-holders were admitted to high Sunday mass. This passing detail resurfaced in a discussion of the worldliness of American religion in *AC*, II, p. 592.

disparate interests of the German, Irish and working class were smoothly absorbed into the platform while vital issues like tariffs were only gingerly touched upon, and innocuous and temporising measures were passed with the invocation of Jefferson, Jackson and divine providence. He was fascinated and mesmerised for he had now found his motif and grasped at once the 'subterranean forces' guiding the surface of events. Meanwhile convention business was swiftly and formally despatched:

> This is said to be the effect of the good wire-pulling of the morning; the quietness of the speeches to be because 'tis felt to be an occasion of business, not declamation . . .. The whole thing helps one to realise more vividly the working of their system, and especially the extreme party solidarity: party feeling is the strongest sentiment these men have.[86]

Weeks later, steaming down the Mississippi, he fell into the company of a Welsh farmer, who expressed contempt for all politicians and considered the party system useful only in so far as it neutralised rapacity. Another passenger, the editor of *The Soldier's Record*, proved non-partisan for quite another reason. His paper was dedicated to furthering the cause of veterans' pensions and their rights to office, and by keeping it independent he could exact higher bids from both parties. Such chance encounters and many like them were recorded and eventually found their way into his book.[87] A more bumpy and relevant introduction to American public life could hardly be imagined: a fixed party convention, a disenchanted independent and a shrewd lobbyist and deliverer of bloc votes all illuminating the tangled and pervasive pull of party. Here in microcosm, stored to resurface again much later, were all the various strands and preoccupations which were to come together and aid him in the formulation of those vital questions which shaped his work — the causes of entrenched corruption and of a pervasive public submission.

One example — of the character and politics of the west — shows especially Bryce's ingenuity and resourcefulness in

---

[86] *1870 Journal*, pp. 78, 79, 164. AC, II, p. 100. The *1870 Journal* has been published in *The New England Quarterly*, June 1977, ed. by Allan B. and Barbara F. Lefcowitz, pp. 314 – 31.
[87] *1870 Journal*, p. 53.

facing and surmounting the limitations imposed by a paucity of material as his sources became scarcest beyond the Mississippi. By chance Charles Eliot's son, Sam, was then a minister in Washington territory and could report *via* his father; Herbert Baxter Adams of Johns Hopkins contacted one of his graduates, Albert Shaw, who had returned to Minneapolis, and a visit by Jesse Macy, Professor of Politics at Grinnell in Iowa, to Oxford in 1887 provided a further contact who could furnish useful information on farmers and protest movements in the mid-west.[88] But it was to California, which he visited in 1881 and again in 1883, that he looked for a symbol of the raucous lawlessness of the last American frontier and to Denis Kearney and his Sand Lot party and the State constitution of 1879 as indicative of the 'ill-considered innovations and a readiness to try wild experiments' characteristic of the west. Kearneyism, however, was not then susceptible to cool reappraisal; the proximity of events and the strong feelings they aroused made citizens afraid or ashamed to speak, while the huge newspaper files through which Bryce worked were notoriously partisan and inaccurate. Instead he fell back on accounts by leading actors in the drama, such as Henry George, much as Bryce deplored his unorthodox economics and socialist leanings, and, with the second edition of 1889, of Kearney himself, who addressed a letter to the author bulging with misspellings and injured pride. Kearney argued that Bryce's reliance on George, his political enemy, was highly tendentious and accused him of an advanced prejudice against him which had been carried into the book. Comparison with George's own article on the episode shows Bryce using his source material in a generally fair and even-handed way, despite the fact that many of his own conclusions differed from those of George. Specifically, Bryce played down George's conviction that the élitist vigilante committees — whose leader, William Coleman, Bryce knew personally — first irritated class conflict and then over-reacted to Kearneyism, and, secondly, that neither the agitation nor the State Constitution of 1879 which followed it was genuinely

[88] Letter from Samuel Eliot to C. W. Eliot passed on to Bryce, 3 January 1888, Ms. Bryce USA 24. Samuel Eliot to Bryce, 18 January 1894, Ms. Bryce Misc. Shaw was especially informative on regulatory legislation in the mid-west; e.g. Bryce to Shaw, 3 January 1886, Shaw Papers, and Lloyd J. Graybar's *Albert Shaw of the Review of Reviews*. Macy to Shaw, 13 December 1887, 13 October 1888, 11 November 1890, 16 September 1891, Ms. Bryce USA 8.

radical or socialist.[89] Amid this confusion and conflict of personality, Bryce turned to the relatively detached authority of an academic friend, Bernard Moses, who had taught at Berkeley since 1876, and who was better able to sift through the misinformation provided by George — who was 'not likely to be impartial or very wise' — and Kearney.[90]

Again when he turned to unravel the railroad interests that dominated California and looked upon the state as their bailiwick, he was able to go beyond such official publications as the United Stated Pacific Commission to inside information at the very top, for Henry Villard, chairman of the Northern Pacific from 1889 to 1893, brother-in-law of Wendell Phillips Garrison and owner of the *New York Evening Post*, was his chief informant. Without attributing the source or specifying individuals or states in his text, Villard, in a detailed and vivid correspondence, identified Senator Edmunds of Maine among those who protected rail companies in return for retainers, and New York and Pennnsylvania as among those states most easily and regularly bought off.[91]

Through Villard's invitation to the 'stupendous picnic' on the Northern Pacific in 1883 Bryce renewed and extended his personal experience of every state and territory in the west, rounding out his composite picture and illuminating his text. On this journey he met the sad, defeated figure of Sitting Bull, the once mighty Sioux chieftain, brought forward for display before the grand European dignitaries beside the railway tracks in Dakota; he symbolised the passing of a warrior race; he observed the restless activity of western life when he woke at 7.0 a.m. in Seattle to find the new town alive with people going about their business; he alighted upon a Welshman among his

[89]   *AC*, II, pp. 451, 388 n. 1, 401 n. 1. Henry George in *Popular Science Monthly*, August 1880, pp. 433 – 53.

[90]   Moses to Bryce, 19 April 1885, Ms. Bryce USA 25, and *AC*, II, pp. 389, 404. Bryce also used an article by a colleague of Moses, Theodore Hittell, which appeared in *The Berkeley Quarterly* for July 1880. Kearney's letter (*AC*, II, pp. 747 – 50) is still extant, and possibly his threat — omitted in the printed version — to turn Bryce's informants out of town led Bryce to cite Moses in the Preface only.

[91]   *AC*, I, pp. 579 – 80, 581 n. 1. *AC*, II, pp. 154 n. 2, 152 n. 3. Villard to Bryce, 15 July 1888, Ms. Bryce USA 10. Bryce made full use of the 'Report of the US Pacific Railway Commission', but added that 'in America there is much to be learnt . . . from conversation with judicious observers outside politics and typical representatives of political sections and social classes, which the most diligent study of the press will not give'. Villard is referred to as 'the president of a great Western railroad' (*AC*, II, pp. 154 n. 2, 267, 155 n. 1).

band of fifty wandering disciples in Washington territory who believed his two sons to be the incarnation of Christ and John the Baptist; this prompted the reflection that the west was the last refuge of the eccentric religious outcast.[92] But the west also symbolised the dignity of the individual and the absence of deference which Bryce considered part of the essential pleasantness of American life. He recounts the occasion when a station master took him out on his locomotive to admire some nearby scenery. That evening he met the driver again, who apologised for the engine not being 'fixed up' properly for the illustrious guest; 'He talked with intelligence, and we had some pleasant chat together. It was fortunate that I had resisted in the forenoon the British impulse to bestow a gratuity.' Most of all he captured the confident days of the frontier; the mile trek to the state capitol in Bismarck, North Dakota, over an empty prairie, spoke volumes on the west's boom and vitality. He even managed to evoke the smell of the west, for a footnote recalls how the paper money in Wisconsin had acquired a marked smell from the constant handling of skins and furs by trappers.[93] Such graphic details show that Bryce could employ the inductive method imaginatively, using the insight of casual minor encounters to shed light on the complex functions of the nation's social and political arrangements. And, because he trusted so much in the insight and intuition personal connections yielded, it is worth studying the impact of his American friendships more fully.

Bryce's American friendships

Visiting America did not mean having to leave the world of liberalism which Bryce conceived of as a transatlantic phenomenon; the mugwump was simply a Gladstonian abroad, so that Bryce's circle of American friends was virtually formed for him even before he set foot on the continent. As Dicey put it in a letter to Eliot: 'The way of looking at things is the really important matter in friendship.' Dress, manner, the tone of discussion and shared assumptions were the medium of recognition and Bryce naturally gravitated to the 'best men', the

---

[92] James to Minnie Bryce, 13 Sept 1883, Ms. Bryce 82. *AC*, II, pp. 697, 703, 594 n 2.
[93] *AC*, II, pp. 679 n. 1, 703, 302 n. 2.

intellectual patrician class of the eastern seaboard.[94] Once
launched it was difficult to break out of this self-contained
coterie and its particular way of looking at the world. As Leslie
Stephen suggested, choice of friends entailed certain limitations
which were then unquestioningly reinforced:

> The traveller in any country is surrounded by an invisible
> atmosphere, composed partly of his preconceived prejudices,
> and partly of those who have naturally gathered round him
> and look at everything through a more or less delusive
> medium. In America there are certain special facilities for the
> process. One man falls into a Republican, and another into a
> Democratic connection; he is naturally handed on to sym-
> pathising friends, and enveloped in a magic circle of which he
> is only partially conscious. Before he knows it, he has
> adopted a certain set of arguments, and has learned the
> proper parry for every thrust of his antagonist.[95]

In Bryce's case it was not that he adopted the rhetoric of one
party as against another, for he quickly appreciated that there
was little to distinguish them, and, although the majority of his
friends were Republicans, most were Republicans who had in
1884 bolted to the Democrats. Far more useful was Bryce's
distinction between an 'inner circle' for whom politics was a
full-time profession and an 'outer circle' of mainly independent
reformers who, lacking the *raison d'être* of party place, engaged
in politics out of a sense of public duty. And, in so far as he
measured the health of the commonwealth in terms of the
preponderance of the latter over the former, he can be seen as
moving almost entirely among the 'outer circle', adopting its
concerns and advocating its panaceas.[96]

Yet *The American Commonwealth* is peopled by the boss and the
wirepuller; these were the men who worked the political system
— the independent reformer constituted the hoped-for future.
Since his observation of Tweed at the Rochester Convention he
was both repelled and fascinated by the boss. To grasp the
realities of American politics he had to fix a steady eye on the
slippery principles and camaraderie which held the system
together, to penetrate the motives and actions of the stalwart

[94] 24 Sept 1918, Eliot Papers.
[95] *Cornhill*, March 1869, p. 337.
[96] AC, II, p. 60.

cohorts. Yet his upbringing, his Presbyterian conscience and the American circles in which he moved, all combined to restrict his empathy and regard them other than *de haut en bas*: essentially he surveyed this class from the elevated heights of a Henry Adams rather than from below in Graziano's Shoeshine Parlor, where George Washington Plunkitt held daily court. For the America he entered did not centre on the ward districts or working man's clubs or immigrant aid societies, but rather on civil service reform commissions, universities, reform clubs and the editorial offices of genteel journals. His attempt to come to grips was genuine enough, but his approach was vicarious and through intermediaries and this distanced his perspective and bestowed a distinct tone of stiff disapprobation. He granted a certain 'shrewdness, a sort of rough good fellowship . . . and loyalty to their chiefs', but generally the professional exhibited 'a low tone, with laxity in pecuniary matters, with a propensity to commit or to excuse jobs, with a deficient sense of the dignity which public office confers and the responsibility it implies . . .. They have of course no comprehension of political questions or zeal for political principles; politics mean to them merely a scramble for places. They are usually vulgar, sometimes brutal, more rarely criminal, or at least the associates of criminals'.[97]

His direct contacts with this class were few. He might provide Senator Conkling of New York with a card to the National Liberal Club, visit the Brooklyn Sachem of Tammany in 1890 or, in the same year, attend his first Constitutional convention in Kentucky, but he readily admitted that he had witnessed only the 'outside' activity 'which meant comparatively little'. Friends could be prim and obstructive, as when he called upon Ivins, a city chamberlain of New York, to investigate the Tweed ring; for this he was sharply reprimanded by Bucklin Bishop of *The Nation*, reminded of Ivins' close connections with Boss Platt and told that 'his name is not an advantage to your book'.[98] When faced with a pro-party tract like D. G. Thompson's *Politics in a Democracy*, he was merely bemused — 'it is an odd little book which purports to defend Tammany by showing that it gives the

[97]   *AC*, II, pp. 61–2. As Denis Brogan wrote, in an unpublished Introduction to the *AC*, Bryce 'knew nothing of the Tenderloin or the Barbary Coast'.
[98]   Bryce to Conkling, 18 June 1896, Ms. Bryce USA 24. Bryce to Bowker of the Brooklyn Institute, 20 Oct 1890, Bowker Papers. Bryce to Nicholas Murray Butler, President of Columbia, 30 May 1916, Butler Papers. Bishop to Bryce, 25 May [1893?], Ms. Bryce USA 24. William Mills Ivins (1851–1915) had associated with Platt but was anti-Tammany and had rendered great service to the city, particularly in the field of Public Service Commissions.

New York masses the sort of government they desire and deserve'. To make up for the lack of close contacts with lobbyists, speculators and fixers on Capitol Hill, he had to rely on academic studies like Woodrow Wilson's *Congressional Government*, to such an extent indeed that Wilson was prompted to write to a friend: 'How remorselessly *Congressional Government* . . . is swallowed up in Part I of Bryce: was I not "nice" not to say anything about it?'[99] This over-reliance is especially worrying in that Wilson was at the time a distinct 'outer circle' man who had never himself visited Congress or met a single congressman. More than one critical review of *The American Commonwealth* singled out Bryce's dependence on mugwumps 'of secondary influence and parasitic vigour', and suggested that the book would have benefited from closer contact with 'the strictly political class' like Conkling, Blaine and John Sherman.[100]

Only after *The American Commonwealth* appeared did Bryce come into memorable but unfortunate conflict with that strictly political class. The first, Denis Kearney, was a powerless and forgotten figure by then despite his disavowals ('this must not be considered a voice from the tomb. I am a young man . . . chock full of vitality, and a great deal of experience'),[101] but Oakey Hall, or 'Elegant Oakey' as he was called because of his flashy dress and dandyism, was quite a different proposition, having served as top level Tammany associate and one-time mayor in the golden days of Tweed.

For reasons of copyright and because he lacked sufficient information himself Bryce asked Frank Goodnow of Columbia to contribute a chapter on the ring. When the book appeared Hall issued a writ of libel and claimed £10,000 in damages. In his defence Bryce reiterated each and every one of Goodnow's assertions in chapter 88, namely that Hall was a member of the ring and mayor from 1869 to 1871 when over $30 million was milked from public funds; that embezzlement had taken place on a stupendous scale and the fact that Hall was an accomplice

99 *AC*, 1910, II, p. 398 n. 2. Wilson to Munroe Smith, 7 Jan 1889, quoted in *Woodrow Wilson Papers*, VI, p. 45. As Wendell Phillips Garrison wrote to Bryce concerning Thompson's book: 'He is little known in this office and very lightly esteemed, & you are safe in treating him as a negligible quantity' (20 Dec 1893, Ms. Bryce USA 4).

100 An anonymous review in the protectionist *American Economist*, 18 Jan 1889, p. 18.

101 Kearney to Bryce, 22 July 1889, Ms. Bryce USA 24. *AC*, II, p. 747.

'had been been for many years a matter of public notoriety, discussion and interest'. Goodnow argued that Hall was attempting blackmail and taking the opportunity, now that most of the protagonists of the 1870s were dead, to whitewash his past career; that any changes made to the chapter would merely encourage Hall to demand further damages and might in the event prejudice the jury against Bryce. Hall's bluff should be called.[102] Meanwhile the great success of the first edition and the demand for a reprint in 1889 made Macmillan's, the publishers, afraid of having a suit of their hands too. Urging caution on the grounds that Hall's suit was imminent, Bryce wrote to Goodnow requesting authority 'to modify the chapter in any way that may seem needful', while at the same time assuring him that he had complete faith in the correctness and integrity of his chapter and promising to restore it intact when the court proceedings were over. Goodnow was obviously upset by this decision but reluctantly consented. In the event the chapter was omitted from the second edition altogether.[103]

By 1891 the trial was still pending and Hall's lawyer, Lewis, offered to withdraw from litigation if Bryce apologised, withdrew his plea of justification and paid his client's costs. At this point Bryce was tempted to pay; collecting evidence for the trial was proving extremely expensive and, even if he were to win the case, he would receive no compensation for Hall was a pauper. But most tellingly Bryce feared for his public reputation; as he wrote to Godkin, 'the world would be apt merely to remember that one had been successfully blackmailed'.[104] Supported by Godkin, he decided to refuse to pay Hall's costs without exacting a release from all restrictions and an acknowledgement that he could republish the offending chapter without further interference. Hall refused, the costly commission continued and the trial was still pending when, in 1893, a new Anglo-American Copyright Act led Bryce and Macmillan's

---

[102] Bryce to Goodnow, 13 July and 9 Nov 1889. Goodnow to Bryce, 21 August 1889, Goodnow Papers. These papers contain typed copies of Goodnow's letters to Bryce. The unexpurgated chapter in *AC*, 1888 ed., III, pp. 173 – 98, renders the first edition a bibliographical rarity.

[103] Bryce to Goodnow, 10 Oct 1889, Ms. Bryce USA 25. Goodnow to Bryce, 4 Dec 1889, Goodnow Papers, and Ms. Bryce USA 25. Bryce explained the omission in his Introduction to the 2nd edition (1889) on grounds of the chapter 'having become the subject of litigation which is now before the Courts' (*AC*, I, p. ix n. 1).

[104] Bryce to Goodnow, 18 Feb 1891, Goodnow Papers. Bryce to Godkin, 18 Feb 1891, Godkin Papers.

to push for a revised third edition. At this juncture Bryce convinced himself that a revision of Goodnow's chapter was permissible because the commission had failed to implicate Hall in the direct filching of funds and because the new edition called for 'such improvements as seem proper'. So under pressure from publisher and lawyer he rewrote the chapter himself, changing its title to 'The Tammany Ring in New York City', which extended the time span and glossed over Hall and the Tweed era. Thus from an unequivocal statement of active complicity Bryce shuffled his ground to one of general neglect; Hall became one of four Tammany leaders to whom 'more or less, though not necessarily in equal measure, the credit or discredit for its acts attach'; he also stressed that Hall has survived three trials relatively unscathed, 'a man to whom no share in the booty was ever traced, and who may not have received any'.[105]

Bryce's American friends congratulated him on his granite steadfastness. In fact, the case illustrates a series of decisive concessions to Hall and, simultaneously, a succession of tactical withdrawals from his initial guaranteed commitment to Goodnow's chapter. It shows him in direct and painful contact with that class of which he writes so persuasively in his book and being outmanoeuvred at every turn. It also indicates the degree of support he could always call upon from the ranks of the 'outer circle'. Godkin scoured for evidence in the *Nation* files, Goodnow contacted Thomas Nast, the famed anti-Tweed cartoonist; George Curtis and John Bigelow offered their services on the witness stand and, while Hall had only one witness and colleague to fall back on, Paul Sweeney, Bryce could summon twenty-three of the 'best men' to his support. 'Should [Hall] ever open his lips on the subject of the suit', Garrison wrote, 'you may be sure we shall let him hear from us.' Finally offers of hard financial assistance came from Godkin, Villard and Chauncey Depew, Senator for New York,

---

[105] Bryce to Godkin, 18 March 1891, Godkin Papers. Bryce gave the same assurance to Goodnow and his lawyer, Notman, 14 March 1891, Goodnow Papers, Bryce to Goodnow, 24 June 1891, 10 Aug 1893, 6 Sept 1894, Goodnow Papers. Cecil Coward, Bryce's lawyer, to Bryce, 17 Nov 1893. Bryce to Coward, 25 Dec 1893, Ms. Bryce USA 24. Broaching the matter of the rewritten chapter Bryce wrote: 'I have thought it best to write the new article on somewhat different lines, so as to avoid the necessity of saying much about Hall, or describing the ring frauds in detail' (20 Oct 1894, Goodnow Paper). *AC*, 1910, II, pp. 388, 396, 393.

even though Godkin kept this secret in case Hall claimed martyrdom at the hands of persecuting plutocrats.[106]

Mugwumps could unite in support of Bryce but were divided among themselves on questions of strategy. Their attempt to create an independent party under Greeley in 1872 had signally failed; given their small numbers the independents were forced to choose between 'bolting' tactically, which the majority of them did in 1884, or staying loyally within the party in the hope of converting from within. The bolt from Republican to Democrat in 1884 took on a mythical importance to the independents similar to 1931 for the Labour Party, and it served as a purifying rite and as a definition of uncontaminated mugwumpery. The bolt not only sustained ideological purity but, with Cleveland's election, a political victory into the bargain. Roosevelt and Henry Cabot Lodge, while unhappy about Blaine's candidature, remained loyally to fight another day.

Between them Godkin and Roosevelt decisively shaped the political stance of *The American Commonwealth*. Reflecting wider issues of temperament and political ethics both can be seen as fighting for Bryce's soul, and that struggle was all the sharper because of the venomous personal quarrel between the two in which Bryce became embroiled. As the advocate of strenuosity and the bully times of the bar-room brawl Roosevelt accused the 'goo goo's' of party disloyalty while still expecting to command party allegiance, of refusing to work with party reformers in fusing tickets and of holding out for an 'impossible good' which often gave victory to the enemy. Nurturing their political purity they and not the political bosses, were the chief obstacle to his clarion call for activism and engagement. It was especially Godkin's invidious negativism, his discouragement to militant reformers, that he found unforgivable. As he put it to Bryce: 'Godkin did all his abilities would allow to discourage young men from going into public life, and banish them when they had

---

[106] Goodnow to Bryce, 10 Oct 1889, 2 Oct 1891, Ms. Bryce USA 25. John Bigelow to Bryce, 12 Dec 1889, Ms. Bryce USA 24. Bryce to Godkin, 20 Sept 1891, 28 Dec 1889, 8 Feb 1890, Godkin Papers. Garrison to Bryce, 22 Sept 1891, Ms. Bryce USA 4. Bryce knew, however, that a Mr Wingate's article in the *North American Review*, Oct 1874, had indicted Hall without contradiction or legal retaliation, and two modern authorities have substantiated Wingate's — and Goodnow's — conclusions. Cf. Alexander Callow Jr., *The Tweed Ring*, pp. 284–6, and Coswell Bowen, *The Elegant Oakey*, pp. 249–63.

gone in.'[107] He had succeeded in dividing politicians into two sorts, one containing 'nice, well-behaved, well-meaning little men, with receding chins and small feet, men who mean well and who if they are insulted feel shocked and want to go home', and the other 'robust and efficient creatures who do not mean well at all'. Roosevelt's plea was simple: 'I want to see our side — the side of decency — including men who have not the slightest fear of the people on the other side . . . my plea is for the virtue that shall be strong.'[108]

As such he was determined not to allow a work of such lasting influence as *The American Commonwealth* to bear the imprint of Godkin's defeatism on its every page. After meeting Bryce in London in 1887 he poured out letters on New York city politics emphasising the fact that in the better brownstone districts it was possible for a decent man like himself to work with machines which were not invariably corrupt, corruption usually resulting from reformist inactivity; that to the New York poor the bosses' liberality more than made up for any wobbliness regarding the eighth commandment. In 1890 he went out of his way to initiate Bryce into the mysteries of Capitol Hill, introducing him to Speaker Reed, McKinley, Joe Cannon and others.

He grasped at once the distinction between these men who *do* things, and the others who only think or talk about how they ought to be done. I think his visit here will be a needed antiseptic for he now goes to visit Godkin and Eliot. He ended his letter of thanks when he left 'I won't let myself be captured by excessive mugwumpery after your warnings'; so you see I did some good missionary work.[109]

Godkin remained churlish and unimpressed: 'The whole Lodge-Roosevelt creed is a humbug.' Those two great reforms of the century — the repeal of the corn laws and the abolition of slavery — had not been achieved by compromise, but by sustained independent zeal and pressure. As a disciple of Mill

107 Roosevelt to Bryce, 2 Dec 1895 and 19 Dec 1903, Ms. Bryce Misc. Roosevelt to Bryce, 12 March 1897, Ms. Bryce USA 9.
108 Quoted in Christopher Lasch, *The Strenuous Life* (unpublished Bowdoin Prize Essay, Harvard, 1954, p. 21).
109 Roosevelt to Bryce, 5 Feb 1888, Ms. Bryce USA 9. Roosevelt to Lodge, 23 and 27 Aug 1890, quoted in Elting Morison (ed.), *Letters of Theodore Roosevelt*, I, pp. 230 – 1.

he fervently believed in the renovation of society by an enlightened clerisy. Settling in America in 1856 he hoped for the regeneration of the old world by the new, and initially dedicated *The Nation* to continue the spirit of Garrison's *Liberator* into the post-bellum world. His co-editor, Wendell Phillips Garrison, son of the abolitionist, personified this tradition. Like the moral suasionists before him, Godkin called for a new moral infusion into the torpor of gilded age politics and the complete regeneration of a decayed party system by dedicated outsiders. Godkin was *The Nation* and *The Nation* in turned created the '*Nation* man', standing 'for something definite in the social order . . . the pages furnished a trusty bond of congeniality when strangers came together with no other introduction'.[110] Bryce and Dicey joined the ranks and made it international by representing the 'English arm' of the paper and from 1870 onwards contributing over 300 articles each to its pages.

The bond between Bryce and Godkin was far closer than that between Bryce and Roosevelt; the former was one of intimacy, the latter one of admiration and esteem. Godkin's indelible mark on *The American Commonwealth* can be measured by his conspicuous absence from both dedication and preface. Godkin felt aggrieved, but Bryce replied that he:

should have liked to say in this preface how much more I am indebted to you than to any other source for the views I have formed both to your letters and talk and to the *Nation* articles, but thought it would be more prudent not to do so because all the set of people whom you have been battling against all these years would at once lay hold of the statement and say (not without truth) that I was reproducing the *Evening Post* and Mugwumpism.[111]

[110] Godkin to Eliot, 24 January [?], Eliot Papers. Garrison in *NYN*, 13 July 1903, p. 30. To James Ford Rhodes Godkin was 'a man whom you would like to meet at dinner, accompany on a long walk, or cross the Atlantic with' and William James referred to his 'towering influence in all thought concerning public affairs' and how, indirectly, he 'determined the whole current of discussion'. (*Historical Essays*, p. 269. William James to Mrs Godkin, 21 May 1902, Godkin Papers).

[111] Bryce to Godkin, 22 October 1888, Godkin Papers. Unappeased, Bryce reiterated the point: 'It was because I thought that any little help my book could give the cause of reform would be best given if it gave no sign of connection with the leading reformers'. (24 Jan 1889, Godkin Papers). An acknowledgement to Godkin was added in the 1889 and subsequent edition.

This was a feeble shield which stalwart papers like *The New York Herald* and *The American Economist* easily saw through. For Bryce had borrowed heavily from *Nation* editorials believing, as Godkin believed, that radical change in the party system would never come from the politicians who profited from it, but from the disinterested outsider; 'instructive critics' and 'philanthropic reformers' who, though a minority, could, by holding fast rather than courting easy popularity, triumph from an inviolate position. Conditions were auspicious because of America's large number of 'philosophically judicial observers of politics' who, combining together, could 'create new centres of force and motion and [nourish] young causes and unpopular doctrines into self-confident aggressiveness'.[112] This rosy assessment was kept buoyant by the euphoria of 1884 when Bryce wrote congratulating Godkin on having unhorsed the plumed knight 'which I believe was largely due to yourself and the *Post*'.[113]

Yet the enemy regrouped, Tammany had nine lives like a cat and the mugwump disenchantment with Cleveland grew. Did the independents not overestimate their importance, Bryce wondered, and were they not asking too much of the Democrats so long deprived of the fruits of patronage? Bryce remained cautious and non-committal; he showered praise on Cleveland in his correspondence with Richard Watson Gilder of *The Century* while, at the same time, Godkin and Schurz traced for him that administration's growing deviation from the faith. Godkin appealed to the don in Bryce, Roosevelt to the politician who more and more found Dicey's stiff and easy integrity from within All Souls as irksome as Roosevelt must have found the *Nation*'s editorials. The howling of the Cambridge dogs in tune with Godkin's and C. E. Norton's almost pathological whining promised only sterility and the paralysis of reform.[114] Bryce

---

112 *The American Economist*, 18 Jan 1889, p. 18. George W. Smalley in *The New York Herald*, 8 September 1895, p. 299. *AC*, II, pp. 47, 352 – 3, 253 – 4, 4, 270. *AC*, I, p. 65.

13 Bryce to Godkin, 12 Nov 1884, Godkin Papers. Even during the subsequent disenchantment with Cleveland, Bryce was convinced he found 'a growing disposition to quote and defer to intellectual and moral eminence' (to Godkin, 6 Feb 1886, Godkin Papers).

114 Cf. Bryce's correspondence with Gilder, Godkin and Schurz in *The Century Collection*, Godkin Papers and Schurz Papers. Eliot to Bryce, 8 August 1921, Eliot Papers. Dying in Leamington Spa, Alice James bravely reflected upon Godkin's self-pity: 'But any impossible strain upon humanity is the asking that it should reflect any illumination other than the individual or personal one' (*Diary of Alice James*, 31 Oct 1891, p. 221).

increasingly admired Roosevelt's wholesome participation and was never entirely immune from the hero-worship that afflicted his timid English admirers; indeed, when Bucklin Bishop prepared his biography of Roosevelt in 1920 Bryce was embarrassed to reread his extravagant praises and hoped they might be deleted.[115] Nevertheless here was a fellow politician who had decisively entered the ring and left his mark taking 'public spirited' followers with him into the 'muddy whirlpool' of the state legislature. In many chapters, particularly 'The War Against Bossdom', Bryce urged Rooseveltian tactics: a frontal attack on party-controlled primaries which defeated the professionals at their own game; he was dismissive of creating wholly new party organisations — travelling on rails was more sensible than constructing your own railroad to travel on — which divided the opposition; he opposed abstention and scratching of party tickets, which relieved feelings but was of little positive value.[116] Exerting leverage against the existing party system and using its full weight for one's own advantage offered worthwhile piecemeal rewards. Such 'rough and toilsome' work required tact as well as vigour, but he was withering in his condemnation of the 'best men' inexcusably absenting themselves from public life on the grounds that politics were vulgar — that 'pseudo-European American complaint' — when their very absence ensured the continuation of that which they most deplored.[117]

This studied balancing act between Godkin and Roosevelt reveals the essential Bryce — 'Scot, lawyer and therefore cautious', as Freeman put it. Holding closer to Godkin's vision of the future he nevertheless appreciated that Roosevelt's methods were more likely to achieve them in the short run. It

[115] Bishop to Bryce, 2 Dec 1919, Ms. Bryce USA 11. Bryce to Bishop, 13 Feb 1920, Bishop Papers. *Theodore Roosevelt and His Times*, II, pp. 134–5.
[116] AC, II, pp. 163–4. The chapter entitled 'The War Against Bossdom' is especially Rooseveltian. Bryce quoted or referred to Roosevelt's *Century* article of April 1885 many times (AC, I, pp. 516; AC, II, pp. 109 n. 1, and 169 n. 1) and referred to him as 'one of the ablest and most vivacious of the younger generation of American politicians' (AC, I, p. 516).
[117] AC, II, pp. 69–70. In the 1890s Bryce increasingly expressed doubts about the reliability of the *NYN*, and after Roosevelt's death deprecated the mugwump attacks that had dogged his career: 'In one way that criticism was unjust. It never allowed for the inevitable difficulties of politicians, when you must occasionally work through, or even with, persons of whom you had a bad opinion' (Bryce to Roosevelt, 27 Feb 1897, Roosevelt Papers. Bryce to W. R. Thayer, 27 March 1919, Thayer Papers).

illustrates too Bryce's combination of detachment and sympathy. *The American Commonwealth* was not a work of scientific objectivity; operating within the limitations of his motives and methods Bryce failed entirely to attain or maintain that level of strictly neutral observation he craved. But this is to state a truism. In fact, the book derives greater value and coherence from certain biases its author failed to acknowledge. From its subjectivity the reader gains fresh insights into transatlantic liberalism, and from its high standards of objectivity a greater understanding of America. As Dicey wrote in his review of the book: 'Freedom from prejudice means want of sympathy, and a critic without sympathy must . . . be a critic without insight.'[118] In *The American Commonwealth* Bryce displays both sympathy and understanding.

---

[118] Freeman to Liddon, 1 Nov 1876, quoted in Shannon, *Gladstone and the Bulgarian Agitation, 1876*, p. 225. *Edinburgh Review*, April 1889, p. 483

4

The Formal Constitution

There is no good in arguing with the inevitable. The only argument available with a nine wind is to put on your overcoat. — James Russell Lowell, *Democracy*

Constitutional comparisons

Bryce began reading for the bar at Lincoln's Inn in 1864 sharing rooms with an Oxford friend, Kenelm Digby, and reading in Sir John Holker's chambers. In 1867 he was called to the bar and travelled on the Northern Circuit. But his commitment to the practice of law remained uncertain, while his love of its academic study grew. He complained of 'interminable records of minute facts through which it is not easy to trace the course of a consistent and clarifying principle', and eagerly pursued alternative distractions.[1] In 1866 he took up the appointment of Assistant Commissioner for the Taunton Schools Enquiry, continued to write for journals, took extensive time off for climbing and travel in Europe in the company of friends like Courtney Ilbert and Leslie Stephen, lectured at Owen's College, Manchester, and continued to hold his Oriel fellowship. In 1870 he was appointed Regius Professor of Civil Law at Oxford.

This brief period in the legal profession served to reinforce a mind already profoundly legalistic in approach. He was especially attracted to constitutional analysis, of which he was 'morbidly fond', and many years later he was observed perspiring in silent agony out of deference to President Roosevelt who was holding forth loudly but erroneously on the American Constitution. In such matters Bryce was an acknowledged expert and the President very much a layman.[2] Some

---

[1]   Fisher, I, p. 63.
[2]   Dicey to Bryce, 4 April 1887, Ms. Bryce 2. *Holmes-Laski Letters*, I, p. 313.

critics objected to *The American Commonwealth*'s 'too legal interpretation', but as a legalist observing an America created by laws, by lawyers and thoroughly imbued with the legalistic spirit Bryce would have found this criticism pointless. He had an immense reverence for constitutions as embodiments of the genius of races, mystically linking past with present and shaping the future, but, as structures of rare intricacy and accumulated achievement, he believed they were also highly vulnerable. Just as Dicey insisted that home rule would destroy the British Constitution at a stroke, so Bryce believed that the acquisition of the Philippines might fatally over-extend the American Constitution.[3]

At Oxford in 1884 Bryce gave a series of lectures on 'Flexible and Rigid Constitutions' which heavily influenced Sir Henry Sumner Maine's *Popular Government* and Dicey's *Law of the Constitution* which appeared the following year and which in turn profoundly altered Britain's understanding of America.[4] Earlier writers had provided Bryce with clues for his lectures. Tocqueville, for example, in a discussion of American judicial powers, established that 'Americans have acknowledged the right of judges to found their decisions on the *Constitution* rather than on the *laws*', and went on to expand upon this insight through comparisons:

> An American constitution is not supposed to be immutable, as in France; nor is it susceptible of modification by the ordinary powers of society, as in England. It constitutes a detached whole, which, as it represents the will of the whole people, is no less binding on the legislator than on the private citizen . . . as it is the first of laws, it cannot be modified by a law.[5]

Building on Tocqueville, Mill spoke of the 'remarkable consequences' of the Supreme Court's interpretative role, and

[3]   *Atlantic Monthly*, March 1889, p. 420. *Studies in History and Jurisprudence*, I, pp. 146, 185.

[4]   The lectures were published in *History and Jurisprudence*, 1901. Dicey employed the classification in print in 1885, but Bryce had already written and circulated his analysis of National Government by then. See Frederic Harrison's evidence in *The Nineteenth Century*, Jan 1889, p. 144. Also *LC*, pp. 87, 124, n. 1; *AC*, I, p. 240.

[5]   Phillips Bradley's ed. of *Democracy in America*, I, pp. 104–5.

Bagehot made an instructive distinction between 'simple' and 'composite' constitutions, observing that in America; 'The "Constitution" cannot be altered by any authorities within the constitution, but only by authorities without it.'[6] But these were merely hints and suggestions which Bryce was to clarify and enlarge upon.

Bryce started by inventing new terms for a new mode of classification which superseded the unsatisfactory traditional distinction of 'written' and 'unwritten' constitutions — unsatisfactory because blurred and indistinct. Unwritten constitutions could theoretically be reduced to written codes and Dicey attempted precisely this in his *Law of the Constitution*. Moreover, in that book Dicey argued that the constitution was riddled with unwritten 'conventions' — the existence of a cabinet and its responsibility to parliament and public opinion, for example — which carried the full sanction of written laws, while many written laws, such as the crown's veto on legislation, had fallen into abeyance. Bryce's classification of rigid and flexible constitutions defined the former in terms of a dual system of laws, one of them a higher, fundamental law above and beyond and ultimately constraining the law-making body which it created; the latter characterised by a system of laws, constituent as well as legislative, emanating from one single law-making sovereign.' Britain best exemplified a flexible constitution whose legislative body, parliament, was sovereign and whose acts and statutes could recreate or destroy its constitution — which was no more than the accumulation of previous parliamentary acts — in the course of a session. The United States in turn was the pre-eminent example of a rigid constitution, creating its forms of government — the executive and law-making branches and its own interpreter, the Supreme Court — but standing quite apart from, and deriving its powers from a source quite distinct from, legislators. Its constitution was doubly rigid not only because it was beyond the reach of mere legislators but also because it imposed a deliberately cumbersome process of amendment procedure. Dicey located sovereignty in the amending power of three-fourths of the states as representative of the sovereign will. But public opinion was a sovereign hard to rouse: 'A federal constitution is capable of change, but for all that a federal

---

6   Mill, *Three Essays*, p. 393. Bagehot's *English Constitution* (Fontana ed.), p. 218.
7   *History and Jurisprudence*, I, pp. 145 – 254. LC, pp. 361 – 416.

constitution is apt to be unchangeable.' Britain had undergone far more revolutionary change than America since 1787: while the President, for example, had retained entire his right of veto, the crown's prerogatives, on which the American executive was partly modelled in the eighteenth century, had dwindled to insignificance.[8] Thus Dicey concluded that a rigid constitution bestowed a degree of permanence and stability unknown under flexible constitutions. Dicey's over-formal linking of rigid constitutions with legislative inertia and his determined attempt to define sovereignty in a dualistic federal system appears surprising, coming as it does from the classic expositor of informal 'conventions', but with regard to America he was driven by an Austinian compulsion to locate an ultimate and indivisible sovereignty while, at the same time, emphasising its diffusion in America as against its unique concentration in Britain. He did appreciate, in principle, the growth of extra-legal 'conventions' in the United States — that the president served a maximum of two terms, that the Electoral College split on strictly party lines — but simple lack of personal experience or understanding of America's intangible politics prevented him from breaking out of his static analysis. Instead, his conclusion that American federalism was conservative, legalistic and weak owed far more to abstract extrapolations and *a priori* reasoning. Bryce, on the other hand, was able to detach America from a general model of federalism, allow for degrees of latitude and variety, and, paradoxically, suggest a flexibility inherent within America's rigid structure. Responding to social and economic forces, constitutional change by amendment, interpretation and usage — what he called 'Flexible parasites growing upon a Rigid stem' — bestowed a surprising resilience and capacity for growth in the United States.[9]

Late-Victorian constitutionalists were intoxicated by the possibilities of federalism. It was, Dicey said, 'the latest invention of constitutional science', one which possessed 'extraordinary prestige' and which seemed to offer 'the panacea for all social ills, and all political perplexities'. British enthusiasts researched the intricacies of the Swiss cantonal system as avidly and systematically as they scaled the Alpine summits of Europe's playground. Bryce and Dicey wrote a large number of articles on

[8]   *LC*, pp. 145, 124 – 5. *AC*, I, pp. 33, 348, 56.
[9]   *History and Jurisprudence*, I, pp. 221, 233. *AC*, I, pp. 353 – 4. *LC*, pp. 167 – 70, 125 n. 1.

this topic and encouraged Sir Francis Adams and C. D. Cunningham in their joint study of the *Swiss Confederation*. But Switzerland was small, of heterogeneous race and language, and with a continental feudal tradition which it had only gradually overcome.[10] The example of America with its size and decidedly democratic Anglo-Saxon heritage offered the closest parallels to Britain and was, in Sidgwick's phrase, 'the decisive model of federality'. Yet having rediscovered federalism commentators were far from sure what to make of it. Was it a good thing or a bad? Neither or both? Was it an intermediate stage on the path towards unionism or towards greater fragmentation? Or did it constitute the culmination of inexorable political processes?[11]

Though no one did more to popularise the topic Dicey remained dubious about the benefits to be gained from federalism. He complained that the new faith in federalism as a political solution was a faith without knowledge, and emphasised its transitory and precarious character. 'Federalism when successful has generally been a stage towards mature government. In other words, federalism tends to pass into nationalism . . .. The United States . . . has been described as a nation concealed under the form of a federation.' If unionism were inevitable it followed that federalism must be a temporary phenomenon which, while it lasted, must also be restricting, even repressive: 'A truly federal government is the denial of national independence to every state of the federation'.[12] But the main thrust of his critique rested on the grounds of federalism's inherent complexity and weakness. The dual demands of independence and unity required of public opinion made for an ambivalent and unstable equipoise; Americans 'must desire union, and must not desire unity'. Furthermore definition

10   Dicey, *England's Case Against Home Rule*, p. 160. *LC*, pp. 475 – 7, 135 n. 1. *The Swiss Confederation* appeared in 1889, and Bryce and Dicey were thanked in the Preface. See also *AC*, I, p. 400, Dicey in *NYN*, 18 Nov 1886, p. 410, and Maine's *Popular Government*, p. 39.

11   *The Development of European Polity*, p. 430. Dicey spoke of the Union as 'the most completely developed type of federalism. All the features which mark that scheme of government . . . are there exhibited in their most salient and perfect form' (*LC*, pp. 134 – 5). Sidgwick changed his mind completely — from centralism to federalism — between his *Elements of Politics* of 1891 (p. 519) and *European Polity* (pp. 438 – 9), which appeared, posthumously, in 1903.

12   *LC*, p. 475. *England's Case*, p. 192. *LC*, 8th ed., pp. lxxvi, lxxix. *The Law Quarterly Review*, Jan 1885, p. 80.

destroyed; in its elaborate distribution of powers, federalism formalised, subdivided and restrained:

> Federalism is unfavourable to the interference or to the activity of government . . . a Federal constitution implies an elaborate distribution and definition of political powers: . . . it is from its very nature a sort of compromise between the claims of rival authorities . . . (while) under all the formality, the antiquarianism, the sham of the British Constitution, there lies latent an element of power which has been the true source of its life and growth . . . in point of pliability, power of development, freedom of action, English constitutionalism far excels the federalism of the United States.[13]

Bryce conceded that purposeful fragmentation was a characteristic of the American Constitution. There was, he admitted 'a want of unity. Its branches are unconnected; their efforts are not directed to one aim, do not produce one harmonious result . . ... There is a loss of force by friction'.[14] He went on to suggest further limitations. Congress, while denying sole initiative to the executive, lacked control over administration; the executive and legislative branches interlocked in such a way as to make it impossible to locate personal responsibility and public accountability. It was difficult for the President to act positively; isolated and tied to the strings of party, he could only exercise a negative power of veto which could be over-ridden by a two-thirds majority in Congress. Most glaringly absent to a British observer like Bryce was a form of cabinet. The President's administration was merely a group answerable each individually to the President, but devoid of a joint policy or collective responsibility. Forbidden to sit in Congress, hold themselves accountable to that body or resign on losing its confidence, ministers were incapable of gaining the fullest co-operation of the legislature or initiating bold executive measures.[15] Yet despite its deliberate atomism Bryce denied that endemic weakness and atrophy were synonymous with federalism. 'History', he asserted, 'does not warrant so broad a proposition.' On the contrary, the very

---

[13] *Law Quarterly Review*, Jan 1885, pp. 81 ff. *England's Case*, p. 160. *Contemporary Review*, July 1882, pp. 74–6.

[14] AC, I, p. 287. Bryce's 'exquisite equipoise' of federalism was dismissed by Dicey as 'a curious and complicated piece of legal mechanism' (AC, I, p. 281. *Law Quarterly Review*, Jan 1885, p. 80).

[15] AC, I, pp. 64, 69, 220–1, 286–7, 87–9.

flexibility of the bonds — bonds which could be loosened or tightened as occasion demanded — gave federalism that degree of adaptability which ensured its survival and which, by 'uniting commonwealths into one nation under one national government without extinguishing their separate administrations, legislatures, and local patriotisms', avoided destruction. Even with the supreme crisis of the civil war a stronger unionism had emerged, and the United States continued to stand as a magnificent refutation of dire prophecies concerning federalism's impermanence.[16]

Running counter to all these distinctions, less obvious Anglo-American similarities were revealed, for, while distinct forms of government divided, underlying principles united the Anglo-Americans. The foremost unifying principle was the rule of law. Inherited from the English, the Americans extended it when the colonial state assemblies bowed to the ultimate fiat of royal charters; 'thus the idea of an instrument superior to the legislature and the laws it passed became familiar', achieving its apotheosis in the Constitution of 1787.[17] Dicey conceded that 'while the formal differences between the constitution of the American republic and the constitution of the English monarchy are . . . immense, the institutions of America are in their spirit little else than a gigantic development of the ideas which lie at the basis of the political and legal institutions of England'.[18] Bryce went further in suggesting that America's adoption of rigid federalism indicated an advanced democracy. Backward polities could not reach beyond custom to conceive of fundamental laws; only in progressive democracies could the sovereign people appeal over the heads of their governors to a superior law which embodied their will.[19] And in welding federalism and democracy together Bryce went on to link both to race and thereby implicitly counter Dicey's criticism that federalism made impossible demands upon its citizens. Meeting just such demands could be said to characterise and define the Anglo-American, for 'the devices which we admire in the (American) Constitution might prove unworkable among a people less patriotic and self-reliant, less law-loving and law-

---

16   AC, I, pp. 335, 340 – 1, 342.
17   *History and Jurisprudence*, I, pp. 146 – 200.
18   LC, p. 135.
19   *History and Jurisprudence*, I, p. 161. Bryce continued: 'A documentary Constitution appears to the people as the immediate outcome of their power, the visible image of their sovereignty' (p. 237).

abiding, than are *the English of America*.[20] Like federalism, the Anglo-American was resourceful, and the possibilities for constitutional cross-reference substantial. Forms as unique as the American Supreme Court or the British cabinet were not inevitable concomitants of rigid and flexible structures. A degree of modification and innovation was possible, and just as Woodrow Wilson was to dream of grafting an English cabinet on to Congress, so Bryce's plans for Irish home rule, with the precedent of the Privy Council's judicial council before him, conceived of a form of Supreme Court along American lines.[21] As the breach of 1776 healed and the English and Americans came closer together, so the possibility of Britain's borrowing from the United States could be explored to advantage, much as the United States had previously borrowed from the mother country.

Britain's constitutional revolution

Throughout the 1880s, in his many anonymous contributions in the *New York Nation* and in private letters to English and American friends, especially E. L. Godkin, a new note enters Bryce's writing. It is a jarring note of worry and concern; a preoccupation with imminent crisis, of disenchantment with the present and growing gloom about future prospects. As an MP (for Tower Hamlets, 1880–5; for South Aberdeen thereafter), he now observed politics from inside and on the whole he was profoundly concerned about what he saw. Born outside the governing classes, he had the newcomer's heightened sense of the dignity of parliament, imagining it to be a noble forum of national debate, a chamber of senatorial wisdom, and, just because his preconceptions were historical and idealised rather than instinctive, he could be pained by his colleagues' cavalier manners and their easy betrayal of long-established traditions. Those colleagues in turn never full accepted the unclubbable and pedantic 'professor' into their ranks. Fed on the writings of Bagehot and Mill, who had lent an air of magisterial permanence to a brief period of parliamentary ascendancy between the

[20] *AC*, I, p. 349. 'No people except the choicest children of England, long trained by the practice of local self-government at home and in the colonies before their revolt, could have succeeded half so well' (*AC*, II, p. 467). 'A love for what is old and established is in their English blood' (*AC*, II, p. 283).

[21] *History and Jurisprudence*, I, p. 172. *AC*, I, pp. 342–3.

crown's eclipse and the emergence of party and executive control, Bryce was especially sensitive to the waning independence of parliament and its members in the face of extra-parliamentary democracy on the one hand and party whips on the other. It was not that he had grown especially reactionary with middle age. Admittedly the bubbling optimism and youthful radicalism had gone to be replaced by a livelier caution, but this was rather because politics had changed while his own principles remained firmly and unchangebly rooted. His Second Reform bill radicalism left him a main-line liberal by 1884. He continued to believe in the politics of consent filtered through representative government, but while he rested his faith on popular opinion he continued to entertain doubts about that trust and was rather wary of it as a source of power. As his fears concerning direct democracy grew in the 1880s so too did his doubts about the capacity of a flawed and vulnerable representative government to survive the assaults of extra-parliamentary forces.

Added to these nagging concerns was the revelation, gleaned from Anglo-American comparisons, of Britain's potentially revolutionary constitution: 'The democratisation of England proceeds with alarming speed', he wrote to Godkin in 1889, 'unluckily we construct no safeguards.'[22] Yet no one appreciated more than he the difficulty of erecting such safeguards under an infinitely flexible constitution subject to a sovereign parliament dominated by two parties outbidding each other in their attempts to gain the support of a volatile and often ignorant electorate. 'The English Constitution', Dicey wrote, 'is a machine which for good or bad gives effect to the opinion of the governing class — now a wide electorate — more immediately than any polity . . . . It has always been from a legal point of view liable to revolution by Act of Parliament.' This being the case, the political problem of the age was how to construct 'conservative democracies . . . to give to constitutions resting on the will of the people the stability and permanence which has hitherto been found only in monarchical or aristocractic states'.[23] Bryce's solution, offered in his 1884 lectures, was to reinforce the independence of parliament and hope its MPs would be

22 Bryce to Godkin, 1 March 1889, Godkin Papers.
23 *Contemporary Review*, April 1890, p. 505.*NYN*, 16 Dec 1886, p. 494. And Bryce: 'The British Constitution is just what the British Parliament pleases' (*AC*, I, p. 351 n. 1).

equal to their task of disinterested guardianship of the constitution:

> The best instances of Flexible constitutions have been those which grew up and lived on in nations of a conservative temper, nations which respected antiquity, which valued precedent, which liked to go on doing a thing in the way their fathers had done it before them . . . . The very fact that the legal right to make extensive change has long existed, and has not been abused, disposes an assembly to be cautious and moderate in the use of that right. Those who have always enjoyed power are least likely to abuse it . . . . Flexible constitutions have a natural affinity for an aristocratic structure of government . . . . It needs a good deal of knowledge skill and experience to work a Flexible constitution safely, and it is only in the educated classes that these qualities can be looked for. The masses of a modern nation seldom appreciate the worth of ancient usages and forms, or the methods of applying precedent.

The effect of such a constitution was to 'polish and mature in the governing class a sort of tact and judgement and subtlety of discrimination and a skill in applying old principles to new combinations of facts which make it safe for a people to leave wide powers to their magistrates or their governing assembly'.[24]

So much for the patrician ideal. In practice, within the House of Commons itself, Bryce found such a political caste conspicuously absent and the last remnants of established parliamentary traditions assailed from all quarters. Too late he realised that while the advance of democracy nominally increased parliament's prestige in actuality it undermined that very authority by rendering representation superfluous and reducing it to the passive role of delegation and the validation of the public will. While the independent representative constituted in Acton's words 'the innermost barrier against the reign of democratic force', 'the more truly the House of Commons comes to represent the real nation the more it must fall under opinion out of doors'.[25] The emergence of powerful extra-parliamentary organisations, the careful presentation of party

24 *History and Jurisprudence*, I, pp. 178 – 9, 166 – 7, 186.
25 Quoted in David Mathew, *Lord Acton and His Times*, p. 298, and *Acton-Drew Letters*, p. 81. Bryce in *The Contemporary Review*, Nov 1884, pp. 724, 728, and *NYN*, 3 Feb 1881, p. 72.

platforms and programmes, the novel concept of a popular mandate and the careful assessment of by-elections as indicators of public support or disapproval, all indicated the same trend. Even the House of Lords, that seeming bastion of hereditary anti-democratic rule, had become virtually an instrument of popular control, for in rejecting a bill it could force the dissolution of parliament and send a ministry back to the sovereign electorate for a renewed mandate.[26] At the same time democracy by delegation required more stringent party discipline and a more active legislative programme which strengthened the hand of the executive and the party whips at the expense of the independent MP. As long as they retained the confidence of the electorate ministries could treat the once-respected back benchers as mere voting fodder: 'To say that at present the cabinet legislates with the advice and consent of Parliament would hardly be an exaggeration', Bryce sourly concluded. If parliament was sovereign the cabinet 'so unified, so strong, so capable of swiftly and irresistibly accomplishing the purposes of a transitory majority, as we now perceive it to be' had gone far since Bagehot's discovery in concentrating that sovereignty in itself.[27]

Of course the insights of comparative politics did not create 'parliamentary sovereignty'; Bryce had long appreciated that the British Constitution was precisely what parliament within reason chose to make it. What Anglo-American comparison did do was reinforce a sense of constitutional vulnerability at a time when parliament was displaying frightening signs of disintegration and a decline in morale and integrity. Various ominous portents seemed to reach a climax and find their confirmation in the extended parliamentary crisis of 1884 – 6. The Third Reform bill which initiated that crisis was not, as the 1867 bill had been, preceded by extended debate on the theoretical justification for change; instead the bill was introduced suddenly and without preliminaries just, Bryce wrote 'when the impulse to change will be greatest, with a House full of new members, largely Radicals'. In place of measured debate each party jockeyed for advantage, used empty dialogue to disguise devious strategy and raised unquestioned the radical implications of redistribution alongside the original purpose of extending the franchise.

[26] Bryce to Eliot, 30 Jan 1917, Ms. Bryce USA 2. Bryce to Dicey, 6 Jan 1919, Ms. Bryce 4. Bryce in *NYN*, 3 Feb 1881, p. 73, and 31 May 1883, p. 46.
[27] Bryce's annotation of Lowell's *Government of England*, Lowell Papers. *AC*, I, p. 279.

What most clearly emerged from this managed debate was the adroit contrivance of the two party leaders, Salisbury and Gladstone, and the relative impotence of rank and file MPs.[28]

Under the new franchise eighty-five Irish nationalist MPs were returned to parliament and the preconcerted obstruction of procedure began to reach its peak. Bryce was frankly appalled by their determined unscrupulousness and vandalism: 'An Irish leader holds his post on condition of perpetual combat', and his followers had 'raised obstruction to the dignity of a science . . ..
It has been plain for months past that their sole game is to stop the wheels, to attack and weaken every Government because it is a Government.'[29] The House with its informal codes and conventions made no allowance for those who refused to play by established rules and parliament was uniquely unprepared for the Irish onslaught. Nor was that all, for the Irish nationalists brutally illustrated the weaknesses of a party system under a flexible constitution; deadlock, the absence of a clear majority in the House, a destructive minority holding the balance, a brief alliance between the nationalists and one of the two parties for temporary advantage, could result in irreparable damage and inject an element of permanent instability into parliamentary affairs. The indecorous game of barter was already being played. Gladstone's rapid about-turn from coercion to the Kilmainham treaty with Parnell, the Tories' cobbled compromise with the Irish during the Maamtrasna debate, indicated a new humiliating order of enslavement to a purposeful minority. The passage of the second reading of the Liberals' Coercion bill was, Bryce considered, the most painful in his parliamentary career: 'It now seems to me to have marked the end of an epoch, the end of the old, dignified, constitutionally regular, and gentlemanly House of Commons, in which everyone was on his good behaviour and felt the force of great traditions.' Afterwards he overheard an MP declare: 'The game of Law and Order is up.'[30]

Bryce was not alone in his fears. Academic observers, jittery at the best of times, were distinctly unnerved by the crisis.

[28]   Bryce to Mrs Whitman, 7 Oct 1884, Ms. Bryce USA 22. Bryce in *NYN*, 3 April 1884, pp. 291–292; 14 Aug 1884, pp. 131–2; 11 Dec 1884, p. 499.
[29]   *NYN*, 13 July 1882, p. 29, and 13 April 1882, p. 310. Bryce to Goldwin Smith, 29 June 1884, Ms. Bryce 17. Smith to Bryce, 24 Jan 1881 and 27 Sept 1885, Ms. Bryce 16. Bryce to Freeman, 18 Feb 1887, Ms. Bryce 9, and *The Nineteenth Century*, Feb 1886, pp. 6, 9.
[30]   Fisher, I, pp. 205, 210.

Sidgwick records Maine's concern in November 1884: 'the genuine alarm that he seems to feel at the existing state of things in England impressed me much', as did Dicey's consternation expressed some months later.[31] In the short run Bryce could only suggest piecemeal measures to avoid the total disruption of parliamentary procedure. He proposed a reduction in proliferating Private Members' bills, and supported the introduction of the 'closure' when freedom of debate was being grossly abused, for 'a governing assembly cannot suffer itself to be paralysed'; it must, at whatever risk to minorities, find some method of despatching its business'.[32]

When he looked at the United States he discerned similar discouraging trends. As in Britain the strength of representative government was yielding to the direct influence of public opinion:

> Congress has not become any more distinctly than in earlier days the dominant power in the State, the organ of national sovereignty, the irresistible exponent of the national will. In a country ruled by public opinion, it could hold this position only in virtue of its capacity of leading opinion, that is to say of its courage, promptitude, and wisdom. Since it grows in no one of these qualities, it wins no greater ascendancy; indeed its power, as compared with that of public opinion, seems rather to decline.[33]

Indeed America had gone further in displaying an almost universal contempt for legislative government. Substantial powers were granted to mayors and state governors to act as a curb on the people's legislative representatives; the trend was from annual to biennial legislative sessions, and the perpetual revision and increasing length of State constitutions was indicative not, as observers believed, of a republican desire for change in itself, but a wish to extend still further the area of enumerated cases placed beyond legislative control and return it either to popular control or invest it in chosen executives. Article 4, Section 25, of the California Constitution of 1879, for example, enumerated thirty-three such prohibitory clauses and was essentially a method of initiative and referendum consonant

---

[31]   *Sidgwick Memoirs*, pp. 393, 488.
[32]   Bryce to Gladstone, 12 Dec 1880, 24 Nov 1882, Ms. Bryce 10. Bryce in *NYN*, 13 April 1882, p. 310, and *North American Review*, Oct 1890, pp. 385 – 98.
[33]   *AC*, II, p. 712.

with the growing demand for direct legislation.[34] But, although at first sight America offered small cause for optimism to the English parliamentarian, further research suggested that built into its constitution were possible antidotes to growing Anglo-American experiments in the dangerous realms of extra-parliamentary democracy. And these both liberal and tory were to seize upon in desperation in the 1880s.

America's constitutional conservatism

It was during the 1880s that the sublime wisdom of America's founding fathers was rediscovered and exalted. Frederick Bancroft's deification of the constitution-makers in his *History of the Formation of the Constitution* appeared in 1882 and John Fiske's *Critical Period of American History* — which told a tale of the republic brought back from the edge of anarchy in 1786 by sage patricians — was published in the same year as *The American Commonwealth*. Sir Henry Sumner Maine might gibe at 'the nauseous grandiloquence of the American panegyric historians', yet he too, while dismissing democracy in general, ended by extravagantly praising American democracy in particular.[35] Gladstone, not to be outdone in matters of intellectual fashion, averred that if Britain's informal conventions had grown under divine guidance, the American Constitution was the single greatest achievement of the eighteenth century Enlightenment and 'the most wonderful work ever struck off at a given time by the brain and purpose of man'. If the 'Americomania' which Bryce and Dicey did so much to encourage flourished in England it was because it appealed to a profound yearning for immutability and permanence in a world of accelerated change and political flux, a yearning reinforced by a sharper appreciation of a potentially permanent state of parliamentary revolution. That both writers exaggerated American stability and British impermanence served only to make the contrast more tantalising. Macaulay's aphorism that America was all sails and no anchor was now applied to Britain, and John

[34]   AC, I, pp. 435 – 7, 439, 510, 535, 691, 683 – 724. AC, II, pp. 406 – 8. *History and Jurisprudence*, I, p. 235.
[35]   George W. Smalley referred to *Popular Government* as 'a protest against Democracy, and a panegyric on Democracy in America.' (*Nineteenth Century*, Jan/June 1887, p. 221).

Morley suggested, instead, that the American ship of state had proved itself no mere kedge.[36]

Furthermore, the fact that the American example could excite both Maine and Gladstone was evidence that the phenomenon was strictly non-partisan, and its indiscriminate appeal was to the cautious temperament, whatever its party persuasion. As Bryce observed: 'The march of democracy in England has disposed English writers and politicians of the very school which thirty or twenty years ago pointed to America as a terrible example, now to discover that her republic possesses elements of stability wanting in the monarchy of the mother country.' 'The establishment in Britain of a species of rigid constitution has begun to be advocated by the persons least inclined to trust democracy.'[37] Dicey spelt the matter out with even greater clarity:

> The plain truth is that educated Englishmen are slowly learning that the American republic affords the best example of a conservative democracy; and now that England is becoming democratic, respectable Englishmen are beginning to consider whether the Constitution of the United States may not afford means by which, under new democratic forms, may be preserved the political conservatism dear and habitual to the governing classes of England.[38]

Sir Henry Sumner Maine ranks as perhaps the outstanding late-Victorian conservative theorist, possessing an immense academic prestige which even Lord Acton deferred to and which he exploited in his ferocious rearguard action against what he termed 'Gladstonian revolution' up till his death in 1888. As chief advocate of the historical method and trained in the stern school of the Indian civil service, his temperament and mode of thinking was deeply authoritarian and establishmentarian; his aim, as Acton perceived it, was 'to exercise power, and to find good reasons for adopted policy'.[39] Anonymously in the pages

---

36 Gladstone in *North American Review*, Sept/Oct 1878, p. 185. Edward Phelps took issue with Gladstone and insisted that the Constitution Bryce depicted displayed a 'better than human intervention' (*Quarterly Review*, 1889, Vol. 169, p. 261). Morley quoted in Michael Weinberg, *The Liberal Image of America in France and England, 1789–1890* (unpublished Harvard Ph.D.) p. 256.

37 *AC*, I, p. 249. *History and Jurisprudence*, I, p. 241.

38 *NYN*, 21 Jan 1886, p. 53.

39 *Acton-Drew Letters*, p. 26.

of the *Pall Mall Gazette* and the *Quarterly Review* he launched a sustained assault on Gladstonian liberalism whose radical and irresponsible policies would, he believed, lead first to the loss of Ireland and, with it, the loss of India, the destruction of the British empire and the disintegration of parliamentary sovereignty. His *Quarterly Review* articles published as *Popular Government* in 1885 constituted, in Henry Sidgwick's estimation, 'the best anti-democratic writing that we have had . . . seemed really concerned that we have no proper constitution in England: thinks it would be a real gain to have a constitutional code settled by Act of Parliament'. So impressed was Sidgwick that when he came to read Bryce's draft manuscript he insisted that Bryce must take full account of Maine and 'the question whether America should be our model in efforts to guard against the dangers of democracy'.[40]

There is a certain irony in all this, for essentially Maine was lifting wholesale material which Bryce and Dicey had made commonplace and welding it into a formidable anti-liberal polemic. Both had already sketched in all the peculiar virtues which Maine discerned in American institutions. The dates in Sidgwick's *Diaries* — 1884, 1885, 1886 — show that Bryce's chapters on the American Constitution were being circulated, read and discussed openly in intellectual circles. Bryce's Oxford lectures in 1884 were well known and Dicey had written on American federalism in the first number of *The Law Quarterly Review* and incorporated the article into his *Law of the Constitution*, published in 1885, the same year as *Popular Government*. Maine's emphasis on the derivation of the American from the English model was unexceptional. The statement that 'the spirit of 1787 was an English spirit, and therefore a conservative spirit, inaugurating the least democratic of democracies' could have come from Maine, though it is in fact Bryce's. But Maine went on to reflect that these links were slow to be recognised by Englishmen because, while America's written copy of the English model had remained substantially unaltered, firmly rooted in its robust eighteenth century origins, the English model had changed beyond recognition since 1776. The president of the United States retained the full plenitude of his monarchical prerogatives; the Senate held firm to its original form of equal state representation and indirect election which

---

[40]   *Sidgwick Memoirs*, pp. 392 – 3. Sidgwick to Bryce, 26 Aug 1884, 22 Jan 1885, Ms. Bryce 15.

was 'a denial or a doubt of the proposition that the voice of the people is the voice of God', and the Supreme Court guarded and perpetuated the Constitution's anti-democratic bias.[41]

Maine's liberal opponents did not — could not — object to his plagiarism as such, but to the ends to which his material was deployed, for he contended that democracy was neither the best form of government nor inevitable; that in a human history dominated by custom and inertia sustained progress might be aberrant and not part of the ineluctable order of things. Most unforgivably he stood the liberals' faith in progress on its head by suggesting that popular government, in forging an alliance with the state, had retreated from free 'contract' (the true measure of advancement) to a socialistic 'status' of dependence. In suggesting that liberals might unwittingly be inaugurating a régime based on the collectivist, monolithic state, Maine deftly managed to shake the confidence of his opponents and sow the seeds of self-doubt. His careful field study of ancient Indian law and his masterly use of historical jurisprudence enabled him to claim empirical evidence based on strict scholarship — a verifiable past and present — and expose liberalism's over-dependence on future prospects; in reality popular governments displayed frightening symptoms of anarchy and impermanence. And if Godkin objected to his loading the dice unfairly in taking Latin American republics as paragons of democracy, and Morley that it was absurd to conclude that English democracy must be frail because thirteen out of Bolivia's last fourteen Presidents had either been assassinated or forced into exile, Maine could retort that this only served to reduce the number of examples still further. Even Bryce's inductive methodology left him open to the charge that America's uniqueness confirmed the ancient anti-democratic argument of 'propitious circumstances' which Maine resurrected, and such was the prestige of the historical method that it did not occur to Bryce to reply that democratic scarcity was not, in itself, evidence of democracy's undesirability.[42]

Instead Bryce concentrated on Maine's faulty logic and dubious extrapolations which reflected a facile style which he

---

[41]   *AC*, I, p. 300. *Popular Government*, pp. 179, 196 – 254.
[42]   Cf. George Feaver, *From Status to Contract*, especially pp. 228 – 323, and his article in *The Journal of Politics*, 1965, Vol. 27, p. 304. E. L. Godkin, *Problems of Modern Democracy*, p. 80, and Maine's reply, *The Nineteenth Century*, March 1886, p. 379. Morley quoted in Collini *et al.*, *That Noble Science of Politics*, p. 235.

found 'provokingly vague and loosely expressed'. Acton insisted that the book was vitiated by gross partisanship; it was 'an assault on the Government', 'a rattling Tory pamphlet', 'a Manual of Unacknowledged Conservatism', all the more seductive for being cloaked in the guise of objective scholarship. As Leslie Stephen commented: 'Democrats naturally regarded his obstensible impartiality as a mask for thorough distrust of popular impulses.'[43] But what his opponents could not do was dismiss the book entirely, for it revealed, only too clearly, the nagging doubts they themselves harboured. As in 1867, the heat of combat was generated by the proximate friction of two factions who felt they should be considerably further apart. Instead the strategy was to render the book innocuous by pointing to its marked unoriginality and lack of fresh insights. It was the peculiar and defining task of the liberal to appreciate the fullest implications and drawbacks of democracy — this is what distinguished him from those who blindly opposed, and pure democrats who as blindly conceded all — before considering the erection of safeguards. Thus *Popular Government* 'was not a new departure, and every good Liberal ought to have discounted the argument of that work, and more besides, before avowing himself a Liberal'.[44] Lord Acton had nothing to learn from Maine on the question of original sin.

Yet all Englishmen of whatever persuasion might learn much from America's example, for the republic seemed to have attained to an ideal state of immutability resulting from an almost unchanging constitution and a passive public opinion. Dicey had located political and legal sovereignty in the only body formally capable of amending the Constitution — three-quarters of the State legislatures or conventions — and it followed from this that 'the sovereign is in a federal state a despot hard to rouse. He is not, like the English Parliament, an ever-wakeful legislator, but a monarch who slumbers and sleeps'.[45] Bryce, with his greater appreciation of the many

---

43   *Studies in Contemporary Biography*, p. 309. *Acton-Drew Letters*, p. 26, and Acton quoted in Feaver, pp. 236 – 7. Leslie Stephen in the *DNB*, XXXV, p. 345. Dicey confirmed this general mistrust: 'With Maine, as with most Englishmen, political theories were too closely connected with the controversies which divided English parties' (*National Review*, 1893, Vol. 21, p. 784).

44   Acton quoted in Feaver, p. 254. Likewise Bryce: 'There is a better case to be made against democracy than [Maine] has made' (Bryce to Sidgwick, 12 Sept 1887, Ms. Bryce 15).

45   *LC*, p. 145.

informal ways in which the constitution could be modified and adapted through interpretation, custom and usage, applied Dicey's concept of 'conventions' much more realistically to an American scene which reflected a transient Gilded Age torpor rather than any permanent characteristics of federalism, 'for the present at least — it may not always be so — (America) sails upon a summer sea'.[46] Despite this he reached broadly Diceyan conclusions with regard to federalism in general and the United States in particular. Americans, he wrote 'are conservative in their fundamental beliefs, in the structure of their governments, in their social and domestic usages. They are like a tree whose pendulous shoots quiver and rustle with the lightest breeze, while its roots enfold the rock with a grasp which storms cannot loosen'. This assumption so suffused *The American Commonwealth* that Acton could suggest that a quotation from Justice Thomas Cooley contained its 'brief abstract':

America is not so much an example in her liberty as in the covenanted and enduring securities which are intended to prevent liberty degenerating into licence, and to establish a feeling of trust and repose under a beneficent government, whose excellence, so obvious in its freedom, is still more conspicuous in its careful provision for permanence and stability.

Yet Acton in his review omitted the words immediately preceding Cooley's address which were an equally relevant 'abstract': 'America has become the leader and example for all enlightened nations. England and France alike look across the ocean for lessons which may form and guide their people.'[47]
There was a broad area of agreement in one area at least concerning the 'lessons' to be derived from a rigid constitution's capacity to withstand the assaults of collectivism. The Fifth Amendment and Chief Justice Marshall's reassertion of contractual obligation in *Dartmouth College v. Woodward* — 'the bulwark of American individualism against democratic impatience and Socialist fantasy', as Maine termed it — provoked the tantalising belief that similar guarantees written into a fundamental British

---

[46] *AC*, I, p. 303. Maine referred to American democracy 'as calm as water in a great artificial reservoir', and rejoiced in a legislative inertia that had failed to arouse itself since the Bland-Allison Act of 1878 (*Popular Government*, p. 111. *Nineteenth Century*, March 1886, p. 379).
[47] *AC*, II, p. 284. *History of Liberty*, p. 580. *AC*, I, p. 302.

Constitution would have reduced Gladstone's confiscatory Irish Church Act of 1869 and Land Acts of 1870 and 1881 to so much waste paper. From this Dicey drew the obvious conclusion:

> Radicalism . . . has ceased to occupy itself deeply with America. A nation whose habits and polity are based upon individual freedom, and whose Constitution guarantees respect for the sanctity of contract, does not in any sense realise the ideals of statesmen who hope . . . to accomplish great things for the mass of the people by means of the intervention of the State.[48]

Where liberals differed was in their objection to conservatives adopting aspects of American rigidity without its concomitant democracy; instead liberals argued for minor adoptions of American-inspired checks to moderate the advent of British democracy. Direct grafting was unscientific and unworkable. A presidential executive beyond the sway of party votes might be stabilising but would conflict with the crown and paralyse the unique joint functions of the cabinet. The Lords could be reformed along senatorial lines, but who and what would the new Senate represent, and what was to be done with the hereditary principle? A rigid constitution had its appeal but would politicise an independent interpreting judiciary and destroy parliamentary sovereignty and the pliancy of 'conventions'. Advocates demanded a Supreme Court to guard the constitution, but what constitution, Bryce asked, were they to guard?[49]

Bryce's more moderate approach can be most clearly seen in his adoption of senatorial reform for the Lords and in his opposition to Dicey's radical advocacy of the referendum. The Reform Bill of 1884 had once more brought the anomaly of the Lords to the fore in liberal thinking and clarified the observable absurdity of a lower house dedicated to curbing privileges depending on that bastion of privilege to effect the change. It was, Bryce argued, unrealistic to expect elevated and disinterested action from a chamber full of peers 'anxious to defend all

[48] *Popular Government*, p. 248. *LC*, pp. 169–70. *NYN*, 21 Jan 1886, p. 53.
[49] See Dicey's 'Can the English Constitution be Americanised?' (*NYN*, 28 Jan 1886, pp. 73–4). Bryce conceded the appeal of a rigid constitution to anti-democrats, but concluded that the erection of judicial safeguards would result in 'the extinction of the present British Parliament and the erection of a wholly different body or bodies in its room' (*AC*, II, p. 490, and *AC*, I, pp. 249–50).

the advantages and prerogatives of great proprietors'. Consisting almost entirely of tory partisans the upper house served to perpetuate and exacerbate party squabbles which, when there was a liberal majority in the Commons, became as predictable as harvest in August and fog in November. The reinforcement of the hereditary principle in the democratic age was indefensible, and in retreat, aware of its precarious existence yet surviving, the Lords were positively dangerous; dependent — on privilege, on class, on party, on public opinion — it could act as a drag on progressive reform yet, in its weakness, be unable to restrain, might even incite, revolutionary measures.[50]

An extensive correspondence with E. L. Godkin and Carl Schurz throughout 1884 encouraged Bryce to propose senatorial reforms, for his aim was to strengthen not weaken the Lords and by so doing ensure its survival against radicals who wished to abolish it and conservatives, like Lord Salisbury, who, in proposing the entrenchment of the hereditary principle, condemned the Lords to a similar fate. A genuine bicameralism was all the more essential as the Commons reflected a 'popular dictatorship'. Enjoying practical supremacy since 1867 'who can tell', Bryce asked, 'that (public opinion) will not soon discover it, and will not be intoxicated by the discovery?'.[51] The Lords remained the sole counter to this growing popular encroachment, and Acton, like Bryce, clearly looked to America as a model for safeguards. 'The more perfect the representative system the more necessary is some other aid to stability . . .. To "sweep away" the House of Lords would be a terrible revolution . . .. As we have none of the other resources proper to unmixed governments, a real veto, a federation of states, or a constitution above the legislature, we must treasure the one security we possess.'[52] The Senate with its fixed and longer term of service, its indirect elections, its veto, its shared executive powers and its reputation as 'a centre of gravity' and 'sheet anchor' offered a solution. Bryce especially wished to emulate the Senate's stabilising influence, its advisory and revisory

---

50   NYN, 21 Sept 1882, pp. 238 – 9; 30 April 1868, p. 34; 14 May 1868, p. 390.
     AC, I, p. 111: 'The upper house', Dicey wrote, 'represents neither the nation nor the empire, but the will of the Tory leaders' (NYN, 28 Jan 1886, p. 74).
51   Bryce to Schurz, 27 Sept 1884, Schurz Papers. Schurz to Bryce, 9 Nov 1884, Mrs. Bryce USA 18. Bryce to Godkin, 27 Sept 1884, Godkin Papers. Godkin to Bryce, 17 Oct 1884, Ms. Bryce USA 4. Bryce in *Contemporary Review*, Nov 1884, p. 725.
52   *Acton-Drew Letters*, p. 81.

functions, and its capacity, at the very least, to buy time for reconsideration. His reformed House would 'stem the torrent of democratic change, arrest revolutionary propensities, and either defeat them by appealing to the sober judgement of the country, or at least secure full time for their consideration and mitigation by delaying them till there can be no more room for doubt as to the will of the nation'.[53] There were problems: how far would the Commons allow genuine competition and a rival infallibility? Nominated or appointed peers would tend to be 'stiff, timid, querulous', but if they were to be elected, elected by whom, and for what? Bryce never resolved these difficulties though we find him attempting a senatorial solution in the draft bill for Irish home rule in 1893, again 'with infinite worry' in 1906, and as Chairman of the Committee on Second Chamber Reform in 1918.[54]

A direct appeal to the nation was another means by which the revolutionary consequences of parliamentary sovereignty could be averted. Practically the Lords' veto was tantamount to a call for a referendum. Constitutionally Dicey argued that the Commons' legal sovereignty had usurped the nation's political sovereignty and that convention required redress through the countervailing force of crown, Lords and public opinion. 'Americomaniacs' seized on the referendum as an instrument of delay and obstruction because it appeared to conform to democratic principles and because it would graft the ailing power of the Lords on to the supposed will of the nation. But these conservative motives presumed an equally conservative public will, and, while Dicey and Maine managed to discover evidence that the referendum was a reactionary instrument in Switzerland and the United States, Bryce remained sceptical.[55]

He was wary of drawing general conclusions from the Swiss example. Bound together in close-knit rural communities,

---

53 *Contemporary Review*, Nov 1884, pp. 730, 724. AC, I, pp. 110, 184.
54 *Contemporary Review*, Nov 1884, pp. 733, 730, 728. NYN, 21 Sept 1882, p. 239. David Lindsay Keir, *The Constitutional History of Modern Britain*, p. 483. *Hansard*, 4th Series, Vol. 8, c. 1431. Both Balfour and Eustace Percy were amused by Bryce's Tory defence of the Lords (Fisher, I, p. 192. Percy to Bryce, 3 Jan 1914, Ms. Bryce Misc.).
55 LC, pp. 376 – 80, 406. On the Swiss referendum cf. *Popular Government*, pp. 39 – 40, 68, and Dicey in NYN, 8 Oct 1885, pp. 297 – 8. The referendum, Dicey wrote, 'is democratic, for it is in reality, as also on the face thereof, an appeal to the people. It is conservative since it ensures the maintenance of any law or institution which the majority of electors effectively wish to preserve' (LC, 8th ed., p. xcviii).

enjoying uniquely benign political conditions, Switzerland's inertia merely reflected the quiet contentment of those who would be foolish to attempt to change the *status quo*. An analysis of American State governments at first inclined Bryce to agree with Dicey and Maine, but further observation led him to the conclusion that the referendum was a dangerous innovation which might act as spur rather than check.[56] Again it was vital to consider the instrument in its American context; traditionally the United States had drawn its sovereignty from the people, from below, and the average American was trained to political responsibility. British tradition was very different. If final authority were removed from parliament the Commons might well be goaded into irresponsible action and the government exploit a form of tyranny by plebiscite. The acceptance of the referendum was a recognition of direct democracy and the destruction of representative government, and while this might appeal to an academic like Dicey who would clutch at any straw to obstruct the liberal government's enactment of home rule, it could only be viewed with extreme distaste by a traditionalist and parliamentarian of Bryce's mould. Furthermore, this innovation set a hazardous precedent; once conceded nothing need stop direct democracy being taken to its logical conclusion as in America, with the initiative and recall being extended even into the sacrosanct sphere of judicial appointment and dismissal. In replying to Dicey, Bryce pointed out that there was no reason to believe that mass opinion would confirm Dicey's opinions or indeed use the referendum only for the limited ends he required:

> I wish I could agree with you about the referendum as applied to England, but I have not enough faith in the popular vote to avert the dangers we foresee . . .. When a weapon is put into a man's hand, you cannot be sure he will use it only for the specified purposes for which it was handed to him . . . What an engine for prompt and drastic change you have in that.[57]

Dicey's continued advocacy points readily to the selectivity and inconsistencies inherent in 'Americomania'; the writer who

56 *History and Jurisprudence*, I, p. 167. *AC*, I, pp. 455, 457. *AC*, I, 1910, pp. 480, 475 – 6.
57 Bryce to Dicey, 28 Nov 1909, 26 Dec 1910, 12 Jan 1911, Ms. Bryce 4. Bryce to Lowell, 14 Dec 1917, 1 March 1918, Lowell Papers.

most powerfully asserted parliamentary plenitude and dismissed the 'singular superstition' embodied in the maxim *vox populi vox Dei* was forced to resort to an American-style referendum in order to escape from a trap he had set himself. He could do this because he distinguished between legal and political sovereignty and could conjure up the 'convention' of the popular will as countervailing force to neutralise the usurped powers of the Commons: he appealed to the referendum as an appeal to democracy to veto home rule. But increasingly throughout the century 'convention' delegated popular sovereignty to the representatives of the people in the House of Commons. To Dicey the concept of parliamentary sovereignty was both appealing and appalling at the same time: appealing when an administration of which he approved inherited the mantle of illimitable powers, appalling when those same powers fell into the hands of a ministry of whose policies he profoundly disapproved, such as the liberal government after 1905. Again, in holding to the principle that no parliament could bind its successor, that, for example, a ministry was under no legal obligation to uphold a home rule bill passed by its predecessor, he had, at the same time, and of necessity, to assert the right of that predecessor to enact home rule in the first place.[58] As early as 1888 he was tinkering with the idea of investing the Prime Minister with presidential powers, a fixed term of office and a right of veto. In the extended constitutional crisis of 1909 – 14 he spoke of reviving the crown's reserved powers to dissolve parliament with the aid of the Lords and hold a referendum on the issue of home rule.[59] Even the saner and more level-headed Bryce in his plans for a senatorial Lords was compelled to make a dubious distinction between a destructive and transient public will on the one hand and a constructive groundswell on the other to which the unflurried Lords would appeal. Yet at the same time he attacked parties for reflecting that public will only too faithfully.[60] His bicameralism was a bid for moderate liberal reform, a wish to maintain the prestige and activism of the Commons without excessive obstruction from the Lords, yet sufficient to act as a brake on the representative chamber's revolutionary potential. Bryce and

[58]   *LC*, 8th ed., p. lxii, *LC*, pp. 372 – 6. *England's Case*, pp. 29, 96, 39, 42 – 43.
[59]   *Sidgwick Memoirs*, p. 488. *LC*, pp. 406 – 12. 'The prerogatives of the Crown have become the privileges of the people' (*LC*, p. 411).
[60]   *Contemporary Review*, April 1890, p. 506. *Modern Democracies*, II, p. 454.

Dicey's selective rifling of the American model suggests not only anti-democratic impulses but also an appreciation of federal devices as oppositional weapons of destruction. The negative, limiting elements of federalism, its highly developed system of checks and balances, attracted both unionist and federalist.

America offered them one other dazzling example. Having asserted the absolute supremacy of parliament in the first section of his *Law of the Constitution* Dicey had then to square this with the three general principles of the rule of law: the first was the absence of arbitrary governmental powers, the second the subjection of every citizen to ordinary laws administered by ordinary tribunals, and the third, the enforcement of these rights by ordinary laws rather than through documents stating general constitutional principles. This appeared at first sight to align the written constitutions of the United States and France. But just as Bryce had detached American organicism from France's revolutionary republicanism so, legally, Dicey did the same, for France failed to meet the requirements demanded by the rule of law on all three grounds, while the Constitution of the United States perfected it. The *Droit Administratif* with its whiff of Napoleonic despotism and Jacobin arbitrariness failed just as the French tradition of immutable constitutions and mutable revolutions historically reinforced the Gallic error of writing imperishable abstract rights into fundamental documents which proved to be only too perishable; that which political bodies gave, political bodies could take away. England's Bill of Rights and the first ten amendments to the Constitution of the United States were superficially similar, but while universalist and libertarian in language they were, in substance, specific and pragmatic rightings of particular legislative wrongs. The Anglo-American Common Law tradition, in marked contrast to the continental variety, progressed through ordinary courts, dealing with specific cases based on judge-made decisions adhering to case precedent. Because of this the apparent contradiction of parliamentary sovereignty and the rule of law in Britain was 'delusive', for parliament and courts jointly perceived and enforced the Common Law so that there ran through the British Constitution 'that inseparable connection between the means of enforcing a right and the right to be enforced which is the strength of judicial legislation'.[61]

[61]   *LC*, pp. 179–201, 322–60, 350, 195.

Dicey took great pains to ground American law in its English origins. Numerous examples of direct transmission such as judicial review, the English privy council as part model for the Supreme Court, the expansion of the Constitution by judge-made precedent, exemplified a joint legal tradition which made 'the institutions of the English people on both side of the Atlantic rest upon the same notions of law'.[62] The implications of this analysis for Anglo-American unity were crucial. Practically, Bryce had to remind English judges that their dicta carried weight from the Bay of Fundy to San Francisco and that 'the interests of the higher class of American lawyers in the English law is wonderfully fresh and keen. An English barrister, if properly authenticated, is welcomed as a brother of the art, and finds the law reports of his own country as sedulously read and as acutely criticised as he would in the Temple'.[63] Personally, there was a particular intimacy between leading English legalists and the Harvard Law School. In September 1870 Bryce and Dicey sat down to dinner with Justice Holmes, Judge Horace Gray and Arthur Sedgwick; the talk was legal and the evening 'very pleasant'. In time both extended their acquaintance with other members of the faculty — James Ames, Christopher Langdell, James B. Thayer — all of them, in Dicey's opinion, 'apostles of English law' teaching at the greatest legal institution in the English-speaking world.[64] Their theoretical belief in the uniformity of Anglo-American law (Dicey even suggested a common Anglo-American citizenship based on it) stemmed from their conviction that the uniqueness of the Common Law tradition reflected the uniqueness of the Anglo-American character. They felt especially confident in asserting this because it was a Frenchmen, Tocqueville, who first elucidated it when he wrote that 'in the United States and in England there seems to be more liberty in the customs than in the laws of the people. In Switzerland there seems to be more

---

62 *LC*, pp. 136, 160, 414.
63 *Macmillan's Magazine*, Jan 1872, p. 211. *AC*, II, p. 514. The law, Bryce concluded, was 'one of the links which best serves to bind the United States to England' (*AC*, II, p. 507).
64 *1870 Journal*, p. 20. Ms. Bryce Misc. Holmes (1841 – 1935) was working on the 12th ed. of Kent's *Commentaries*. Gray (1828 – 1902) was the Senior Justice of the Massachusetts' Supreme Court. Sedgwick (1844 – 1915) was joint editor with Holmes of *The American Law Review*. Dicey in *Contemporary Review*, Nov 1899, p. 748. *AC*, II, pp. 503, 504 n. 1. Dicey dedicated his *Law and Public Opinion* to Eliot and the Professors of the Law School. See also Richard A. Cosgrove, *Harvard Library Bulletin*, July 1978, pp. 325 – 35.

liberty in the laws than in the customs of the people.' Dicey expressed this principle with its profound implications thus: 'Each man's individual rights are far less the result of our constitution than the basis on which the constitution is founded.'[65] So, while Goldwin Smith and Freeman stressed racial unity and Gladstone ethical unity, Bryce and Dicey borrowed from all three but added the ties of law, with England's increasingly universal legal system emulating, in the modern world, Roman law in the ancient.[66]

But they went further in illustrating how the Americans, having inherited the Common Law, proceeded to embody its principles in an imperishable document placed forever beyond political whim and destructive change. Consequently American society was based on a unique legalism and held an unprecedented respect for the rule of law; its citizens were acquiescent constitutionalists who deferred to the supremacy of judges. It followed that the extraordinary powers bestowed on the Supreme Court made it almost master as well as guardian of the polity. 'It is technically correct to say that the Supreme Court acts only as interpreter of the Constitution, but we must not be deceived by fictions. The Supreme Court has legislated as truly, and perhaps more effectively, than Congress.' 'The American tribunals have dealt with matters of supreme consequence.'[67] The impact on public opinion was likewise immense. It bred a legal spirit in the masses and imbued them with a reverence for the law. In a society where litigation had replaced legislation this reverence, reinforced by the cumbersome method of popular amendment, became self-perpetuating: 'The difficulty of altering the Constitution produced conservative sentiment, and national conservatism doubles the difficulty of altering the Constitution.'[68] The appeal of a vast republic run on the lines of a solicitor's office in Lincoln's Inn, guided by the safety of precedent and the unquestioning acceptance of judicial

---

[65] *Contemporary Review*, April 1897, p. 470. *LC*, p. 182, and *LC*, 8th ed., p. xxxvii. Woodrow Wilson, in his review of the *AC*, adapted the formula: 'America has democracy because she is free; she is not free because she has democracy' (reprinted in *Brooks*, p. 187).

[66] *History and Jurisprudence*, I, pp. 230–1.

[67] *England's Case*, p. 186. *LC*, p. 158. *History and Jurisprudence*, I, pp. 230–1. *AC*, I, pp. 225–70.

[68] *LC*, pp. 175, 169. 'That a federal system . . . can flourish only among commuities imbued with a legal spirit and trained to reverence the law is as certain as can be any conclusion of political speculation' (*LC*, p. 175).

decisions, held obvious allure for Bryce and enabled him to conjure afresh the vision of a harmonious community removed from the messy squabbles of Westminster.[69]

This was especially so because Bryce idealised the legal profession and unquestioningly accepted the abstract justice of judicial decisions. Judges were, to him, 'stewards of sacred mysteries', a priesthood whose external trappings of authority reflected the authority of their judgements. He spoke of the 'cool, dry atmosphere of judicial determination', of the Supreme Court as 'a pure organ of law, commissioned to do justice between man and man, but to do nothing more'. His greatest veneration was reserved for Chief Justice Marshall — 'a special gift of favouring Providence' — whose god-like achievement was 'honestly and logically to unfold the meaning' of the constitution so that it 'seemed not so much to rise under his hands to its full stature, as to be gradually unveiled by him till it stood revealed in the harmonious perfection of the form which its framers had designed'.[70] This hagiography was in contrast to his lurid portrayal of Marshall's political opponent and kinsman, Jefferson, who, in inaugurating party spoils, wirepulling and 'acrid partisanship', had precipitated America's abrupt decline to Jacksonianism: 'The first generation of statesmen whose authority had restrained the masses had just quitted the stage. The anarchic teachings of Jefferson had borne fruit. Administration and legislation, hitherto left to the educated classes, had been seized by the rude hand of men of low social position and scanty knowledge.' It was Jefferson, and thereafter Jackson, who had assaulted judicial independence in an attempt to level the courts and embroiled them in party conflict and political debate. The election and dismissal of the judiciary and its control by party or purse led inevitably to the decline of the New York bar from the palmy days of Chancellor Kent and Justice Story to Justices Barnard and Cardozo, 'two of the most remarkable sights in the city', both in the pay of the Tweed ring, whom Bryce met in 1870.[71] Marshall's singular achievement was

---

69 AC, I, pp. 237–54.
70 *Macmillan's Magazine*, Jan 1872, p. 213. AC, I, pp. 250, 257, 261, 251, 375. 'No one vindicated more strenuously the duty of the court to establish the authority of the fundamental law of the land, no one abstained more scrupulously from trespassing on the field of executive administration or political controversy' (AC, I, p. 261).
71 AC, II, pp. 364, 343, 515–16. The two Tweed judges were named in the 1910 edition (AC, 1910, II, p. 391).

to fight a long Federalist rearguard action against democratic excess during America's darkest days, and to preserve and embody the judicial ideal in the Supreme Court.

The task of the bench and bar, for which Bryce had inordinate respect, was to sustain this same ideal, especially as the major bulwark of representative government sank lower and lower in esteem. In its role as cautious interpreter and constraining power it held public opinion and legislatures in check. The remarkable provisions of the founding fathers meant that 'the consciences of the people ... have resolved to restrain themselves from hasty or unjust action by placing their representatives under the restriction of a permanent law ... finding the interpreter and enforcer thereof set high above the assaults of faction'.[72] The unique responsibility of the American judiciary was to maintain this legal and conservative spirit.

The American example and Ireland

That the 'Americomania' of the 1880s was prompted by Irish considerations seemed so obvious to Dicey that it barely required mention, for 'the success ... of the Federal system in reconciling many Englishmen to the proposal for the establishment of Home Rule in Ireland is too patent to anyone who has followed the stream of English politics'.[73] Insofar as Ireland became an obsessional matter the American example correspondingly encroached on English political discourse. Dicey himself perfectly illustrates the preoccupying and neurotic quality of that debate: in December 1886 he wrote of a high table dinner at All Souls: 'we are at a supreme crisis, yet last night not a single person talked a word of politics . . .. There is something in me which makes Home Rule and its evils possess my mind.' And this virus was contagious. When Godkin reported to Bryce that Lecky was writing abrasive anti-home rule propaganda in the *North American Review* Bryce urged Morley to pen a reply. Undaunted, Lecky returned to the battlefield in his *Democracy and Liberty*, and on this occasion Godkin replied directly: 'One might call Mr. Lecky's book an attempt to pay democracy off for suggesting or assisting the Irish land laws and home rule movement.' Even the cosmopolitan Acton was not immune to

---

[72] *AC*, I, p. 266.
[73] *NYN*, 20 Jan 1898, p. 46.

this creeping paranoia, for he discerned in von Holst's massive work on America a subtle counter-offensive against German, and hence British, federalism.[74]

Acton, along with Bryce and Morley, found himself intellectually stranded in a debate in which the heavyweights supported the Unionist cause. Anchored on the rock of paternalism and humane despotism the Unionist response was that much more visceral because Ireland raised far more than dusty constitutional matters; it raised, first and foremost, the question of self-determination for a nation for whom the vast majority of Englishmen felt complete contempt. Dicey conceded his countrymen's inveterate bias — 'I say this with the greatest shame and regret' — and then proceeded to ignore it.[75] A deep-seated English phobia towards Catholic Ireland — Ulstermen were always honourably exempt — helps explain why, as parliament granted varying degrees of self-determination to dominions within the empire, similar concessions to Ireland were considered unthinkable. And it was partly because the United States offered the example of an orderly republic despite its large Irish immigrant population that this example was unwelcome to many. Less welcome still was the wider lesson of democracy. 'This belief in the virtues of self-government', Dicey wrote in 1885, 'is confirmed by the teaching of American critics, who hold that the recent experience of the United States presents a clue by which Englishmen may find a path out of the labyrinth of their present perplexities.'[76]

But what, precisely, were the clues, and how were they to be interpreted? To discover them American history was plundered and substantive argument gave rise to counter-argument. Was her revolution proof, if proof were needed, of the inexorable triumph of determined revolutions for self-government as Godkin argued, or merely a moral for Britons to assert stronger if more benign ties over her empire, as Seeley believed? Throughout the critical months of 1885 and 1886 Gladstone retreated to his library and immersed himself in Burke,

---

[74]   Rait, p. 101. Godkin to Bryce, 5 March 1891, Ms. Bryce USA 5. Roosevelt to Bryce, 13 March 1891, Ms. Bryce USA 9. Morley, *Oracles on Man and Government*, p. 49. Godkin, *Problems of Modern Democracy*, pp. 280, 40 – 3. *Correspondence of Lord Acton*, p. 190.

[75]   *NYN*, 20 Jan 1881, p. 41. Bryce characterised English rule in Ireland as 'hereditary arrogance and hatred' (Introduction to George Sigerson's *Political Prisoners at Home and Abroad*, p. vii).

[76]   *NYN*, 20 Jan 1898, p. 46.

emerging to report on Burke's 'magazine of wisdom on Ireland and America'. The Duke of Argyll drew the obvious conclusion: 'Of course your reference to Burke indicates a tendency to compare our position as regards Ireland to the position of George III towards the colonies.'[77] At least Gladstone's interpretation had the advantage of consistency, with his pro-Southern stand during the American civil war reinforcing his advocacy of Irish home rule. Nevertheless Dicey, who could claim an equally consistent unionism, was not disposed to allow the public to forget Gladstone's Newcastle speech, 'spoken at a time when to speak was to act, and when to comfort and encourage the Confederacy was to aid in the destruction of the United States', nor to resist clarifying the implications of that speech for the future integrity of the United Kingdom if left in Gladstone's hands. Likewise Dicey exposed and exploited Bryce's inconsistency, reminding his readers that those same liberals who had supported the Unionists during the civil war were now ardent 'states' righters' with regard to Ireland. But Bryce was not so easily caught out; for him the fact that the Confederacy ultimately failed in its bid for independence pointed to the hopelessness of the Irish nationalist cause outside the United Kingdom, and suggested a peaceable and workable compromise instead.[78]

The moral to be drawn from reconstruction was as confusing and as contradictory as any drawn from the civil war, and had the similar advantage of being sufficiently ample and varied in its details to sustain any interpretation the interpreter wished to put on it. Godkin's contribution to Bryce's *Handbook of Home Rule* drew the conclusion that intimidation and violence, whether by Klansmen or cattle maimers, were inevitable when self-responsibility and self-respect were denied. This conclusion had the added advantage to the Irish-American editor of implying that violence was not a feature unique to the Celtic race. Instead, 'the Irish are not peculiar in their manner of expressing their discontent with a government directed or controlled by the public opinion of another indifferent or semi-hostile community which it is impossible to resist in open

77 Godkin to Bryce, 15 Sept 1882, Ms. Bryce USA 5. Seeley's *Expansion of England*, pp. 141 – 60. Morley's *Life of Gladstone*, III, p. 211 – 12.
78 Dicey, *Contemporary Review*, April 1888, pp. 496 – 7, and *England's Case*, p. 70. 'I say to Ireland what the Liberals or the Republicans of the North said to the Southern States of America — the Union must be preserved' (Bryce in *The Nineteenth Century*, Feb 1886, p. 14).

warfare'.[79] Dicey was more than equal to this challenge with its odious suggestion that subjection alone was responsible for lawlessness. Godkin's logic was obvious and reprehensible; home rule would turn law-breakers into law-makers and gain for the British government a brief respite only at the expense of ignoring justice. He carried his attack further into Godkin's misreading of American history. In emphasising states' rights Godkin ignored the underlying unionist cause of the war and ignored, too, the fact that the result of war and reconstruction was a return to the *status quo ante bellum*, while Irish nationalists radically challenged the *status quo*. He refused to accept that self-government and self-esteem were the lessons to be drawn from reconstruction. The vicious co-operation of Blacks and carpet-baggers had no parallel in Ireland, and the termination of reconstruction in 1877 entailed the complete sacrifice of the North's commitment to Black equality and hence the sacrifice of the rule of law.[80]

Yet Dicey and his fellow Unionists found it harder to deny that the example of the United States confirmed what the British empire had already made clear — that there was nothing constitutionally innovative about Irish home rule. Britain already included two federations, Canada and Australia, within its empire, as well as four self-governing dominions (New Zealand, Cape Colony, Natal and Newfoundland) and when Wickham Stead, the English journalist, argued for the Americanisation of the British constitution in order to avoid the break-up of the empire he was simply echoing his American colleague, Albert Shaw, who insisted that American federalism had, from its beginnings, been 'imperial' in its capacity to absorb constitutionally vast areas of the western hemisphere through equal statehood. It was the example of unity through equality rather than loose confederate dominion that led Sir John Seeley to suggest copying the American union in his *Expansion of England* because it promised 'a system under which an indefinite number of provinces is firmly held together without any of the inconveniences which have been felt in our empire'.[81]

---

[79]   *Handbook of Home Rule*, pp. 1 – 23.
[80]   *England's Case*, pp. 102, 107 – 10.
[81]   Stead, *Contemporary Review*, August 1892, p. 304. Shaw, *Contemporary Review*, Sept 1892, p. 313. *The Expansion of England*, p. 160. Seeley concluded 'when we have accustomed ourselves to contemplate the whole empire together and call it England, we shall see that here too we have a United States' (p. 184).

It was because Seeley and Shaw seemed to be insidiously transforming liberal federalism into a brand of ultra-imperialism that Bryce raised objections. An empire with heterogeneous races at various stages of development could not be subject to uniform laws and legislation as in America. Greater unity within the empire along American lines meant in practice pro-consular coercion — the very negation of what Bryce intended. Such assumptions would lead to Ireland being governed along Indian lines such as Froude proposed.[82]

Yet with specific regard to Ireland America's example remained absolutely central and it is a crowning paradox that Dicey, the most strident of Unionists, should more than anyone have made home rule seem not only plausible but almost inevitable. First, in his *Law of the Constitution*, he had drawn a vital distinction between sovereign and non-sovereign law-making bodies which placed the American Congress in the same constitutional class as the Great Western Railway. In the United States 'no legislature throughout the land is more than a subordinate law-making body capable in strictness of enacting nothing but bye-laws' yet, subject to this limitation, each state within the union was legally supreme within its proper sphere. Morley notes that Gladstone seized upon this chapter for it suggested that Westminster could bestow whatever degree of automony it chose on a newly-created Dublin parliament without impairing its own sovereignty. Dicey's comparison with the Great Western Railway had the effect of making home rule appear not only possible — parliament had already granted a degree of limited sovereignty in the form of the company's bye-laws — but positively innocuous. Having offered a brilliant solution to Anglo-Irish relations he then proceeded to hand Gladstone the weapon by which to implement it — a powerful reassertion of parliamentary omnipotence. Gladstone referred to the licence granted by Dicey in his great home rule speech of 8 April 1886.

No work that I have ever read brings out in a more distinct and emphatic manner the peculiarity of the British Constitution in one point . . . namely the absolute supremacy of Parliament. We have a Parliament to the power of which there are no limits whatever, except such as human nature in a divinely ordained condition of things imposes . . .. There is

[82] Bryce to Albert Shaw, 15 Oct 1892, Shaw Papers. *History and Jurisprudence*, I, pp. 247 – 8.

nothing that controls us, and nothing the compels us, except our conviction of law, of right, and of justice.[83]

Appalled, Dicey sought to escape from the trap he had set himself. For the first time, he insisted, the proposed Anglo-Irish imperial parliament attempted constitutional definition, and definition destroyed: 'The merit of the English constitution is that it is no constitution at all.' Definition destroyed also because in distributing powers it acted quite contrary to a British tradition of unified and concentrated executive power; thus 'federalism as the dissolution of the United Kingdom is absolutely foreign to the history, and . . . instinctive policy of English constitutionalists'.[84] Next he attempted to wrest back the weapon of sovereignty from out of the hands of his adversaries in whom he had placed it. He argued that Parliamentary sovereignty could not restrict itself by passing immutable laws restricting its successors; because 'limited sovereignty' was a contradiction in terms parliament could not so much 'divest' itself of sovereignty as surrender it, either by dissolving itself altogether or by transferring and absorbing itself into a wholly new sovereign body, such as followed the Anglo-Scottish union of 1707. But Dicey denied that the Gladstonian bill was similar to 1707. In Articles 37 and 39 of that bill the liberals had transferred certain inalienable parliamentary powers to a new and separate Anglo-Irish imperial parliament and this, he held, rendered it unconstitutional.[85]

This theoretical discussion of what Bryce called the 'gibbering and unsubstantial ghost' of sovereignty seemed otiose and rarefied in the extreme, but whether the 1886 bill trenched on parliament's powers was the first and fundamental obstacle Gladstone had to face in the House, and in this light an obscure footnote in *The American Commonwealth* took on immense relevance. For in that footnote Bryce commented on the maxim *Delegata potestas non delegatur* and concluded, John Locke and Judge Thomas Cooley notwithstanding, that in practice parliament had delegated large legislative powers to various authorities such as the Crown in Council and had generally displayed a

---

[83] LC, pp. 83 – 176, 145 – 6. Morley's *Life of Gladstone*, III, p. 211. *Hansard*, 3rd Series, 304, c. 1048. Dicey wrote in LC that 'The one fundamental dogma of English constitutional law is the absolute legislative authority or depotism of the King in Parliament' (p. 141).
[84] NYN, 4 Sept 1873, p. 240. LC, 8th ed., p. xc.
[85] LC, p. 65 n. 1. *England's Case*, pp. 243 ff.

far greater degree of pliancy than was generally admitted. By the Act of Union with Ireland, for example (39 and 40 Geo. III, c.67), parliament had guaranteed the established Church of Ireland, but that Church was disestablished in 1869 'with as much ease as though this provision had never existed'. In essence, Bryce's retort to the Diceyan formula that sovereignty could not divest itself of its illimitable powers was that parliament could do precisely that because it was sovereign. Making a distinction between legal and moral delegation he concluded in parliament that 'we shall retain, as a matter of pure right, the power to legislate for Ireland for all purposes whatever, for the simple reason that we cannot divest ourselves of it'.[86] Dicey retaliated with a three page footnote in the next edition of his *Law of the Constitution* but was incapable of escaping from a dilemma of his own making, for in attempting to declare the 1886 bill unconstitutional he was explicitly destroying his own analysis, for, as Justice Holmes pointed out, Dicey had 'done more than any living person to disprove the idea of unconstitutionality'.[87]

Having argued that Gladstonian reform was feasible Bryce had then to go on to suggest that it was also right; to insist that the federation of the United Kingdom would solve England's as well as Ireland's problems and resolve, once and for all, the fearful liberal equation of liberty's opposition to democracy. But, pragmatist as he was, he concentrated on empirical evidence and on the demonstrable fact that federalism was both practical and workable. His historical analogies and geographical citations proliferated tediously. Dicey found his conclusions based on 'the scanty inhabitants of a desolate Island' — Iceland — remarkable for ingenuity rather than discrimination, and Hansard records an even sharper impatience with the professor's pedantry in the House:

(Bryce)   I will give another instance, which is rather a curious one — I mean the case of Iceland.
(Cries of 'Oh!' from the Opposition).[88]

---

[86]   *AC,* I, pp. 451 n. 1, 359 n. 1. *Hansard,* 3rd Series, 305, c. 1218.
[87]   *LC,* p. 65 n. 1. *Holmes-Laski Letters,* I, p. 421. Holmes was referring specifically to Dicey's stand on the Parliament Act of 1911, but the principle is the same. Dicey himself wrote that, while acts could oppose the spirit of the constitution, 'it cannot mean that the Act is either a breach of law or is void' (*LC,* p. 464).
[88]   Dicey, *NYN,* 3 June 1886, p. 463. *Hansard,* 3rd Series, 305, cc. 1223–1224.

But there were other and more relevant cases, and two days after this speech Henry James wrote congratulating Bryce: 'I feel an American has a tolerably unerring feeling of what a big democracy can and can't do. One wants to cry bravo! when an old friend has scored.' Bryce organised and regrouped American opinion in favour of home rule and kept up a steady transatlantic pressure group. Friends — Theodore Roosevelt, Seth Low, Albert Shaw, Charles Eliot — wrote, and Godkin in particular was wheeled on to put the American case for home rule in English publications, and collect round robins from distinguished academics such as William Thayer of Harvard and William Graham Sumner of Yale to keep up the pressure. Bryce even quoted his American friends directly in a chapter on 'The Strength of American Democracy' in his *American Commonwealth*, repeating their home rule views as indicative of the wisdom of America's patrician class, and in terms comfortingly Gladstonian. It was especially important to tap this source in order to convince British opinion that American support for home rule was based on principles ('As an American', Albert Shaw wrote, 'I believe in Home Rule for Ireland as a matter of course'), and not on anti-British or pro-Irish prejudice.[89]

But pre-eminently Bryce's most solid contribution rested on his detailed illustration of successful devolution in his *American Commonwealth*, each page illuminating the wider issues of self-government, dual sovereignty and practical federalism in action, all of obvious and explicit applicability to Ireland. In this sense his obligatory rider that 'no fact has been either stated or suppressed, and no opinion put forward, with the purpose of serving any English party doctrine, or in any way furnishing arguments for use in any English controversy' seems disingenuous.[90] It was impossible for the public to read about the United States without thinking of Ireland, just as the author could not remain unaware of his book's pertinence even had he wished it otherwise.

---

[89] Henry James to Bryce, 19 May [1886], Ms. Bryce Misc. Godkin contributed 'An American View of Ireland', 'American Home Rule' and 'American Opinion on the Irish Question' in *The Nineteenth Century* in August 1882, June 1886 and August 1887. The first two articles were reprinted in Bryce's *Handbook* and the results of the round robin in the August 1887 article, pp. 285 – 92. Most Americans, Bryce concluded, wanted 'all such self-government as might be compatible with the maintenance of ultimate imperial control and imperial unity' (*AC*, II, p. 484). Shaw in *Contemporary Review*, Sept 1892, p. 305.

[90] *AC*, I, p. 8.

But how separate this discourse was from discussions in the corridors of parliament and the shifting sands of party strategy Bryce grasped when, on his way to a Committee room after the fall of the liberal government in June 1885, he momentarily glimpsed Rowland Winn, the tory whip, in deep conversation with Parnell. Out of this discussion emerged a brief conservative-Irish Nationalist pact which carried the Maamtrasna debate for the conservatives and acted as a catalyst in turning Gladstone and Spencer to home rule and a watershed in history. Power, party, personal contact, provisional pacts, were of the essence of government and reduced the endless and finely-drawn constitutional dissections to a dry irrelevance. As politician and academic Bryce wished to bridge the two worlds, and having dealt with the formalities of American government his ambition in *The American Commonwealth* was to probe and lay bare, for the first time, the political currency of party.[91]

91   Fisher, I, p. 210.

5

The Informal Party

An argument from the United States to England is necessarily unsafe, and often directly fallacious.   — Leslie Stephen

Public opinion

To James Bryce the United States offered a novel political phenomenon. Advancing beyond the direct democracy of ancient Athens and Britain's representative government, America signalled the emergence of mass participatory democracy. Subject to the dominion of a public opinion which not only reigned but governed, the absolute authority of the popular will was symbolised in a constitution which entrenched their will in a written document and placed it beyond the reach of its governors.[1] Conservative critics had long argued that the conspicuous debasement of American political life reflected the general debasement of her people. In a review of Henry Adams's *Democracy* in 1882 Bryce conceded the corrupt and un-English characteristics of the American party system, but then proceeded to dismiss American political life generally as insignificant and peripheral, 'a kind of side channel encumbered by weeds and bushes', in a nation of self-suffcient citizens substantially untouched by governmental rules and regulations. But in his *American Commonwealth* Bryce could not evade the centrality of politics to American life or fail to recognise that American politics was a matter, above all else, of party politics, and the more he laid bare the arcane apparatus of control and the corroding influence of party the more he was faced by what he termed the 'cardinal problem' of his book: 'Where political life is all-pervading, can practical politics be on a lower level than public opinion? How can a free people which tolerates

[1] *AC*, II, pp. 247 – 54, 255 – 6.

137

gross evils be a pure people?' After thorough investigation he reached the conclusion that these two propositions were entirely compatible and explicable in specifically American terms; that, to adopt Goldwin Smith's aphorism, America's grocers were statesmen and her statesmen grocers. The underlying purpose of the section on 'Public Opinion' was to confirm his conviction that under the advantageous circumstances of popular government America's grocers were indeed pure.[2]

For Bryce the purpose of America was to illustrate the unfolding advance of liberal principles. If the purpose of liberalism was to advance the freedom of the individual, to give free will full play, it followed that the granting of maximum power to a collective opinion was the nearest means of reflecting and implementing that will. A mechanism which bestowed authority upon a numerical majority was necessarily imperfect; it gave weight to numbers over wisdom, placed equality above liberty. Yet at the same time, while the individual, separately, might be selfish and acquisitive, he also possessed a common co-operative humanity, the gift of reason and a desire for harmony. Liberals, Bryce suggested, 'have faith in the power of reason to conquer ignorance and of generosity to overbear selfishness. They are therefore disposed to leave the individual alone, and to entrust the masses with power'.[3] This belief did not amount to the worship of an infallible majority, but rather the cautious acceptance of a sifting process between divergent opinions from which emerged a vague consensus and rough wisdom. Theoretically at least majoritarianism offset the threat of political fragmentation on the one hand and despotic centralism on the other. It also resolved the central problem of coercion; in an open and responsive democracy the distinction between governors and governed dissolved; the state ceased to repress or serve one divisive interest as against another, and became instead the individual enlarged and possessed of all the decisive energy of unity. Majoritarianism also legitimised party politics, serving to uphold the rights of minorities when in opposition, and enact the wishes of the majority when in

[2] Goldwin Smith, *Reminiscences*, p. 406. Bryce, *Fortnightly Review*, Nov 1882, p. 639. AC, II, p. 231.
[3] AC, II, p. 17. As Acton, the high priest of liberalism, put it: 'Our conscience exists and acts for ourselves. It exists in each of us. It is limited by the consciences of others . . . therefore it tends to restrict authority and to enlarge liberty. It is the law of self-government' (quoted in F. E. Fasnacht, *Acton's Political Philosophy*, p. 40).

power. A two party system offered choice and alternative principles. One such principle, Bryce indicated, which distinguished liberals from their conservative counterparts was a greater confidence in the masses. Gladstone had been profoundly impressed by the self-sacrifice of the Lancashire cotton mill workers during the American civil war and defined liberalism as 'trust in the people qualified by prudence. The principle of conservatism is mistrust of the people qualified by fear'. Similarly Bryce in a chapter significantly headed 'How Far American Experience is Available for Europe' suggested that 'the masses of the people are wiser, fairer, and more temperate in any matter to which they can be induced to bend their minds than most European philosophers have believed it possible for the masses of the people to be'.[4]

Yet for all his theoretical confidence Bryce's analysis of public opinion remains unsatisfactory. This is partly because, in a pre-psephological age, he was forced to resort to impressionistic generalisations and use strictly unverifiable conjecture — methods which he did not like using and which he was not especially good at using. But in one respect at least Graham Wallas's criticism (in his *Human Nature in Politics*) of Bryce's overly sanguine approach is unjust, for the pages of *The American Commonwealth*, especially those dealing with party, are far from confirming the essential benignity of human nature. If Bryce insisted on remaining a 'professional optimist' it was because he wished to remain optimistic despite his seasoned awareness of the irrational and habit-ridden in man. In a chapter which graphically reconstructs the formation of one individual's opinion in the course of a day, he stresses the unthinking response, the inbred and ineradicable prejudices which leave 'our businessman . . . no time to reason at breakfast'. He assigned a negative and limited role to public opinion. Its task was to determine the general areas of debate, contribute sentiment rather than thought, and formulate desired goals rather than the specific means for implementing them. Public opinion was salutary only as long as it appreciated its limitations and left the business of initiative and practice to the politician

---

[4]   *AC*, II, pp. 247 – 54. Gladstone quoted in Elizabeth Wallace, *Goldwin Smith*, p. 135. *AC*, II, p. 493. Public opinion 'can bend all its resources to the accomplishment of its collective ends. The friction that exists in countries where the law or institutions handed down from former generations are incompatible with the feelings and wishes of the people has disappeared. A key has been found that will unlock every door' (*AC*, II, p. 252).

and the informed observer of the political 'outer circle'. Paradoxically American democracy failed in as much as the average capacity of its citizens was so high. It was precisely because the majority of Americans were sufficiently shrewd and intelligent that they did not leave government to better men; instead, confusing equality of rights with equality of capacity, they failed in the matter of leadership. He welcomed the blessings of equality but was fully aware of the follies committed in its name.[5] Running throughout *The American Commonwealth* is an implied criticism of the United States for not conforming to Britain's representative model, but it remains implied. Bryce had seen the future in America in 1870 and, a decade later, it still appeared to work beyond all liberal hopes. The immense stability of popular government, the equilibrium of freedom and order symbolised by Jefferson and Hamilton, and the curative educational power of freedom, all contributed to raise the standard of responsible citizenship.[6]

In stark contrast to Europe class conflict was mercifully absent in the United States and, insofar as there were growing symptoms of discontent intruding into the classless republic, such as strikes and labour unions, he held responsible European immigrants who, ignorant of American ways, attempted to recreate old world struggles through labour militancy. What differences of opinion there were tended to split along vertical and occupational rather than horizontal lines — 'what the employer thinks, his workman thinks' — so that political discourse and party difference were spared the intensity of venomous class hatred. He made no attempt to ignore or deny the presence of large disparities in wealth and property, indeed he forecast their increase, but he interpreted such distinctions as a spur to positive self-improvement rather than negative discontent. In place of sullen resentment there was an admiration for those who had created wealth and a healthy desire to emulate them. Each citizen, having achieved legal equality, considered himself the equal of every other citizen. Unencumbered mobility and the unrestricted advance of the able reflected a just and open society which amply rewarded aspirations and

---

[5]   *Human Nature in Politics*, pp. 128, 126 – 7. Bryce's Introduction to Ostrogorski, *Democracy and the Organisation of Political Parties*, p. xliii. *AC*, II, pp. 240 – 2, 469, 472, 271 – 2. In the light of 1867 he concluded the 'History does not support the doctrine that the mere enjoyment of power fits large masses of men . . . for its exercise' (*AC*, II, p. 357).

[6]   *AC*,II, pp. 244, 344, 283. *AC*, I, pp. 635, 457.

success and gave each American 'the sense of a vast future to be laboured for'.[7] 'There are', he wrote, 'no struggles between privileged and under-privileged orders, not even the perpetual strife of rich and poor which is the oldest disease of civilised states . . . instead of suspicion, jealousy and arrogance embittering the race of classes, good feeling and kindliness reign.'[8]

He illustrated the upward thrusting mobility of the professional classes by the absence of rigid distinctions between barristers and attorneys which exemplified the unique absence in America of restrictive barriers, an example, he added, 'on which anyone who is accustomed to watch the career of the swarm of young men, who annually press into the Temple or Lincoln's Inn full of bright hopes, may be pardoned for dwelling'.[9] Again, typically, when he came to define what he termed the essential 'pleasantness' of American life and its ameliorative effect on manner and standards, he did not take an abstract Actonian definition of 'liberty' as his yardstick, or lay stress, as his conservative counterparts would have, on the blessings of an ordered and stable society, but rather a simple material measure of physical comfort. The absence of poverty, of physical squalor and pauperism contributed more than anything else to the level of American civilisation.

> The fog and soot flakes of an English town, as well as its squalor, are wanting; you are in a new world, and a world which knows the sun. It is impossible not to feel warmed, cheered, invigorated by the sense of such material well-being all around one, impossible not to be infected by the buoyancy and hopefulness of the people. The wretchedness of Europe lies far behind; the weight of its problems seems lifted from the mind . . .. To some Europeans this may seem fanciful. I doubt if any European can realise till he has been in America how much difference it makes to the happiness of anyone not wholly devoid of sympathy with his fellow-beings, to feel that all round him, in all classes of society and all parts of the country, there exists in such ample measure so many of the

---

[7] AC, II, pp. 289 n. 1, 479, 261, 617, 622, 333.

[8] AC, II, p. 479. In 1910 Bryce reconsidered these paragraphs and wondered whether they were not 'too roseate'; on balance he thought not (AC, 1910, II, p. 648).

[9] AC, II, p. 500. 'A man without capital or friends has a better chance than in Europe' (AC, II, p. 68).

external conditions of happiness: abundance of the necessaries of life, easy command of education and books, amusements and leisure to enjoy them, comparatively few temptations to intemperance and vice.[10]

This 'pleasantness' reflected far more than the frequently cited propitious circumstances of the continent; they were the direct consequence of a benevolent political system whose task it was to respond to the wishes of its people and enhance a sense of equality through participation. The word 'equality' had, Bryce admitted, an 'odious sound' to Europeans; it evoked images of obtrusiveness and bad manners, of a dirty fellow elbowing his betters or a villager shaking his fist at the parson and squire. 'The exact contrary is the truth. Equality improves manners, for it strengthens the basis of all good manners, respect for other man and women simply as men and women, irrespective of their station in life.'[11]
Bryce also took the opportunity to refute the conservative myth of democratic inertia. Maine had depicted popular government in terms of the reign of mediocrity and the extinction of creative powers; under a democracy, he insisted, there would have been no Reformation, change of dynasty or toleration of dissent; no threshing machines, power looms or spinning jennies. But such a list seemed especially inept when applied to the Yankee's genius for technical innovation. On the contrary, America had produced a whole continent of Franklins, Stephensons and Watts and proved conclusively to Bryce that democracies unleashed vast reservoirs of energy and human resources hitherto frustrated by the 'unaspiringness' of feudal hindrance.[12] The same force which created an Eli Whitney or a Thomas Edison also provided a much needed unity to offset the fragmenting checks and balances of the constitution and a much needed purifying political agent too. Public opinion was 'a sort of atmosphere, fresh, keen and full of sunlight . . . and this sunlight kills many of those noxious germs which are hatched where politicians congregate. Selfishness, injustice, cruelty,

[10] *AC*, II, pp. 677–8.
[11] *AC*, II, p. 678.
[12] *Popular Government*, pp. 98, 36. Mill, in his 'Repesentative Government', had only to quote extracts from the *Report of the English Commissioners to the New York Exhibition* to illustrate the innovative dynamism of democracy, and implicitly refute Maine. (*Three Essays*, pp. 275 n. 1, 194–5). Also *AC*, II, pp. 251–4, 354–64.

tricks and jobs of all sorts shun the light; to expose them is to defeat them'. This immense force was not the irresponsible and levelling revolutionary mob English conservatives delighted to evoke. A study of the constitution had already revealed the essential moderation of the American 'who relished little of that haste, that recklessness, that love of change for the sake of change with which English theorists . . . have been wont to credit democracy', and he discerned a similar moderation in most aspects of American life and in American history. Having never suffered under feudal oppression, Americans had progressed steadily and without convulsions to an advanced stage of popular control; a tradition of continuity, a benevolent government, a widespread diffusion of wealth and property and the blessings of religious freedom had removed most of the vexations of the old world.[13]

A far more formidable obstacle to Bryce's optimistic appraisal of America was the spectre of majoritarian tyranny which had haunted Tocqueville and which had passed into European demonology; more formidable because it threatened those principles which lay at the heart of liberal belief — the supremacy of individual freedom, of mutual toleration and the leavening influence of the creative minority. Tocqueville's final judgement was damning: 'I know of no country in which, generally speaking, there is less independence of mind and true freedom of discussion than in America.' Bryce decided to meet the challenge head on and boldly assert the contrary: '[Americans] have a boundless faith in free enquiry and full discussion.'[14] Tocqueville's conclusion had rested on a thorough analysis of legal, social, political and material equality in the United States. In a brief and highly anecdotal chapter Bryce dismissed the matter of legal equality as no longer relevant and concentrated instead on the current trends towards or away from social equality. His discussion of the craze for genealogy, the First Families of Virginia and 'the 400' on the one hand and the average American's dislike of social ostentation on the other tended to blunt and trivialise Tocqueville's larger perceptions. Searching for evidence of legislative tyranny (the least likely area of abuse in Tocqueville's estimation) he discovered a few

[13] *AC*, II, p. 355. *AC*, I, p. 457.
[14] *Democracy in America*, I, p. 273. *AC*, II, p. 359. And again: 'Public opinion grows more temperate, more mellow, and assuredly more tolerant. Its very strength disposes it to bear with opposition or remonstrance. It respects itself too much to wish to silence any voice' (*AC*, II, p. 364).

'dark corners' of social persecution, specifically the anti-Chinese legislation in California and the ostracism of Prudence Crandall in Connecticut, but the extraordinary omission of the Southern question from the first two editions excluded comparable examples from that section.[15]

Bryce insisted that Tocqueville's grim hypotheses were based on the transient, youthful intolerance of Jacksonian democracy. Since then the maturer American had passed on to the 'absolute freedom and tolerance of today'. Again, struck by the enormous power of general opinion, Tocqueville had attributed too much of the submissiveness which he observed to the active coercion of the majority, and too little to the minorities' willing acquiescence. Thus the curtain falls on the 'tyranny of the majority' only to rise again in the shape of 'the fatalism of the multitude' where, because the minority is quiescent and passive, active compulsion on the part of the majority is unnecessary. Indeed the element of coercion is almost entirely absent because the majority itself chooses to be passive rather than active: 'In the fatalism of the multitude there is neither legal nor moral compulsion; there is merely a loss of resisting power, a diminished sense of personal responsibility and of the duty to battle for one's own opinions, such as has been bred in some peoples by the belief in an overmastering fate.' To talk of 'tyranny' at all, except possibly in the short run, was erroneous, for given the average American's honesty and good sense, his capacity to reach a reasonably sensible consensus, the distinction of 'majority' and 'minority' appeared both abstract and unreal.[16]

To support these contentions Bryce cited the example of the abolitionists who, faced initially by a hostile and indifferent majority, ultimately succeeded in winning over that majority to its cause: 'this . . . had been deemed a ground for holding that all minorities who have right on their side will bring round their antagonists, and in the long run win by voting power'. Similarly, if a minority were in error a righteous majority was certain to prevail, as when the Klan outrages ceased, when the North recognised that military reconstruction was unnecessary and the South was 'redeemed'. Such examples were intended to reassure, but in fact they undermined his case; the success of

---

[15] *AC*, II, pp. 615 – 26, 457 – 60, 340, 342. Bryce insisted that the Chinese were not technically a minority, for they were not US citizens (*AC*, II, p. 340).

[16] *AC*, II, pp. 342, 332.

the abolitionist cause was achieved through the outcome of war and not by the ballot, while, in the case of the Klan, the North's abandonment of radical reconstruction through the informal disfranchisement of the Black removed the Klan's rationale.[17]

Bryce undoubtedly believed that Tocqueville had genuinely misplaced his emphasis, exaggerating coercion at the cost of underrating aquiescence, and that it was important to strike the right balance. He was equally convinced that public opinion had grown more tolerant and understanding since the rude and boisterous 1830s. But his bland prediction that 'in no imaginable future is there likely to be any attempt to repress either by law or by opinion the free exercise and expression of speculative thought on morals, on religion, and indeed on every other matter not within the immediate range of current politics' suggests another, barely concealed, purpose.[18] That purpose was to remove the blemish of intolerance and enforced conformity of which majoritarian democracy stood accused. And to do this he had not only to lose sight temporarily of his dynamic American and replace him with a passive, unresisting individual, but also, in implying the ultimate and inevitable correctness of majority decisions, force himself into a deterministic straitjacket. But more damaging still was his blunt misreading of Tocqueville, a misreading which paradoxically undermined his strategy of exoneration. For Tocqueville had gone to great lengths to emphasise that negative oppression, the oppression of the soul not the body, rather than positive physical coercion, was the greater and more insidious form of tyranny.[19] In finding little evidence of active oppression, and stressing instead a majority omnipotence so total and pervasive as to brook not even nominal opposition, Bryce's 'fatalism' hints at a far subtler and absolute compulsion. He himself wrote that 'many submit willingly; some unwillingly, yet they submit. Rarely does anyone hold out and venture to tell the great majority of his countrymen that they are wrong'. Yet when he says in conclusion that 'what the individual loses as an individual he seems in a measure to regain as one of the multitude' he seems unaware that in shifting the balance of his liberal principles he has also precisely defined what Tocqueville

---

[17] *AC*, II, pp. 275, 477 – 8.
[18] *AC*, II, p. 344.
[19] *Democracy in America*, I, p. 274. Modern tyranny, Tocqueville insisted, had dispensed with the clumsy weapons of chains and hangmen.

implied by egalitarian tyranny.[20]

Nor does his intellectual confusion end there. If public opinion was omnicompetent it was also indeterminate; diffused through the atmosphere, it was amorphous and vague, and as difficult to discern as it was hard to interpret. This disparity between Bryce's theorising on popular sovereignty and his signal failure to provide precise evidence of this sovereignty in action is borne out by the paucity of examples provided in his chapter on 'Organs of Public Opinion', especially following as it does on a chapter entitled 'How Public Opinion Rules in America'. He specifies three organs which transmit the wishes of the electorate. The first and greatest, party, is depicted as an alien imposition rather than a channel of communication; the second, the press, panders to the whims rather than to the wisdom of the people, follows rather than leads, confirms prejudices rather than initiating change; the third, organised lobbies, mainly served selfish interest groups more often opposed to the general well-being of the community.[21] Yet if, as he had asserted, public opinion governed and not merely reigned, and if, as he had likewise asserted, American politics were party politics, he should have accepted that the answer to the 'cardinal problem' was that American public opinion was no more than moderately enlightened: that the grocers were just grocers, not statesmen. But such a solution was unacceptable to him. In fairness he does state the case for the opposition against himself: 'Assuming, as a European is apt to do, that the working of political machinery fairly reflects the temper, ideas, and moral standards of the governing class, and knowing that America is governed by the whole people, he may form a low opinion of the people.'[22] Yet he states the case only to dismiss it. At the same time he could not resort to general political apathy to explain the debasement of American politics. On the contrary, the frequency and multiplicity of elections, the exceptionally high turnout, far higher he noted than in Britain, and his depiction of politicians hastening to fulfil every wish and whim of their constituents, all argued an exceptionally high level of engagement. To escape from this self-imposed conundrum he had recourse to the argument that public opinion

---

[20]   AC, II, p. 335. See also Jack Lively, *The Social and Political Thought of Alexis de Tocqueville*, p. 234, and James T. Schleifer, *The Making of Tocqueville's 'Democracy in America'*, p. 202.

[21]   AC, II, pp. 262, 271, 255 – 72, 315, 355.

[22]   AC, II, p. 230.

was frequently misread or manipulated; its 'uncertain sound' was not always clearly interpreted; like other valuable articles it was surrounded by many counterfeits. But, despite this, 'a sovereign is not the less a sovereign because his commands are sometimes misheard or misreported . . . (politicians) . . . take the course which they believe the people at the moment desire'.[23] More practically he suggested narrower organisational and technical reasons such as the party establishment's stranglehold on vital primaries to suggest that, while a generally sound electorate wished for change, party contrived to make that change difficult. By such means the people were vindicated and the politicians indicted in their place. Public opinion remained wholesome and unsullied, but the channels by which that essential soundness was conveyed to the politicians were frequently blocked. Much of this analysis of political malaise and malfunctioning was correct and his solutions became textbook examples for progressive change. But modern research indicates an element of strained artificiality in his general diagnosis. If American public opinion governed then it followed that the American electorate got approximately the party system it wanted, and the 'cardinal problem' disappeared. But then the problem was partly contrived, and was the consequence of Bryce's own conviction that Americans did not get the type of party system he wanted or approved. But to appreciate his criticism of the American system it is necessary to consider Bryce's understanding of the British equivalent and his theories about the function of party government in general.

The British party system

Suspended uncertainly between the twin roles of political scientist and politician, Bryce shared to some extent the former's endemic distrust of party and the two party system, while in his latter capacity he had to justify his intense involvement. The intellectual's high rectitude, his conviction that truth was always and everywhere indivisible, encouraged a scientific distaste for political relativism, temperate adjustments and the insincere advocacy of adversarial debate. In a political world made up of counsel for the prosecution and counsel for the defence, he yearned for the Olympian detachment of the bench.

[23]   AC, II, pp. 271, 345, 311–26, 271.

How, he asked, could politics claim the status of a science if there were a variety of truths and a variety of solutions which a party system might legitimately reflect? If, then, truth were indivisible and absolute, then party artificially manufactured divisions and splits and exploited a potentially unified national will; in this sense formal opposition constituted a species of treason, a 'moral rebellion against the authority of the nation', as Dicey phrased it.[24] Maine, for example, scorned an irrational system of government which 'consisted in half the cleverest men in the country taking the utmost pains to prevent the other half from governing', and could explain it only in terms of a primitive and atavistic male combativeness. Henry Sidgwick deplored the institutionalised obstructionism, the replacement of intellectual conviction by arid rhetoric and unthinking loyalty, and the overall 'force of resistance which this machine of party government presents to the influence of enlightened and rational opinion'.[25]

Paradoxically, however, the intelligentsia's yearning for a single national party or, put another way, a partyless national state, merely intensified and perpetuated two party combat, and contributed to late nineteenth century debate an ideological inflexibility and doctrinaire rancour absent in the main from the disputes of the politicians themselves. Because each intellectual had differing but strongly held opinions as to what constituted an ideal party, he naturally attacked any other party which dared to challenge that supremacy, or offer any other alternative, with venomous severity. All of them — Acton, Dicey, Lecky, Froude, Sidgwick, Maine — deplored party government: all, without exception, were vociferous partisans and ideological shock troopers in their party's cause. This was no less true than when, undergoing intense conversion, as so many liberal unionists did in 1886, they crossed party lines, carrying the ark of the covenant with them. Lord Acton was an extreme but not

---

24 Dicey to Eliot, 5 Jan 1908, Eliot Papers. Dicey to Lowell, 19 June 1910, Lowell Papers. Ultimately 'party' became a reflex hate-word to Dicey. 'The Parliament Act is the last and greatest triumph of party government' (*LC*, 8th ed., p. ci).

25 *Popular Government*, p. 99. *Sidgwick Memoirs*, p. 442. Like forensic advocates, party professionals were required 'to make the worse seem the better reason' and thus degrade politics (*Elements of Politics*, p. 573). Also Froude: 'Nature has created us with two eyes, but in matters of state, either of necessity or deliberately, we must extinguish one' (*Short Studies on Great Subjects*, IV, pp. 326 – 7).

untypical example. In leaping from his youthful whiggism to his maturer liberalism, he suppressed or forgot his earlier damning judgements of Gladstone, (his 'utmost intellectual duplicity', his 'fatal instability of purpose'), and praised him instead in sycophantic letters to Mary Drew, the Prime Minister's daughter. This change was admittedly one between factions within a party and not a change from one party to another. Nevertheless, in Actonian terms, the leap from whig to liberal was as wide as it was possible for any thinker to jump, yet not once, after this *volte face*, did he cease to believe that the principles to which he happened to adhere possessed a monopoly of legitimacy nor that, as a corollary, the principles he had abandoned were thereafter illegitimate. As early as 1863 Acton had singled out Thomas Erskine May's praise of two party democracy for attack. In his *Constitutional History of England*, May had asserted that 'government without party is absolutism, that rulers without opposition may be despots'. Acton firmly rejected this in favour of a single 'constitutional' party ideal:

> Our political system is founded on definite principles, not on compact or compromise. Every compromise marks an imperfect realisation of principle — a surrender of right to interest or force. The constitution stands by its own strength, not by the equal strain of opposite forces. The idea of harmony proceeding from discord — of a balance between contending elements — is derived from a mechanical notion of the State, which refuses to regard it as a physiological organism, formed on distinct principles and regulated by its own laws.[26]

Thus to Acton, as to Dicey, party opposition was a species of treason, the invasion of a foreign body from without. Even a national party was only justified in the short term before achieving its ultimate goal which was the absolute transcendence of party itself. 'Progress depends not only on the victory, the uncertain and intermittent victory, of Liberals over Conservatives, but on the permeation of Conservatism with Liberal ideas . . . the gradual desertion of the Conservative masses by

---

[26] Acton's *Essays on Church and State*, pp. 481, 399 – 400. Acton's review of Erskine May's *Constitutional History* appeared in the *Home and Foreign Review*, July 1863.

their chiefs.' In speaking of conversion Acton emphasised that party principles were sacred dogmas, that politics was an arena of moral imperatives and moral absolutes, and party struggles a form of latter day religious crusade. 'Have you not discovered', he wrote to Mary Drew, 'have I never betrayed, what a narrow doctrinaire I am, under a thin disguise of levity? . . . Politics come nearer religion with me, a party is more like a church, error more like heresy, prejudice more like a sin, than I find it to be with better men.' These last words carry an intentional ring of irony for they hint at the intellectual's contempt for party compromise and politicians' expediencies, of having 'to defend in public what they condemn in private and to make no real secret of their real sentiments to their opponents'.[27]

No one ever accused Bryce of such laxity, but as a party politician of some twenty-seven years' standing he could not indulge in Acton's notorious austerity. Instead he cultivated an elaborate pose of unworldly semi-detachment with his intellectual colleagues. Staying on the Vanderbilt's luxurious Biltmore estate placed a strain on his 'philosophic ascetic' temperament, and in a long and elegaic correspondence with Justice Holmes he chose to play the role of scholar entangled in political distractions longing for the tranquillity of the library. 'I feel as if death would suddenly find one over a pile of not yet answered trivial business letters, saying to oneself that, when the replies have gone to be mailed, we would have time to think about truths and poetry and live free for happy restful thoughts with friends.'[28] More realistic perhaps is his more ambivalent appraisal of political ambition in a letter to his mother: 'How tiresome it is to care enough for a thing to regret its absence, and not enough to make fervent efforts for it, which is how I feel about success.' Yet political success was what he strove for. He was petulant about his party's failure to recognise and use his 'special knowledge' and its shallow under-estimation of his true worth. Goaded, he fought tooth and nail, holding out for a cabinet seat when Gladstone offered him the Duchy of Lancaster, and getting it. Yet, having got it, he felt it necessary to make light of his accomplishment, writing to his wife that it did

---

27 *Acton-Drew Letters*, pp. 200, 199. Acton quoted in Lionel Kochan, *Acton on History*, p. 86. Dicey agreed with Acton: 'You will never triumph unless you make a kind of religion of your politics, or turn your politics into a kind of religion' (Rait, p. 115).
28 Bryce to Minnie Bryce, 28 Sept 1904, Ms. Bryce 82. Bryce to Holmes, 9 August 1890, Holmes Papers.

not represent 'any very considerable achievement. However, it is an opportunity for trying to exercise influence in the right direction'.[29]

An opportunity to exercise influence in the right political direction was the first and most obvious justification for party political involvement. Party was the necessary and inevitable concomitant of popular government, the channel by which a free public opinion could make its influence continuously felt, and in reply to Goldwin Smith's ranting anti-party polemics (his Canadian newspaper, *The Bystander*, had as its motto 'Not Party but the People'), Bryce could not forbear from asking how the people were to be represented if not through party? But party organisation was justified only insofar as it remained a vehicle for formulating and implementing principles; the pursuit of high ideals, the collective furtherance of certain fundamental and distinguishing doctrines, offered the sole salvation of party, and once party ceased to fulfil this task it ceased to be legitimate. 'Party organisation is one of those things which is good or bad according to the spirit with which it is worked.' Parties were merely the means to an end, and must not be allowed to become a self-serving end in themselves. It was Gladstone's Midlothian campaign which first drew Bryce into politics, and it was Irish home rule and altruistic support for the persecuted Armenians which sustained him and which earned him a reputation for crankiness in Rosebery's administration.[30] A firm and settled conviction that you were on the right side and that you were united against the formidable ranks of those who were on the wrong side assisted loyalty and justified organised partisanship. He found his conservative opponents selfish, regressive, habit-ridden and dominated by privileged interest groups. They were held together not by over-riding principles but by expediency and 'closely compacted political organisation'. 'The richer sort in England', he wrote to Mrs Godkin in 1902, 'are now practically all Tories, and Tories of a somewhat sordid type, blatant and inaccessible to the nobler emotions.' 'We can't exist merely as a party as the Tories do and the parties in America . . .

29 Bryce to his mother, 20 March 1873, Ms. Bryce 82. Bryce to Marion Bryce, 11 August 1893, Ms. Bryce 92. Bryce to Gladstone, 16 August 1892, Ms. Bryce 12. Bryce to Marion Bryce, 23 August 1892, Ms. Bryce 92.
30 Smith to Bryce, 7 May 1891, Ms. Bryce 17. Wallace, p. 90. *AC*, II, p. 492. Bryce in *North American Review*, 1893, Vol. 156, p. 118. Peter Stansky, *Ambitions and Strategies*, p. 211. Bryce considered party as necessary but an evil necessity (*AC*, I, p. 70).

and what are Liberals without a policy?' he asked Freeman.[31]

By evoking the higher cause and by genuinely believing that parties in Britain divided along substantive lines, Bryce justified his intense party loyalty both to himself and to his friends. He admitted that in practice throughout a long parliamentary career he encountered surprisingly few crises of conscience, not least because he recognised and accepted the subtle double standards in English public life:

> the one conventional or ideal, the other actual. The conventional finds expression not merely in the pulpit, but also in the speeches of public men, in the articles in leading newspapers and magazines. Assuming the normal British statesman to be patriotic, disinterested, truthful, and magnanimous, it treats every fault as a dereliction from a well-settled standard of duty . . . . The actual morality, as one gathers it in the lobbies of the legislative chambers, or the smoking rooms of political clubs, or committee-rooms at contested elections, is a different affair . . . . Each profession indulges in deviations from the established rule of morals, but takes pains to conceal these deviations from the general public, and continues to talk about itself and its traditions with an air of unsullied virtue. What each profession does for itself most individual men do for themselves. They judge themselves by themselves . . . and thus erect in the inner forum of conscience a more lenient code for their own transgressions than that which they apply to others.[32]

From his unique vantage point he could distinguish the conventional from the actual, know them each for what they were and yet accept and reconcile the two. Dicey once confided to Lowell that, while 'no one writes and thinks more like a "thinker" than Bryce, no one has stood more firmly by a

---

31 *The Past and the Future of the Irish Question*, p. 60. Bryce to Mrs. Godkin, 19 Feb 1902, Godkin Papers. Bryce to Freeman, 22 March, 1874, Ms. Bryce 9. In the light of Freeman's failed candidacy in mid-Somerset, Bryce wrote that 'a great deal remains to be done before true liberalism, not as a party cry, but as the intelligent advocacy of principles, can be understood and establish itself against the powers of darkness' (Bryce to Freeman, 30 Nov 1868, Ms. Bryce 9).

32 AC, II, pp. 234–5.

party'.[33] Yet Bryce (or indeed Dicey had he been more honest with himself) would have seen no contradiction between thinker and party man. His political aim was precisely that of reconciling the two, of formulating long term party aims and of activating the party organisation to implement these aims. He recognised that party politics had its sordid side, its jobbery and its betrayals, but he also held firm to the loyal belief that ideological ends redeemed much short term party intrigue.

His reconciliation of principle with practice is best illustrated by his appointment as Chancellor of the Duchy of Lancaster in 1892: 'Odd work', as he wrote to Justice Holmes, 'chiefly appointing magistrates and presenting clergymen to livings in the Church of England, to which I do not belong.' In 1870 the appointment of JPs in the duchy had been turned over to the Lord Lieutenant, Lord Sefton, who had proceeded to appoint 1,000 unionist JPs as against 300 liberals. In 1893 Bryce revoked the 1870 decision and made thirty-nine liberal appointments after Sefton refused to co-operate. This decision exposed him to a good deal of opposition criticism, 'specially disagreeable', as Fisher wrote, 'to a highly principled and sensitive man'. But Bryce defended his decision in parliament by arguing that in matters such as game law, electoral disturbances, licensing regulations and public rights of way which came up before the local magistrates, liberal and tory magistrates would think and judge differently. Because Sefton's appointments had been political, he felt justified in attempting to establish party parity on the bench: 'I saw an injustice; I had the power to rectify it; I conceived that it was my duty to rectify it.'[34] Yet in doing so Bryce acted contrary to one of his own principal political axioms, that national and local issues ought not to be mixed, for if they were local matters would be sacrificed to national party ends. Deliberate confusion of the two had enabled party machines in America to divert attention from much needed local reforms and tighten the rings' control of the cities. Similarly, in Great Britain

---

[33] 19 June 1910, Lowell Papers. 'No Parliamentary observer would ever have described Bryce as other than a strong party Liberal . . . he took without faltering the Liberal line, to the surprise of some critics, who wondered why a man so learned and cosmopolitan should have been content to deviate so little from the straight way of party orthodoxy' (Fisher, I, p. 191).

[34] Bryce to Holmes, 19 Sept 1892, Ms. Bryce USA 22. Fisher, I, p. 288. *Hansard*, 4th Series, 11, c. 1172. The opposition member for S.W. Lancashire, Mr. Legh, actually accused Bryce of introducing the American spoils system into British government (c. 1147).

Joseph Chamberlain had practised the same obfuscation in order to build up a local power base to advance his own political ambitions and launch a subversive attack on the parliamentary liberal party.

It was the growth of the caucus in the 1860s and 1870s and the springing up of alternative extra-parliamentary centres of political power that most clearly dramatised the increasing hold of party organisation in English public life after 1867. Because of the relative novelty of this phenomenon and because of the pervasive influence of Bagehot and Mill, the study of party had been generally neglected by commentators. Trying to convince the average Englishman of the vital new role of parties was, as Maine put it in 1885, like trying to convince them that the air had weight: 'It enveloped them so evenly and pressed on them so equally that the assertion seemed incredible.'[35] Certainly Bryce, inside parliament, was more alive to this new phenomenon than most political observers, and although hankering after a passing tradition of independence, in practice he gave up a good deal of that independence to achieve unity of party purpose, success at the polls and the implementation of liberal programmes. As an MP he was loyal, approved of strong government, clear party agendas, decisive judgements at general elections and a powerful executive assured of back bench support. The British system had the singular advantage of getting things done. The use of three line whips and the decline of abstentions and cross-voting confirmed the strength of party organisation. 'When you belong to a party you are impelled to play the party game in all things great and small . . . . We vote at the sound of the division bell, as the Party Whips tell us.'[36] It was Bryce's inside appreciation which led him to draw a vital Anglo-American distinction between strong party government in Great Britain as against strong party spirit in America. A long tradition of parliamentary sovereignty linked to a highly effective party organisation made for a potent combination; it meant that 'one set of men united . . . holding one set of opinions, have gained control of the whole machinery of government, and are working

---

[35] *Popular Government*, pp. 98–9.
[36] Bryce to Dicey, 10 Jan 1922, Ms. Bryce 4. A. L. Lowell's statistics in his *Government of England* amply verified this trend (II, pp. 76–7, 81, 85). Also John P. Macintosh, *The British Cabinet*, pp. 204–6. Harold Laski compared Bryce's loyalty to 'the industrious apprentice who always marries his master's daughter and never makes a mistake' (*Holmes-Laski Letters*, I, p. 933).

it in conformity to those opinions'.[37] America, in contrast, had perfected the machinery of party, co-ordinated its ranks of voters and was pre-eminently successful in galvanising public opinion and winning elections, but to what purpose? Strong party spirit in the United States did not result in effective party government, and while British statesmen became directors of policy their American counterparts had become pointless power brokers. Woodrow Wilson had grasped this crucial difference as early as 1885 when he wrote that 'the British system is perfected party government', and Lowell had overwhelmingly confirmed it in 1912 in his *Government of England*: 'though party feeling has generally been stronger in America than England, party government is distinctly weaker.'[38] This perceived distinction was one of the mainsprings of independent progressive reform, and no one did more to give it currency than Bryce.

He further heightened this comparative awareness by perpe-tuating an idealised image of parliament, this despite his private doubts and reservations concerning the integrity of individual MPs. He persuasively depicted the House as a great debating chamber, swayed by elevated emotions and noble rhetoric and dedicated to the disinterested pursuit of high principles. No American statesman since Seward could command the authori-tative influence Parnell exerted over his Irish nationalist cohorts, or Bright over his followers even when out of office. And, towering over all, was Gladstone who, as experienced parlia-mentarian, passionate speaker, consummate tactician and thinker motivated by the most profound personal convictions, served as the epitome of party statesmanship. Beside him the presidential election of 1884 brought forth only Cleveland, 'a shrewd and upright mayor of Buffalo', and Blaine, 'never forgetting a face or a service', both colourless epigoni in comparison.[39] But parliamentary politics was elevated not only by charismatic leadership, but supported and decisely influenced by a large and distinguished 'inner circle' — some 3,500 in all, Bryce calculated — made up of back-benchers and lords, expectant candidates, registration agents and secretaries of political associations. Together this 'inner circle' constituted the 'first set', 'men eminent by rank, wealth and ability, who

[37] *AC*, I, p. 285.
[38] *Congressional Government*, p. 99. *The Government of England*, I, pp. 285 – 6.
[39] *AC*, II, pp. 49, 5, 54, 723 – 4, 466 – 7, 219. 'It would seem that the natural selection of the English parliamentary system . . . has more tendency to bring the highest gifts to the highest place' (*AC*, I, p. 80).

form a sort of governing class, largely hereditary' who bestowed a high tone, conspicuous outward splendour and an exemplary decorum in manners. These classes 'which wear black coats and live in good houses' contributed to public life not for reasons of pecuniary gain or position, but out of a sense of conviction and *noblesse oblige*. They confirmed the fact that 'the political life of the country is its main, its central, its highest social life. It is the chief occupation of the men most conspicuous by rank and practical talents. It is the great game'.[40]

This ideal image of wise patrician rule seems all the more wistful when contrasted with America's political debasement and with the author's dark, private forebodings in the 1880s, and perhaps the comparison was drawn with deliberate starkness, looking backward to Bagehot and Trollope rather than forward to Lowell and Ostrogorski, precisely because Bryce was fully aware that the British parties were afloat on new and uncharted democratic seas after 1867. The liberals' failure at the polls in 1874 led them to resort to a party programme and seek a popular mandate. Gladstone took to the hustings and galvanised his audiences with the rhetoric of class conflict. Rosebery's management of the Midlothian campaign drew on his experience of Tammany Hall and his friendship with 'Elegant' Oakey Hall, and Joseph Chamberlain learnt many lessons from local American-style party organisations as well as marrying an American wife in 1888. His political slogans, 'Free Church, Free Schools, Free Land, Free Labour' and 'Three Acres and a Cow', already had a distinct American populist ring to them, and long after he had deserted them liberals were still attempting to capture the elusive voter by adopting the Newcastle Programme in 1891 along the lines of American party platforms.[41]

This growing party organisation and this reaching out to tap new grass-roots support was partly an inevitable consequence of a post-1884 extended electorate which now had many constituencies with over 2,000 electors. Nevertheless it was anathema to be stigmatised as the party of 'Americanisation' just as it was easy to score off the opposition by accusing it of encouraging the caucus. For it was not just high tories like Maine who deplored the predominance of organisation over doctrine and numbers over opinion in the 1880s; Bryce himself

[40]   *AC*, II, pp. 59, 466. *The Fortnightly Review*, Nov 1882, p. 638.
[41]   Robert Kelley, *The Transatlantic Persuasion*, pp. 211–34. Lowell's *Government of England*, I, p. 525.

would have agreed that 'the antidote to the fundamental
infirmities of democracy was Representation, but the drug
which defeats it has now been found in the Caucus'.[42] Other
liberals, such as Goldwin Smith, pointed to Schnadhorst,
Chamberlain's colleague and party manager, as the first English
boss; Dicey drew direct parallels between the New York and
Birmingham rings, and Godkin cautioned Englishmen to
beware of Chamberlain, 'a charlatan of the American type'.[43]
These Anglo-American parallels culminated in the publication
of Moisei Ostrogorski's Democracy and the Organisation of Political
Parties of 1902 which presumed throughout its two huge
volumes that the Birmingham Liberal Assocation would repro-
duce every single dire aspect of its American counterpart.
Chamberlain had been answering these commonplace accu-
sations as early as 1887 in a series of articles in the Fortnightly
Review where he argued that his Association of 1867 and his
encouragement of the National Liberal Association after 1877
were never intended as copies of such well known American
institutions as the wirepuller and boss, corrupt elections and
managed primaries. He suggested instead that such popular,
progressive local organisations gave the ordinary public greater
voice and influence, that they were genuinely spontaneous and
representative and were in tune with that grass-roots democratic spirit which Tocqueville admired so much in America and
which Britain ought to replicate.[44]

Once more Bryce had publicly to dismiss these misleading
analogies and insist that conditions peculiar to Britain, such as
the absence of pecuniary rewards and party patronage, a
permanent civil service, the sense of patrician duty among
English politicians and of deference among the working class,
combined to prevent any Americanisation of English politics.

[42] The term 'caucus' was first used as a weapon against Chamberlain in The
Times, and Saturday Review, and Chamberlain replied in The Fortnightly
Review, July 1877, pp. 126–34, and Nov 1878, p. 722. Cf. J. L. Garvin's Life
of Joseph Chamberlain, I, p. 262 n. 1. Popular Government, p. 94.
[43] Goldwin Smith, Macmillan's Magazine, Feb 1889, p. 245. Dicey, NYN, 6
April 1882, p. 292. Godkin, NYN, 5 September 1878, p. 142, and Godkin to
Bryce, 17 Oct 1887, Ms. Bryce USA 5. Schnadhorst 'a born organiser, a
master in the art of "wire pulling" ' (Ostrogorski, I, p. 165), was the
founder of the National Liberal League.
[44] Fortnightly Review, Nov 1887, pp. 723–30. Garvin, Chamberlain's biographer, dismissed Ostrogorski's book as 'mathematics tinged with melo-
drama' and 'preconceived in hostility' (Robert McKenzie, British Political
Parties, p. 6 n. 1).

Essentially Ostrogorski had taken over much of Bryce's pioneering material on the British and American party systems without adopting Bryce's strict comparative method, and consequently Bryce proved to be correct and Ostrogorski incorrect. The once terrifying caucus vanished like a bad dream. In 1886 the NLF remained loyal to Gladstone, moved its headquarters to London and became a useful but subservient extension of the parliamentary liberal party. The inchoate Newcastle Programme foundered, the liberals were defeated in 1895 and Campbell-Bannerman was left thereafter to formulate his own parliamentary agenda. Fortified by his own experience and the rich statistical evidence provided by his friend, A. L. Lowell of Harvard, Bryce could then write in his introduction to Ostrogorski's book that the 'caucus' had terrified only the timid during its heydays in the 1880s. But his private correspondence during that decade reveals a very different Bryce, one far more prone to private fears and apprehensions.[45]

For at the time Chamberlain seriously challenged the old liberal guard and threatened to subvert its established order of 'Whigs and Whips'. Bryce himself, a middle of the road liberal, neither whig nor radical, treated his constituents with truly Burkean condescension, refusing to canvass or subscribe to local churches or charities, travelling north to Aberdeen only twice a year and only then for a couple of days to make a single obligatory address and keep a second free for consultation.[46] The NLF's growing local activism, its widening of the popular base and the strengthening of direct democratic controls through local associations, the ominous example of W. E. Forster's collision with the Bradford Association over 'Rule 15' which gave the local party association the right to select and confirm parliamentary candidates, all pointed the way to the caucus's challenge to the liberal patriciate. Bryce noted in *The American Commonwealth* that, whereas up until 1874 most appointed liberal candidates offered themselves to their local party association for confirmation, after 1880, and especially after 1885, most candidates were chosen by their associations or

---

45 *Fortnightly Review*, Oct 1882, pp. 741, 651 – 5. *North American Review*, Jan 1893, pp. 105 – 18. Bryce's Preface to Ostrogorski, pp. xxxix – xlvii. To Lowell, Ostrogorski's book furnished 'an illustration of how a man might know all about a subject without understanding it', and specifically recommended Bryce as an antidote. (Lowell to Bryce, 17 Dec 1902, Ms. Bryce USA 8. *Government of England*, I, p. 481 n. 1).

46 Garvin, I, p. 258. Fisher, I, p. 201.

denounced as interlopers and traitors, 'a curious symptom of the progress of democratic ideas and usages'.[47] Equally threatening to the MPs' traditional independence of extra-parliamentary bodies was Chamberlain's case for merging local and national politics. He argued that because party principles reflected a prevalent habit of mind there was no reason why major issues like foreign policy and defence should not divide the electorate locally in the same way that draining, lighting and education did. While Bryce might in principle have been sympathetic to this point of view, for no one had argued more than he for the unity and cohesion of party principles or applied it with such rigour in the political contest over the appointment of Lancashire magistrates, he remained wary. For he was concerned that the blurring of local and national issues could lead to the invasion of the parliamentarian's traditional domain, provide a dangerous alternative power base in municipal councils, and serve as a springboard for radical and ambitious politicos like Chamberlain.[48] Privately, like Gladstone, Bryce entertained a profound mistrust of Chamberlain's destructive and unscrupulous nature, found him 'ignorant, vulgar, restless — a mere demagogue', and while willing to let 'the radical colts frisk' because he was unable to stop them, declared the NLF 'a disagreeable necessity, a thing to be got over'.[49]

Before 1866 Chamberlain fundamentally challenged Bryce's own concept of party and representative democracy. The caucus threatened not only whigs and whips, not only the independence of parliament and its MPs, but also what he had conceived to be the liberal party's rationale. His loyal identification with Gladstone's crusading politics, the pursuit of possibly fruitless but emotionally satisfying and politically unifying causes such as Ireland would, under Chamberlain's programme, be replaced by practical nuts and bolts domestic reform, by the politics of drains and sewage and radical social improvement. The caucus aimed to divert the party's attention

---

47 Lowell, I, pp. 508 – 9. AC, II, p. 76 n. 2.
48 'Political principle where it is sincere, is to a great extent a prevalent habit of mind' (Chamberlain in *The Fortnightly Review*, Nov 1878, pp. 733 – 4). AC, II, p. 88. *North American Review*, Jan 1893, p. 112. Bryce spoke of the caucus as 'a party machine . . . dictating a policy to the electors on the one hand, and to the cabinet on the other, itself reigning in the spirit of tyranny, but under the forms of the Constitution' (*History and Jursiprudence*, I, p. 177).
49 Bryce to Lowell, 17 Jan 1904, Mrs. Bryce USA 22, and Bryce's annotations of Lowell's *Government of England*, I, p. 458, Lowell Papers.

from aimless obsessions in areas where it could achieve little, like Ulster or Armenia, and, beginning with municipal socialism, concentrate instead on the long neglected task of internal renovation. These new priorities would in turn produce a new class of professional political managers far removed from the moral concerns and doctrinal dogmas which motivated Bryce and statesmen of the old school. In *The American Commonwealth* Bryce would only obliquely point to the consequences of organisation's victory over idealism and of the reign of the wirepuller. The prophylactic he offered American parties could only be liberal and Gladstonian. In Britain these values were threatened but essentially secure for the time being; in the United States they had to be fought for. Without such values there could be no justification for his remaining in politics, no justification to his intellectual friends nor any point in writing a reformist tract for American citizens. There would, if Chamberlain's future came to pass, be no role for the 'theorist' and 'visionary', and the party pundits, 'very well in their libraries, but very ignorant about the "mechanism of government" '; they would, like himself, become redundant.[50]

The American party system

American politics were party politics and as *The American Commonwealth* progresses the shadow of party lengthens across its pages. The founding fathers had intended that republican consensus should obviate faction. Under the Constitution of 1787 the executive was intended to be an Olympian figure cast in the mould of Washington and voted into office indirectly by an independent and non-partisan electoral college. In reality the nomination and election of the president, that 'costly and complicated machinery of agitation', served instead as a unifying ritual and symbol of party domination. Similarly Senate nominations and elections were made on the strictest party lines, and in the House of Representatives open, responsible government had yielded to secret party committees, and its Speaker, whose task it was to distribute the party balance of power as evenly among the committees as possible, had fortuitously become the second if not the first public figure

---

[50] Godkin, *NYN*, 5 September 1878, p. 142. Bryce, *North American Review*, Jan 1893, p. 118.

in the land. 'So hard is it', wrote Bryce, 'to make any scheme of indirect election work according to its original design; so hard is it to keep even a written and rigid constitution from bending and warping under the actual forces of politics.'[51] Party government, a Diceyan 'convention' of immense proportion, had flourished parasitically, subverting the intentions of the constitution-makers, converting 'extra-legal groupings of men' into the mainspring of political activity. Bryce appreciated that:

> the spirit and force of party has in America been as essential to the action of the machinery of government as steam is to a locomotive engine . . . for it is into the hands of the parties that the working of the government has fallen. Their ingenuity, stimulated by incessant rivalry, has turned many of the provisions of the Constitution to unforeseen uses, and given to the legal institutions of the country no small part of their present colour.[52]

As an Irish congressman once said to a friend of Bryce's: 'Shure the Constitootion should never be allowed to come between frinds.' It rarely did.

Party, as in Britain, could be justified in terms of the organised expression of the popular will and opposition as the legitimate recognition of a counter-ideology and of minority opinion, but Bryce's observations led him to conclude that America's party system represented not public opinion, or indeed anything else but itself, and was strong because it was self-regarding and self-perpetuating. A potted history traced the fall from grace, beginning in 1800 when 'the logical and oratorical force of Hamilton's appeal to the reason of the nation told far less than the skill and energy with which Jefferson played on their feelings and prejudices'. This bias culminated in the ascendancy of Jackson, 'a raw, rude Westerner', in 1828, when extreme democratic theory was wedded to profoundly undemocratic practices and the spoils system was inaugurated and perfected. Evasion of the central issue of slavery signalled the demise of the Whigs and the emergence of a Republican party which did not fudge the moral issues involved, but in the wake of the civil

[51] *AC*, I, pp. 66, 96.
[52] *AC*, II, pp. 3, 531. The anecdote was related by Roosevelt.

war's exertions and sacrifices had come 'a season of contentment and lassitude' which enabled party organisation to extend
its control yet further.[53] That control remained total because a
monopoly of power was shared between two parties and a static
equilibrium of dual loyalty, tradition and patronage ensured its
continued survival against any third party competition, which
was either crushed or absorbed by one of the two monoliths.[54]
The cohesive force of joint plunder was easy to grasp; defining
those principles which separated and distinguished each party
was harder. Bryce spoke variously of centrifugal *versus* centripe-
tal forces, of state as opposed to federal powers, of liberty *versus*
order, and of free thinking as against puritan traditions
personified in Jefferson and Adams, Republican and Federalist
respectively. But these historical traditions had grown shadowy
and become empty party slogans by the 1880s. He was in no
doubt that Republican and Democratic reflected distinct tones
and characteristics, that his own friends, 'the philanthropists,
the men of culture, the men of substance', were Republican
almost to a man, while the Democrats with their dependence on
immigrants, especially Irish immigrants, had an air of 'row-
dyism' about them.[55] But what was so patently lacking were the
American equivalents of Britain's conspicuous and defining
party ideologies. In America parties were devoid of programmes, of ideals, of higher aims which gave purpose to
strategy and the holding of power, and herein lay the essence of
his damaging criticism.

Because he believed that the Gilded Age had regressed to a
Jacksonian level, Bryce's perceptions were heavily influenced by
Tocqueville's dialectic of organisation *versus* idealism. Both
conceived of party in European terms, as something which
looked to principles rather than to their consequences, to
general rather than specific policies. 'Minor' parties, unlike
'major', were deficient in political good faith. Because they
were not sustained and dignified by lofty purposes, they
displayed the selfishness of their character in their action: 'They
glow', continued Tocqueville, 'with a factitious zeal; their
language is vehement, but their conduct is timid and irresolute.'
The second American party system reflected a post-revolution-
ary calm, when 'great men seem suddenly to disappear and the

---

[53] *AC*, II, pp. 7, 126, 70.
[54] *AC*, II, pp. 205 – 206.
[55] *AC*, II, pp. 5, 6, 9, 17, 31 – 2.

powers of the human mind to lie concealed. Society is convulsed by great parties, it is only agitated by minor ones; it is torn by the former, by the latter it is degraded; and if the first sometimes saves it by salutary perturbation, the last invariably disturbs it to no good end.'[56]

This distinction chimed perfectly with Bryce's own English perception of party struggle as 'salutary perturbation' much as the Jacksonian calm seemed to parallel exactly America's *post bellum* moral lethargy. Consequently alongside his thorough dissection of American party in its strictly American context there runs a countercurrent based on European presuppositions. Like Tocqueville and Mill before him, he is obsessed with explaining why the 'best men' do not enter politics or become presidents, and why American parties do not duplicate their European models. His analysis assumes that parties deliberately set about creating an ideological vacuum in which they can flourish, avoiding genuine and hence divisive and disruptive issues. The best remembered image in *The American Commonwealth* is of two empty bottles each with a different label marked 'Republican' and 'Democrat'.[57] The ensuing unreality was best measured by the hollowness of stump oratory. 'The commonest American defect is a turgid and inflated style . . . apt to aim at concealing poverty or triteness in thought by exaggeration of statement, by a profusion of ornament, by appeals to sentiment too lofty for the subject or the occasion . . .. American statesmen keep their pockets full of the loose cash of empty compliments and pompous phrases.' This inflated language reflected a devaluation of content and was part of the regrettable phenomenon of 'booming', the self-fulfilling hullabaloo which built railroads in order to create towns and printed newspapers to establish a readership.[58] But in most cases it was a confidence trick played on the expectant emotions of the public which served as a substitute for the fulfilment of extravagant promises. The ritual act of the party nomination conventions was the best

---

[56] *Democracy in America*, I, p. 182.
[57] The simile did not appear till the 1910 edition, and was taken from an 'eminent journalist' (*AC*, 1910, II, p. 29). Woodrow Wilson in his *Congressional Government* had written that party names 'stand for a fact, but scarcely for a reason' (p. 331).
[58] *AC*, II, pp. 668, 203. *AC*, I, p. 143. Bryce partly blamed this inflated rhetoric on the increase of larger audiences and whistle-stop tours. 'A man straining his voice in the open air is apt to strain his phrases also, and command attention by vehemence (*AC*, II, pp. 669, 198 n. 1).

example of a betrayal rather than a fulfilment of the democratic process. Bryce quoted from an observer at the 1884 Republican convention: 'Is there something in the atmosphere of such a place that robs reason of her faculty and transforms humans into some other species? . . .. The fat woman has lifted the little girl on the shoulders of a slim young man, and the child has put her hands together, and is saying, in a high, shrill key, ''God bless James G. Blaine; God bless James G. Blaine'', and we all wonder what for.' Bryce ruefully observed that after such ephemeral gatherings the hastily constructed convention halls were torn down and their materials sold to contractors.[59]

Even architecture reflected the politics of muddle and evasion, for the very shape of Congress made obfuscation tangible. Unlike the Commons' tradition of ministry and opposition facing each other across the floor, Senators and Congressmen merged together in desks fitted around a semi-circular hall. In his diary the parliamentarian recorded his shock and dismay at lax conventions so distinct from the rigid formalities of strict adversarial politics: 'Strikes one as disorderly, people standing up, talking in gangways, hurrying behind, even smoking there, general sense of a sort of hotel hall or large public drawing room, rather than of a deliberative assembly.' From the gallery above this assembly he noticed that it was considered bad form to pay attention to a speaker holding forth for the benefit of his constituents and the pages of the *Congressional Globe* rather than for members present, although the system ran according to its own distorted code of ethics.[60]

He observed that resourcefulness in organisation like sterile rhetoric helped fill the void left by ideology. 'The government counts for less than in Europe, the parties count for more; and the fewer have become their principles . . . the more perfect has become their organisation. The less of nature the more of art; the less spontaneity the more mechanism.'[61] In discussing parties, he frequently resorted to military metaphor. Party government was a 'species of war conducted by ballots instead of bullets'; discipline was more important than numbers 'because scattered voting is even worse than scattered firing'; immigrant votes were 'captured' and kept on a 'war footing'; 'divisions' were 'enlisted' and 'drilled' by 'recruiting agents'

---

59   *AC*, II, pp. 743–4, 688.
60   *1891 Journal*, Ms. Bryce Misc. *AC*, II, p. 467. *AC*, I, p. 140.
61   *AC*, II, p. 5.

and 'inferior officers'.[62] Under this system a premium was placed on blind loyalty and undeviating obedience, its ranks were packed with 'stalwarts', 'regulars' and 'heelers', and because disloyalty was the greatest sin 'sore-heads' and 'kickers' were ostracised. Particular contempt was reserved for the 'mugwump' who 'scratched' the straight party ticket by pasting over the printed official lists with his independent choice.[63] The two parties were tacit allies enjoying the shared fruits of patronage; the minority party was collaborationist, and because the independents were the only genuine reformist counterbalance they were considered the true enemy. The two party monopoly of patronage from the highest federal office down to the lowliest country postmaster gave it the obedience it needed to perpetuate the sterile system of rewards. Put simply, 'the source of power and cohesive force is the desire for office, and for office as a means of gain. All has been lost except office or the hope of it'.[64] In return for cash, jobs or favours the parties accumulated vast revenues by subscription from members and from business, by appropriations from the treasury, from taxes levied on office holders and from proceeds from the sale of office. A system based on financial accumulation and distribution was oiled by corruption ranging from the direct exchange of money to the shadier areas of favouritism in the granting of franchises and contracts. And the public's loyalty was bought just as the loyalty of the party officials was bought, by money, through 'log-rolling', 'special bills' financially advantageous to various localities, and by dispensing hugely inflated pensions from the treasury to a larger number of veterans than had ever served in the war.[65] By means of 'subsoiling' — that is, by carefully preparing the ground in advance — local bosses could retain their firm grip on the vital nominating primaries and elect 'regulars' to party posts. While these primaries were theoretically open to all party members, the rings exploited the complicated election machinery to exclude large numbers of

62 AC, II, pp. 95, 108. *North American Review*, Jan 1893, pp. 105–7. Or again, he referred to the system as feudal, with vassal-voters rendering life-long service, with party nominating conventions serving as medieval pilgrimages to the faithful (AC, II, pp. 108, 112, 184).
63 AC, I, pp. 45–9. AC, II, pp. 79, 83–8, 108, 136, 203. Walter Dean Burnham estimates a two-thirds turnout for the straight party ticket between 1876 and 1896 with a further 10% of eligible voters showing a high degree of loyalty (F. O. Gatell et al., *Readings in American History*, pp. 263–6).
64 AC, II, p. 102.
65 AC, I, pp. 521–2, 85. AC, II, pp. 149–61.

qualified voters and run them on the lines of private clubs. For example, Bryce calculated that in 1880 only six to eight thousand out of a rough total of 58,000 New York Republicans belonged to the organisations and were thus entitled to vote.[66]

Because they were paid to win elections and act as brokers in distributing spoils, America's professional politicians bore no similarity to their European equivalents. 'Politics has now become a gainful occupation, like advocacy, stockbroking, the dry goods trade, or the getting up of companies.' Commercialism and corruption had degraded the ideal of selfless leadership and yielded to astute management and the delivery of voting blocs which debased the calibre of its practitioners. The boss had usually 'grown up in an atmosphere of oaths and cocktails; ideas of honour and purity are as strange to him as ideas about the nature of the currency and the incidence of taxation: politics is merely the means for getting and distributing places'. Even at its highest level the party demanded mediocrity and compliance and presidential nominating conventions looked for a good candidate rather than a good president. An able, vociferous and independently-minded statesman would make enemies and divide the ranks; far better to elect a candidate of the order of Garfield, a third of whose brief tenure of office was given over to dispensing spoils or attempting to avoid the importunity of spoilsmen.[67]

The 'inner circle' of congressmen, federal, state and local office-holders made up a total of some 200,000 who between them effectively excluded the neutral political observers of the 'outer circle'. And, insofar as office-holders or those expectant of office precluded the contribution of independents to political debate and the formulation of policy, so 'the proportion between Outer Circle and Inner Circle men is . . . a sort of ozonometer by which the purity and healthiness of the political atmosphere may be tested'.[68]

Cumulatively Bryce's evidence was highly damaging and his judgement severe, but as always and at each stage of his critique he took pains to identify the specifically American factors at play which shaped the current state of public affairs. This

[66]   AC, II, pp. 97, 98 n. 1. Even ostensibly non-partisan election officers came within the sphere of party patronage (AC, II, p. 139).
[67]   AC, II, pp. 56, 106, 131 n. 1. AC, I, pp. 76, 60 – 1. 'What a party wants is not a good President but a good candidate.' 'The present system makes a wire-puller of him' (AC, I, p. 61. AC, II, p. 180).
[68]   AC, II, p. 60.

method had the advantage of indicating that such evils as there were were not the inevitable consequence of a Tocquevillian democratic spirit but were capable of reform through the application of specifically American antidotes which would eradicate specific evils. Thus he identified a Jeffersonian-Jacksonian tradition which he believed had contributed to the low moral standard of American politics. With its doctrinaire faith in equality it had instigated rotation in office and the election of judges and excluded the more able and scrupulous. But he recognised, too, a countervailing Hamiltonian-Whig tendency which had continually offset the prevailing extreme democratic orthodoxy by advocating élitism and wider discretionary powers being granted to political leaders. More specifically he explained the current exclusion of the more able partly by the vulgar ribaldry of bar-room politics which deterred the fastidious, and partly by the expansion of far more attractive alternative professions such as business, law and higher education. As matters stood, being president of a large railway company or of a university offered far more scope for talent, advancement and solid achievement than the sterile job of chief executive. And, although he dismissed Matthew Arnold's verdict on America as 'uninteresting' as insufferably condescending, Bryce himself shared a residual feeling that the questions which absorbed American political life such as tariffs and currency were dry and tedious, and that the statesman's true *métier* lay in the drama and consequence of foreign policy and domestic reform. Politics was a grubby profession because there was not that conjunction of social and political life as there was in Europe. The dull provincialism and dreary uniformity of Harrisburg or Sacramento held few prospects of brilliant *soirées*, and the United States conspicuously lacked a national capital where 'the forces of rank, wealth, knowledge [and] intellect naturally make such a city a sort of foundry in which opinion is melted and cast, where it receives the definitive shape in which it can be easily and swiftly propagated and diffused through the whole country'.[69]

Federalism's fragmentation conspired with a Jacksonian tradition of narrow delegation of powers to breed an excessive parochialism in the form of residence qualifications and the passing of 'special bills' in congress to reward local interests.

[69] *AC*, II, pp. 65–71, 660. Bryce stated frankly that 'politics are less interesting than in Europe' (*AC*, II, p. 67).

Dicey thought this obsessive localism the greatest revelation of *The American Commonwealth* and Acton drew the conclusion that 'if ten statesmen live in the same street, nine will be thrown out of work'.[70] To Bryce the consequences in terms of tighter party control through the purse, in 'log-rolling' and the arbitrary exclusion of independents were nothing short of catastrophic. Because of the uneven geographical concentration of talent in Boston, Philadelphia, Baltimore and New York, city rings virtually disfranchised able independents like George Curtis, Carl Schurz and Charles Francis Adams Jr. Unfairly disqualified from contributing their weight to national politics, they looked on dismayed while 'many parts of the country [which] do not grow statesmen', as Bryce put it, continued to elect nonentities to the national legislature. The bane of localism placed an arbitrary premium on geography, while the politics of vote-catching and brokerage placed the management of numbers above personal capacity. Even the choice of presidential and vice-presidential candidates depended far more on which state they came from and the number of voters they brought with them to the electoral college. A colourless mediocrity from a large and marginal state such as Ohio, Indiana or Illinois took automatic precedence over a good candidate who had the misfortune to hail from a small, solid one party state such as Vermont (Republican) or Maryland (Democrat).[71]

The parties' grip on cities came in for especially severe criticism. 'There is no denying', Bryce wrote, 'that the government of cities is the one conspicuous failure of the United States . . .. The commonest mistake of Europeans who talk about America is to assume that the political vices of New York are found everywhere. The next most common is to suppose they are found nowhere else.'[72] Accelerated growth, the rich concentration of lucrative pickings, the multiplicity of elections which confused and deadened the electorates' capacity for choice, a large reservoir of ignorant and exploitable immigrants, all contributed to the unique control of parasitic rings in urban centres. And, just as parochialism invaded national politics, so it was to the parties' advantage to neglect vital local issues and enforce regularity by summoning the electorate with national rallying cries. In 1884 in Philadelphia, for example, the Republicans, by raising the controversial matter of tariffs in a highly

[70]   *Edinburgh Review*, April 1889, pp. 499 – 500. *History of Freedom*, p. 579.
[71]   AC, I, pp. 186 – 90. AC, II, pp. 180 – 81.
[72]   AC, I, p. 608.

protectionist city, were able to divert attention from the scandalous depredations of the Gas Ring.[73]

Even today Bryce's interpretation of Gilded Age parties holds inordinate sway, not least because his conclusions are satisfyingly simple and exclusive; his analysis is built up, step by step, on stark contrasts — statesmanship yields to manipulative bosses, ideals to organisation, high tone to the venal morality of party hacks. He states at one point that it is unfair to expect higher, saintlier standards from America just because it is new and republican, that 'the heaven of ideal purity is above the ordinary earth of Boston and Westminster'.[74] Yet the implied contrast with England running throughout is far more indulgent and idealised with regard to Westminster, and the subtler understanding of English double standards and her more insidious forms of moral corruption tend to get lost in the overall impression of an Anglo-American contrast of pure *versus* impure. Bryce remains emphatic in his conviction that party as it exists in the United States is an alien imposition, that it obstructs Congress's genuinely representative role, that, while going through the forms of consultation, it substantially ignores them.[75] It follows that either the general public is excluded from party activities or that it is apathetic and indifferent. Bryce maintains both propositions at various times, and yet both are contradicted by the unusually high level of support and participation revealed in the voting figures. Bryce is dimly aware of this but responds with surprise since 'no party has any benefit to promise to the people which it may not as well get from the other, and where the voter is a keen-witted man, with little reference for the authority of any individual'. As it is, he cannot square what Robert Wiebe has termed the two major political characteristics of the period — 'intense partisanship' and 'massive political indifference'.[76] Yet here Wiebe falls into Bryce's trap. That the political system was intensely partisan is indisputable, but what constitutes 'political indifference' is a normative judgement and can usually be interpreted as meaning indifference to those issues which concern the author. In Bryce's case his preconceptions led him to absolve public

[73] *AC*, I, pp. 541 – 4, 598, 610 – 11. *AC*, II, p. 380.
[74] *AC*, II, pp. 733, 157.
[75] *AC*, I, p. 6. *AC*, II, pp. 94, 101. Bryce to Dicey, 27 April 1909, MS. Bryce 4.
[76] Again the explicit contrast is to Europe, 'where momentous issues inflame men's passions' (*AC*, II, p. 48). Wiebe, *The Search for Order, 1877 – 1920*, p. 27.

opinion and blame parties instead for excluding the 'best men' and discouraging reform and issue politics; to agree with an anonymous observer that there was no longer 'any politics in politics'. But the average American was intensely partisan precisely because he was intensely political, even if indifferent to the political style which Bryce cherished. Because of this his tone is often chastising and disapproving; he approached the ward boss as he might approach a psychopath and dissects the party system as if it were a malignant organism. In harsh terms he condemns the Black as a burden on local rates and the immigrant as unprincipled voting fodder. He can offer an excellent definition of interest politics as 'the art of distributing salaries so as to secure the maximum of support from friends with the minimum of offence to opponents', but can never approve of the pork-barrel: 'To this art able men have been forced to bend their minds.'[77]

He is less than fair to the vital role of brokerage which the parties played in a dynamic and pluralistic system, negotiating a politics of conciliation and consensus which helped create that very stability and unity he so much admired. He made insufficient allowance for the emotional needs that party fulfilled in a time of rapid change and rootlessness, the social focus it provided, and the sense it gave of identity and of communal co-operation in a highly atomistic society. Robert Marcus suggests in his study of the GOP that Americans got exactly the parties they wanted. Much more absorbed in local ethnocultural conflicts, of native against immigrant, Protestant against Catholic, and pietist against ritualist, the electorate repeatedly voted firmly against change, third party alternatives, charismatic leaders and issue-oriented campaigns. 'The leaders of the gilded age', he concludes, ' have long been excoriated for their colourlessness and their failure to confront significant issues. But this accusation — which is wholly just — must be understood in terms of the voting public the politicians represented.'[78] Bryce's call for reform, then, came at a time when most Americans chose to ignore it. When the call was answered much of Bryce's reforms of 1888 seemed rather dated and conservative and went largely unheeded. Yet at the same time *The American Commonwealth* was germinal and a precursor of later progressivism.

---

[77] AC, II, pp. 110, 131.
[78] *Grand Old Party: Political Structure in the Gilded Age, 1880 – 1896*, pp. 3 – 10.

Solutions

The American Commonwealth's underlying optimism reflected a
decade which began in euphoria for its author. Gladstone's
principled stand on the Eastern Question had returned him
triumphantly to office in 1880. Wide ranging liberal reforms, of
Ireland, of the franchise, of the Lords, were in the air, and
among those elected to parliament among a dazzling array of
thinkers such as Grant Duff, Goschen, E. L. Stanley, Harcourt,
Courtney, Henry Fawcett, G. O. Trevelyan and Charles Dilke
was the new member for Tower Hamlets. The aim of elections,
Dicey wrote, was 'to facilitate the approach of men of genius to
the service of the State and . . . Professor Bryce's election . . .
outweights a hundred lamentations over the alleged incapacity
for citizens or shop-keepers to recognise character and ability.'[79]
In America the assassination of Garfield led to the passing of a
limited federal Civil Service Reform bill in 1883, while the
mugwump bolt of the following year appeared to presage the
final emergence of the independents as an effective political
force. And this new spirit was alive at all levels. In Massachusetts Colonel Theodore Lyman, President Eliot's cousin, was
elected to Congress, Ben Butler was defeated in the gubernatorial contest of 1883, and in 1884 Richard H. Dana and Josiah
Quincy pushed through a state Civil Service Reform bill. In 1880
Grover Cleveland was elected mayor of Buffalo, then, as
Governor of New York State, passed his own Civil Service bill.
In Brooklyn Seth Low was elected mayor in 1881, inaugurating a
new era of enlightened municipal administration. Bryce knew
most of the actors in these stirring events and followed each
new triumph with keen interest; he wrote to Colonel Higginson
congratulating him for taking the lead against Blaine, corres-
ponded with John Murray Forbes who helped finance the
Massachusetts bolt, and with Henry Villard who had bought the
New York Evening Post to place at the disposal of the mugwump
cause in 1881. In October 1884 he was writing to Mrs Whitman,
the Boston matriarch, impatient for news of 'the attitude of the
"wise and better" . . . and our independent friends, who I
suppose include most of our common friends'.[80]

---

[79] *NYN*, 20 July 1882, pp. 49–50.
[80] Bryce to Mrs. Whitman, 7 Oct 1884, and to Higginson, 13 Dec 1885, Ms.
Bryce USA 22. The bolt illustrated 'a growing disposition to defer to
intellectual and moral eminence.' (Bryce to Godkin, 6 Feb 1886, Godkin
Papers).

Everywhere the auguries seemed bright, but the victory celebrations were premature. Just as liberal hopes foundered under disasters in Egypt and Ireland, so Cleveland's administration proved disappointing as the president yielded to the importunities of Democrats too long starved of patronage. Even during the excitement of the hour Bryce realised that the victory of 1884 owed more to anti-Blaine feeling than pro-reformist support ('How pleasant it is to congratulate you on Mr. Blaine's defeat — that is better than Mr. Cleveland's success'), and that the bolt would reinforce and not transcend conventional two party politics. He appreciated, too, that Cleveland's carrying of New York State was far more the result of traditional 'favourite son' voting patterns than of Republican defection, that the independents were noisy rather than numerous, 'more important by the intelligence and the social position of the men who composed it than by its numbers', and that without greater popular support permanent achievement was unlikely. Yet despite his misgivings he remained buoyant, partly to sustain the flagging zeal of his American counterparts, and in his *American Commonwealth* contributed his own 'boom' to inspire them in the future.[81]

Although the links between British and United States imperialism and the example of Britain as a model for American progressives have been thoroughly studied, historians have neglected the influence Bryce and his contemporaries exerted in the period immediately preceding 1898. This is partly because mugwump anglophilia has been interpreted in negative, retrograde terms, as yet another example of the mugwumps' backward-looking myopia. The same historians have vigorously distinguished between old mugwumps and new progressives instead of exploring the links and continuities between the two. The futile attempts by Gamaliel Bradford and the young Woodrow Wilson to graft Bagehot and the cabinet system on to American constitutionalism has served to reinforce a conviction that the earlier reformers were abysmally misguided. There was indeed a strong scent of wistful nostalgia in American anglophilia, of looking across the Atlantic to a reassuring replica of the lost early patrician republic. But there was also a more reasoned and positive appreciation of Great Britain and no one did more to encourage this appreciation than Bryce. For to Bryce the

[81] Bryce to Mrs. Whitman, 30 Nov 1884, Ms. Bryce USA 22. *AC*, II, pp. 188 n. 2, 43.

American state appeared hopelessly chaotic, irrational, amateur and ramshackle. The Jeffersonian-Jacksonian tradition had not only poisoned politics, but rendered it inefficient and decentralised, so that by 1888 the United States, on the verge of world power and increasing industrialisation and urbanisation, retained an antiquated structure of government ill-equipped to cope with the modernisation and rationalisation urgently demanded of her. Faced by problems of unprecedented complexity, American legislators were condemned 'to be architects without science, critics without experience, censors without responsibility', while Britain's middle class government was, in the words of Henry Adams, 'the ideal of human progress'.[82] The comparative studies of Bryce and Dicey reinforced the conviction that in Britain, at least, power could be forcefully united with morality and party government, that an omnipotent central government could delegate wide executive powers to statesmen, examples which American had at first partially duplicated then misguidedly dismantled. The Federalists in their wisdom had provided firm foundations for centralism, and one of Bryce's aims, twenty-one years before Herbert Croly, was to reassert a neglected Hamiltonian tradition. 'The people', he wrote, 'when they confer a power, must be deemed to confer a wide discretion as to the means whereby it is to be used in their service.'[83] To amplify his point he contrasted presidential and prime ministerial forms of government, pointing to the long dismal list of innocuous Gilded Age presidents, remarkable only for their total subservience to party, to bosses and to sectional interests. Incapable of initiating positive policies they were hamstrung by irresponsible congressional committees and hedged around by all sorts of balances and checks. As one reader of *The American Commonwealth* wryly observed: 'No man of tolerable talents need despair of having been born a Presidential candidate.' That same reader, Woodrow Wilson, in his *Congressional Government*, emphasised even more starkly than Bryce the tone and force of an English executive: 'The question is not What will Parliament do, but What will Mr. Gladstone do?'; the Prime Minister's phenomenal mastery of parliament and control of the wider constituency of the nation added 'genius and noble oratory to the authority of established

---

[82] *AC*, I, p. 224. Henry Adams' *Education*, p. 33.
[83] *AC*, I, p. 369.

leadership'.[84] The difference in executive style and performance reflected two distinct traditions: federalism's formal distribution of powers left the American president with few resources besides his veto and a careful distribution of patronage, while Britain's contrary tradition of cabinet government as 'nerve centre' fused executive and legislative functions and bestowed power and responsibility equally. Like Henry Adams twenty years earlier, Wilson was unable to detect any similar centre of gravity in American administration. Any power he did locate was found in secret and decentralised committee government in Congress, where the 'hide and seek vagaries of authority' veiled the 'central secret' of irresponsible and unresponsive government.[85] When *The American Commonwealth* appeared Wilson unjustly accused Bryce of cribbing wholesale from his writings when in fact the substitution of cabinet for congressional government was a commonplace nostrum offered by independents at the time. But, unlike the young Wilson, Bryce did not fall into the trap of advocating a palpably unworkable cabinet system as a solution to all America's political ills. The ultimate wisdom Wilson drew from Bryce was that tinkering with machinery and long established constitutional traditions was far less effective in the long run than transforming the spirit of those who operate it; that a strong activating executive could weld together the formal separation of federal powers; that a president cast in the mould of Gladstone rather than of Chester Arthur could emulate the British system and transform the existing party spirit into effective party government.[86]

George Pendleton, who had attempted to introduce a bill giving cabinet members seats in Congress in 1872, also gave his name to America's first major Civil Service Reform ten years later. The Pendleton Act of 1883 owed its success far more to the

[84] *Congressional Government*, pp. 256, 332, 209, 59. Dicey repeatedly urged this point on his American audience: 'The English democracy are amply justified in preferring that the executive should be strong. Parliament has never done its proper work . . . except under vigorous guidance' (*NYN*, 6 April 1882, p. 293).

[85] Brooks, p. 173. *Congressional Government*, pp. 266 – 7, 56, 280, 318 – 19, 284, 213 – 14. Arthur Link, *Woodrow Wilson: The Road to the White House*, p. 13, and Link (ed.), *Papers of Woodrow Wilson*, VI, p. 36. *AC*, I, pp. 209 – 10.

[86] Bryce dismissed the cabinet solution on the obvious grounds that it would destroy the constitutional balance of power (*AC*, I, p. 284). As one reviewer wrote: 'The general conclusion which Professor Bryce reaches is, that the faults which need correction are not so much in our constitutional frame of government as in our method of working it, (*NYN*, 10 Jan 1889, p. 35).

Republican strategy of entrenching its party followers in permanent positions beyond the reach of partisan rotation than to horror following upon Garfield's assassination at the hands of a disgruntled office-seeker. But it was also a first, faltering attempt to copy the British model of a skilled and permanent bureaucracy. Jenckes's abortive bills of 1865 and 1868 closely followed the principles laid down in the Northcote-Trevelyan report of 1853; here, however indistinctly, the high tone of the Indian Civil Service and the writings of James and John Stuart Mill began to enter the mainstream of American political consciousness. Again, after 1870, when Gladstone extended further the area of competitive exams for top civil service posts, President Hayes sent Dorman Eaton to Great Britain to report back. 'I am astonished', he wrote to the President in 1877, 'at the immense length the English have distanced us, in the great cause of honest and efficient administration.'[87] Easton published his *Civil Service in Great Britain: A History of Abuses and Reforms and their Bearing upon American Politics* in 1880, and received every encouragement in his efforts from Bryce, with whom he has struck up a friendship. For the independent Civil Service reform was the reform on which all other reforms must be based. At one stroke it cut off party spoils at their source, replacing party minions by capable bureaucrats, and establishing a tradition of permanent uninterrupted service and cumulative administrative wisdom in place of arbitrary party change. George Washington Plunkitt of Tammany Hall might rail at the foolish notion that being able to give the exact number of grains of sand in the Sahara was sufficient to equip a man for dealing with New York ward politics, and accuse the reformers of setting up an alternative machine, entry to which was based on exams which only they were likely to pass. But his incessant denunciations were a direct measure of the threat which reformers posed to the old political ethic which distinguished between 'honest' and 'dishonest' graft. The replacement of transient political considerations by long term non-partisan objectives, of amateur by professional standards, would, if effectual, dry up the source of ring patronage. It was under popular forms of government that those qualities singled out by Dicey as 'the permanence of tenure, the consistency of action,

---

[87] Garrison to Bryce, 30 Dec 1882, Ms. Bryce USA 4. Eaton quoted in Ari Hoogenboom, *Outlawing the Spoils*, p. 177. Mill and Godkin had both earlier encouraged Jenckes. Cf. *The Collected Works of Mill*, xvi, p. 1572, and n. 3. A. P. Grimes, *The Political Liberalism of the New York Nation*, p. 45.

the scientific knowledge, the devotion of work unrecognised by the public — all those virtues, in short, which would not otherwise be fostered under a parliamentary and democratic constitution' which made this reform so necessary.[88] Even more so the staffing of local administration by dedicated permanent officials was needed to break the endemic corruption of American municipal government.[89] Bryce gave his whole-hearted support to this and other piecemeal reforms — 'home rule' from corrupt state party control and direct responsibility of self-government by the large metropolises, a vigorous counter-attack by independents at the critical primary elections — precisely because he knew that parliamentary solutions were inapplicable. The average American's strong aversion to élitism, his lack of deference, his suspicion of superior expertise and his passion for rough equality and the more direct forms of democratic participation, all helped to reinforce Bryce's opinion that the implanting of non-American solutions was futile.[90]

At the same time he did not believe that any 'mechanical' tinkering was in itself sufficient to bring about the changes in American political life he desired. What was ultimately required was a complete 'ethical' change, a complete renovation of heart and mind and a profound reappraisal in order to reverse the unthinking assumptions underlying pointless party combat. A call for the re-entry of the 'best men' into public life was hardly original, for Tocqueville and Mill had urged the same.[91] But no observer had pressed the case with such resolve before, or focused his attention so unremittingly on those forces which led to the exclusion of this class, or considered in such detail the means by which this class could effect its re-entry into politics. In this matter *The American Commonwealth* was remedial as well as descriptive, and aimed at waking citizens to a sense of their

[88] *NYN*, 7 Dec 1905, p. 467. Garrison in a letter to Bryce of 30 Dec 1882 suggested that if the Pendleton Bill were passed it would be as significant as Britain's 1832 Reform Bill (Ms. Bryce USA 4). See too *AC*, II, p. 489, where Bryce suggests that the extension of Civil Service reform is the chief aim of American reformers.

[89] All of Bryce's informants on city government urged this reform (*AC*, I, pp. 593 – 635), especially Seth Low, former Mayor of Brooklyn, who wrote the chapter on 'Municipal Government'.

[90] *AC*, II, pp. 65 – 71.

[91] *Democracy in America*, II, pp. 256 – 62, 347. Mill wrote of American democracy in his *Representative Government* as 'a most valuable school, but it is a school from which the ablest teachers are excluded' (*Three Essays*, p. 275).

grave responsibilities in ensuring good government. He never underrated the reformer's task; he appreciated the 'Sisyphean labour' required; it was a 'warfare of volunteers against disciplined troops'. 'The machine will not be reformed from within; it must be assailed from without . . . . The powers of evil do not yield without a battle.' As 'a European observer, sympathetic with the aims of the reformers', his plea was a simple one:

> What opinion chiefly needs in America in order to control the politicians is . . . a more sustained activity on the part of the men of vigorously independent minds, a more sedulous effort on their part to impress their views upon the masses, and a disposition on the part of the ordinary well meaning but often inattentive citizens to prefer the realities of good administration to outworn party cries.[92]

In this intangible area of tone and spirit he felt able to point to the superiority of the English model, and, if the picture he painted was a shade idealised and differed from his private misgivings, it could be put down to his wish to provide an example after which Americans could strive. More specifically he wished to show the successful impact in Britain of an enlightened 'outer circle' making its beneficial influence felt, and encourage informed but independent politicians in America first to challenge then to take the 'inner circle' fortress of salaried professionals. This class felt compelled to enter public service out of a sense of *noblesse oblige* not pecuniary gain; their occupations, like their education, manners, breeding, income and conviction confirmed that they were gentlemen. But their very fastidiousness made them unwilling to engage in the rough political trade of politics, and Bryce had to stiffen their resolve and determination by offering examples from his own political experience:

> In every country a politician has to associate with men whom he despises and distrusts . . . .. In every country he is exposed to misrepresentation and abuse, and the most galling misrepresentations are not the coarse and incredible ones, but those which have a semblance of probability, which delicately discolours his motives and ingeniously perverts his

[92]   AC, II, pp. 376, 168, 713. AC, I, pp. 551, 168. AC, II, p. 326.

words. A statesman must soon learn . . . to disregard all this, and rely upon his conscience for his peace of mind, and upon his conduct for the respect of his countrymen.[93]

The message was clear enough and was taken up enthusiastically by the class at which it was aimed. 'The moral is that if good men do not take the matter up, bad men will' (Gamaliel Bradford): 'You, probably, can hardly realise the profound influence your book has made . . .. It is bound to exert a most wholesome influence on our way of seeing ourselves' (Edward Eggleston). Bryce's words 'are stimulants to nobler life; they are instinct with a faith in supreme good; and they force upon every American reader a conviction of this responsibility, not of his good fortune alone' (an anonymous reviewer in the *Atlantic Monthly*) — and so on.[94] But these and other gratifying responses came overwhelmingly from the already converted, while the unregenerate ignored the book or retaliated in critical reviews. Nevertheless sales figures (212,288 copies were sold in American up to 1910) are fairly impressive and suggest that the book reached a wide audience. Impressive enough at least for the Pond's bureau to tout for Bryce, now a 'household word', as lecturer, and there is ample evidence that the book exerted a seminal influence both as textbook and tract in the universities which Bryce particularly wished to reach. There it became the standard students' guide to 'civics' and required reading in History and Politics courses. Jesse Macy assured Bryce that the book had not only become an important political institution in itself, but that every student from Grinnell went East with a copy 'both in his head and in his hand'. Bryce gave every encouragement to publishers and academics who wished to adapt or abridge editions for high school purposes, believing that to nurture civic responsibility at school where children were receptive and impressionable would extend the time span of the book's influence.[95]

---

93 *AC*, II, pp. 55 – 9, 30 – 2, 69 – 70. Chapter headings convey the polemical engagement of the book: 'Remedies for the Faults of State Government', 'Corruption', 'The War Against Bossdom'.

94 Bradford to Bryce, 24 March 1892, Ms. Bryce USA 12. Eggleston to Bryce, 10 July 1889, Ms. Bryce USA 13. *Atlantic Monthly*, March 1889, p. 423.

95 Woodrow Wilson, who used Bryce as a basic text at Bryn Mawr, received this invidious comparison after offering his own services to the bureau (*Papers of Woodrow Wilson*, VII, p. 376). Macy to Bryce, 6 Feb 1891, Ms. Bryce USA 8.

That the independents answered Bryce's call to arms is proved by his voluminous American correspondence which is replete with reports of advances against Tammany, of retreats, reformations and further assaults. The obituaries in the *Proceedings of the Massachusetts' Historical Society*, in the various state bar journals and university alumnus publications are impressive monuments to the ethos of duty and selfless service, and if dedication and effort had been enough the ring and the boss would not have survived the mugwumps' ponderous onslaught. As it is, the independents failed spectacularly in the last years of the nineteenth century, and their conspicuous nonachievement has done nothing to add to their reputation among later historians. A record of failure is never popular or judged lightly by the timid but omniscient historian, and, while a very practical appreciation of what the abolitionist and radical reconstructionist was up against led to a wise reappraisal and rehabilitation by historians during the civil rights campaign, the mugwump has not been absolved but, rather, because of his weak democratic credentials, consigned to oblivion. Having suffered the insidious slights of their contemporaries as 'goo goos', 'men milliners' and 'political flirts', the mugwumps have received the further indignity of being dismissed by posterity as irrelevant. 'Backward looking', 'myopic', with an 'un-American' yearning for deference and patrician leadership, they were, John Sproat concludes, 'reduced to playing the role of querulous aristocrats in a nation that had long since been infatuated with democracy'. Their patent Anglophilia only made them more contemptible in the eyes of parochial and chauvinistic progressive historians like Parrington and Beard. Parrington, for example, presents a gross distortion of Godkin, suggesting that he settled in the United States only after having been spurned by a rigid English caste system, and then only to pursue swifter social advancement and solicit for cheap distinction. There is nothing here of Godkin's youthful idealism, the disciple of Mill and Lincoln or the fervent admirer of Republican virtues.[96] Neo-Beardians like Ari Hoogenboom and Richard Hofstadter have argued that civil service reform was merely a means by which the socially displaced could exert political leverage to retrieve status, power and jobs. But this truth, satisfying in its simplicity

[96] *The Best Men*, p. 281. *Main Currents in American Thought*, III, pp. 156–7. A similar insularity pervaded progressive literary criticism. Van Wyck Brooks' *Pilgrimage of Henry James* (1925) insisted that James's expatriation doomed him to literary sterility.

and easy cynicism, is only partial and strangely shallow coming from historians rightly noted for their psychological insights. Furthermore the thesis merely resolves itself into a tautology, for improvement was necessarily impossible without the power to implement it. The various inbred vices of the American historical profession were only compounded by those who, like Daniel Boorstin and Oscar Handlin, romanticised ethnic society and ward bosses during the Gilded Age, and who did so at the expense of understating the exploitation of the immigrant communities by the rings, and by implication underplaying the rationality and efficiency of a permanent civil service from which everyone, new immigrants included, ultimately benefited.[97]

It is possible to strike a juster balance. Denis Brogan had implied and David Hammack has recently provided ample proof that the 'best men' were not, as Bryce fondly believed, distinct from, but tacitly connected with business and boss in maintaining the *status quo*. The independent distanced himself, socially and ideologically, from the boss, but both were conservative and both wished to manage a docile electorate and avoid disruptive and levelling insurgence from below.[98] Populists and labour unions threatened the luxury of reform politics which was soundly based on financial security and because, like their English counterparts, they adhered to the strictest *laissez-faire* principles, they stopped far short of substantial government intervention to alleviate the material lot of the majority. In any major battle they could be expected to take the side of wealth and privilege against bimetallism and economic regulation. As in 1867 Bryce, as an English 'mugwump', propounded a formula for reform from which the American middle-class professional and not the masses would be the main beneficiaries. The tone of his writing was profoundly élitist and anti-populist and the average voter was assigned the role of numerically prising control from the rings and instead offering it gratefully to the wealthy independent citizen. Throughout he

---

[97] *Outlawing the Spoil*, pp. 20 – 1. *The Age of Reform*, pp. 139 – 140. As Jon C. Teaford, writes in *Reviews of American History*: 'The former king of corruption Boss Tweed shifted from scoundrel to social necessity' (Dec 1982, p. 135).

[98] *An Introduction to American Politics*, p. 130. *Power and Society: Greater New York at the Turn of the Century*, pp. 12 – 15. Bryce did, however, quote Roosevelt on the way in which corporations bought demagogues off by offering money or jobs (*AC*, II, p. 109 n. 1).

argued not for the democratisation of party organisation but only that it should pass into the hands of his own class.[99]

Yet it is important not to exaggerate the negativism of the mugwumps or to think of then as hopelessly out of touch. Their high level of literacy and readability has done their cause a disservice. Beguiled by the voluminous output of the professional malcontents — Henry Adams, Godkin, Charles Eliot Norton — historians have alighted on their predominant note of shrill complaint. The one autobiographical masterpiece of the period, Henry Adams's *Education*, is largely given over to protesting against an American fate which left the grandson and great-grandson of presidents with the offer of the Guatemalan consularship by President Hayes. It was clear to Adams at least that America and not Adams was responsible for this sorry termination of affairs. The image of his brother, Charles Francis Jr's, daily contemplation of the grey seas off Scituate and his resigned exclamation: 'My God, how dreary', sums up this conventional stereotype only too well.[100] Yet if the focus is adjusted slightly from Hofstadter's 'status displacement' to 'occupational dissatisfaction' much of the vented frustration becomes understandable if not wholly justified. The independents were imbued with a deep sense of public service, felt that their more disinterested, scrupulous qualities would enable them to do the job — their job — better, yet, at the same time, they were effectively excluded by the complicity of a two party system which offered no genuine reformist opposition as in Britain. There Mill had provided the engaged liberal with a political justification. Mill's insistence on the creative powers of the principled man and of his leavening influence of reason gave the politically motivated a purposeful role to play. 'One person with a belief is a social power equal to ninety-nine who have only interest', and, grouped together with like-minded men, could provide 'a social support, a *point d'appui*, for individual resistance to the tendencies of the ruling power: a protection, a rallying point for opinions and interests which the ascendant public opinion views with disfavour'.[101] But Bryce's American equivalent was faced with the much more formidable 'Sisyphean labour' of breaking into the charmed 'inner circle', with far weaker weapons at his disposal. Deprived of the solid

[99] Bryce's Preface to Ostrogorski, p. xliii, *AC*, II, pp. 65–77.
[100] Quoted in Geoffrey Blodgett's 'The Mugwump Reputation, 1870 to the Present', *Journal of American History*, March 1980, p. 867.
[101] 'Representative Government', reprinted in *Three Essays*, pp. 155, 262–3.

satisfaction of a responsible and fulfilling life at the highest public level, exclusion from the wider areas of public service entailed a personal deprivation far worse than social displacement or financial loss. Henry Adams returned to Washington after serving as his father's ambassadorial secretary during one of the most momentous periods in Anglo-American affairs only to find that his services were not required, when 'all I wanted was something to support; something that would let itself be supported'. Godkin admitted towards the end that he had passed his best years 'doing a sort of detective work to my infinite distaste. I have not discussed constructive work much, because there has been little or no constructive work to discuss'.[102]

Charles Francis Adams Jr, after an early career as soldier and journalist and various attempts at entering politics, threw himself into the dynamic alternative of the railroad business and served as President of the Union Pacific till ousted by his old enemy, Jay Gould. But it was not this final disaster which hurt most, or the sterility of mere money-making as Charles Eliot suggested, or even his chronic dyspepsia which made him a byword for testy cantankerousness in his old age. His lament over his wasted business years is a lament for abilities unused and capacities misappropriated:

I found no vestige of statesmanship — no observation, philosophy and patience. They were all uneducated strong men — energetic, rough and undisciplined, seeing what was immediately before them very clearly and nothing beyond. They were 'practical men': I was a 'theorist'. To preach the lessons of experience — to point out the inevitable train of events . . . to attempt anything of this sort — stamped you in their eyes as not a 'practical man'.[103]

---

[102] *The Education of Henry Adams*, p. 267. Godkin to Eliot, 5 Dec 1899, Eliot Papers. 'The habitual critic gets a darker or less cheerful view of the social and political state than one does who is actively engaged in efforts to improve that state' Eliot conceded to Godkin (30 Nov 1899, Godkin Papers).

[103] Eliot to Bryce, 8 March 1912, Ms. Bryce USA 1. Adams considered his failure to find a satisfactory niche symbolised the failure of his class, 'the typical college man' (Edward Chase Kirkland, *Charles Francis Adams Jr., 1835 – 1915: The Patrician at Bay*, pp. 94, 127).

Not surprisingly this potentially first class civil servant turned to historical research in compensation.

What all this excessive public self-flagellation tended to disguise was the very active participation of the independents at the lower, local level. It was here that Charles Francis Adams Jr relieved some of his frustration by serving as moderator of the Quincy town meetings, on the School's Committee inaugurating the revolutionary 'Quincy System' of teaching by practical example rather than by rote, participating in the Parks Commission, the Sinking Fund Committee, and for twenty-four years as a vociferous member of the Harvard Board of Overseers and thorn in the side of President Eliot — all of it modest but useful and satisfying work. Locally the independents slowly loosened the party grip on primaries, and, while at the federal level civil service posts yielded reluctantly to competitive appointments, swifter advances were recorded in cities (New York, Brooklyn, Boston) and states.[104] Other reformers excluded from politics turned their attention to their own professions, to law, medicine and journalism, setting new and higher standards of entry and formulating stricter codes of conduct. If the aim was partially to restrict entry, impose a monopoly and raise salaries, it also brought much needed regulation and rationalisation in areas where there had been none before. Biding their time, the perennial zeal of the 'do-gooders' channelled their energies into eminently practical occupations. Oliver Wendell Holmes answered his summons to the Massachusetts Supreme Court from Harvard because, as he wrote to Bryce, he could not 'without moral loss decline any share in the practical struggle of life'. Eliot's own over-riding concerns at Harvard were intensely pragmatic, and during his presidency the long domination of Classics was ended and the vocational postgraduate schools of Business, Law, Medicine and Applied Sciences grew and flourished. Their products were the men who 'push things onward' and pushed them on in the most practical way, for Harvard, Eliot insisted, was not 'a nursery of tradition but a seminary of service'.[105] Similarly when Johns Hopkins was offered a new country site President Herbert Baxter Adams

104 By 1910 Bryce recorded that seven states and nearly 100 cities had adopted the merit system (*AC*, 1910, II, p. 145).
105 Holmes to Bryce, 31 Dec 1882, Ms. Bryce USA 15. William A. Neilson, *C. W. Eliot: The Man and his Beliefs*, p. 542. Eliot to Bryce, 16 March 1904, 14 September 1905, Ms. Bryce USA 1. Eliot's *Address to the Harvard Club of Cincinnati*, 22 April 1908, p. 5.

rejected it because, as he wrote to Bryce, it would have abandoned 'the municipal idea of a university in favour of a rural, isolated, monastic system. We don't care for academic walks and shades . . . so much as we do for some other things'. Bryce himself noted in 1910 that academics were no longer considered impractical, visionary, pharisaical, 'kid-gloved', 'high-toned' and 'un-American' as they had been in 1888.[106]

It was in the universities that many mugwumps took refuge during unpropitious times and armed their students to refight the battles which they had lost. Geoffrey Blodgett's profile shows that the most characteristic mugwump feature was the extraordinarily high proportion with first and postgraduate degrees.[107] Gerald McFarland has stressed the inculcation of the gospel of duty at university as the source of reform motivation and of a desire to carry academic and professional standards into political life. Robert Wiebe has identified the independent as part of the early progressive's search for order in a chaotic and unregulated *post bellum* United States, reintroducing principles of uniformity, rationalisation and non-partisan bureaucracy.[108] This is not to deny that there was a very real split between the *laissez-faire* liberal school and the young progressives. The undeviating Godkin actually tried to get Richard Ely removed from his chair at Madison, Wisconsin, for preaching heterodox interventionist economics. It was in the economic sphere particularly, in their greater sense of social justice, their demand for regulation and federal controls, their conviction that the robber baron and the trust were a greater threat to democracy than ward bosses, that the gulf between new and old guard was widest, and the early twentieth century witnesses a bitter rearguard action by Bryce's friends, such as Lowell at Harvard and Nicholas Murray Butler at Columbia, against the new radicals — with Harold Laski over the Boston police strike, with Felix Frankfurter over the Sacco and Vanzetti trials, and with Charles Beard over academic freedom during the First World War. In their declining years the liberals were tenacious in their wilful hold and exertion of power, increasingly narrow and inelastic in their thinking, and do not present an edifying

---

106 Adams to Bryce, 9 June 1882, Ms. Bryce USA 11. *AC*, 1910, II, p. 307.
107 *Journal of American History*, March 1980, p. 879.
108 *The Search for Order*, pp. 111–13. *Mugwumps, Morals and Politics, 1884–1920*, p. 31, and p. 66 where McFarland notes the usually large number of doctors supporting the New York 'bolt' in 1884.

picture.[109] Yet young and old, rising professional as well as declining patrician, were forced to live uncomfortably together, and in certain areas at least the university ethos bestowed a shared commitment; specifically to recasting the party system and making it more responsive; more generally to a greater deference to order, reason, to the science of politics and belief in the intellectual specialist who knew his job and could initiate practical change and prepare a workable blue print for America's future.

It was because the universities were 'supplying exactly those things which European critics have hitherto found lacking in America: and they are contributing to their political as well as to her contemplative life elements of inestimable worth' that Bryce placed so much faith in their regenerative power. They stood as centres of reason and practical leadership and exerted an enlightening influence on the general public.[110] Bryce shared the liberal's inordinate and unjustified faith in the power of education to transform the individual and eradicate old instinctual prejudices. He believed in rule by a political priesthood; just as the ailing patient would turn to his physician, so the majority would turn for political guidance to a wise clerisy. His Platonic approach was antipathetic to the art of management, duplicity, double talk, small talk and the visceral instincts which sustained the existing two party system. He could not understand why specialist knowledge, which commanded respect in applied science, law or finance, was considered a disadvantage in politics. He shared the independent's passion for order and planning. George Curtis spoke of the 'sanitary' influence of *The Nation*, and Eliot's obsession with venereal disease and physical hygiene betokened a deep psychological need for political cleanliness.[111]

Along with this went the compulsive urge to preach and pontificate. 'I am continually wanting to run up the attic stairs',

109 Ely was supported at Madison by Albert Shaw and Frederick Jackson Turner and Godkin's attacks in *The New York Evening Post* failed. But Godkin was earlier able to congratulate President Gilman on securing Ely's resignation from Johns Hopkins. 'I think he has been for years a discredit to you and mischievous to the community in spite of his extraordinary industry, or rather because of it. Professors of Political Economy preaching their own philanthropic gospel as "Science" are among the most dangerous characters of our time' (William M. Armstrong [ed.], *The Gilded Age Letters of E. L. Godkin*, p. 432).

110 AC, II, p. 569.

111 Curtis quoted in J. F. Rhodes, *Historical Essays*, p. 270.

wrote Charles Francis Adams Jr, 'thrust my . . . head . . . through the skylight, and holler down into the crowded street some objurgatory message.'[112] In a republic that had banished monarchy, Victorian America resurrected that institution in the form of college president. Eliot, wrote a critical pupil, 'was the non-pareil schoolmaster to his age — an age that worshipped the schoolmaster and clung to him'. Eliot was undoubtedly a figure of monarchical proportion; an oracle whose widely sought and publicised opinions on the calibre of presidential candidates were eagerly awaited by the nation; whose impressive profile — taken always from the left to hide a childhood disfigurement — was known to every American girl and boy; who distilled the knowledge of the world into fifty books, the Harvard Classics, and whose pen provided mottoes and inscriptions — for the boy scouts, the Chicago exhibition, the Shaw monument on Boston common — to inspire a democratic people. Throughout his immense tenure of office from 1869 to 1909 his scientific training would not allow him to accept the politics of approximation and temporising. He preached instead the imposition of the just theory: Harvard was to cleanse the world of unreason.[113]

Armed with such complacent self-confidence himself Bryce predicted the replacement of the corrupt organisation by the responsible politician. The solution was to replace the party boss by the independent boss, the old paid professional by the new scientifically trained professionalism. Minorities would always rule majorities, the thinker the unthinking, and the liberals held an ill-concealed admiration for virtuous authoritarianism bringing order out of chaos. G. O. Trevelyan wrote to Roosevelt of Lecky as 'a man of the study, who was infected by, and helped largely to spread, the idea of what men of that sort regard as *strength* in public affairs. It is really a reflex of their own timidity . . .. He was a mild man, desperately afraid of being too liberal, too humane, not enough like Cromwell and Bismarck'. Yet Trevelyan succumbed in turn to a boyish, vicarious admiration of Roosevelt's strenuous style, and Bryce too initially praised

---

[112] Adams to Charles Eliot Norton, 28 Nov 1906, Norton Papers.

[113] The wise pupil was John Jay Chapman. Cf. *Memories and Milestones*, p. 167. Henry Adams presented a copy of his *Education* to the President with all the trepidation of a schoolboy offering up his prep work to a severe headmaster — 'Charles Eliot's sentence will be damnation for ever' (W. C. Ford [ed.], *Letters of Henry Adams, 1892 – 1918*, I, p. 473).

Roosevelt's unshrinking vindication of executive power.[114] Just as the economy had flourished under concentrated power and leadership so Bryce applied the lesson to the political sphere. Just as his friend Seth Low had implemented the methods of Morgan and Carnegie in Brooklyn, so the Commission form of government, first set up to meet the emergency of a tycoon in Galverson, allowed the city to emulate the swift decision-making capacity of a corporation's Board of Directors.[115] Most vital of all, two future presidents confirmed their sense of destiny by what they read in the pages of *The American Commonwealth* of the potential of the executive office. A strong moral president could break the chains of constitutional fragmentation and govern successfully in spite of the lack of a cabinet system. The executive was the visible symbol of the people; he could revivify and inspire the nation, awake the public from its long sleep and use its strength to destroy the old order.

> There may . . . be still undeveloped possibilities of greatness in store for the Presidents of the future . . . . Perhaps no form of government needs great leaders so much as democracy . . . to be thrilled by the emotions which great men can excite, stimulated by the ideals they present, stirred to a loftier sense of what national life may attain . . . the ambition of American statesmen has been schooled to flow in constitutional channels, and the Republic is strong enough to stand any strain to which the rise of heroes may expose her.[116]

---

[114] Trevelyan to Roosevelt, 25 Sept 1905, 30 June 1908, and 13 May 1915, Roosevelt Papers. 'You seem to me to have done more for the advancement of good causes, more to stir the soul of the nation and rouse it to a sense of its incomparable opportunities and high mission, for the whole world as well as for this continent, than many of your predecessors for a century save Abraham Lincoln himself' (Bryce to Roosevelt, 6 March 1909, Roosevelt Papers).

[115] Edward Kirkland shows that big business supported Civil Service reform, and Samuel Hays argues that the business corporation, and not the political party, was the reformer's model (*Dream and Thought in the Business Community, 1860–1900*, p. 141. W. N. Chambers and W. D. Burnham [eds.], *The American Party Systems*, p. 177).

[116] *AC*, II, pp. 713, 473.

6

Epilogue 1888 – 1922

My dear Bryce, you must allow us to know something about
Regent Street.   — Henry Campbell-Bannerman.
We squeeze together into some motor-car or other and we so
talk and talk and what comes of it?   — Henry James

'The American Commonwealth'

The American Commonwealth was instantly recognised as a
classic; read or unread, its citation was obligatory and deference
to its author a necessary formal requirement for anyone
following in his path. Even moderately unlettered Presidents
like Harding and Coolidge felt compelled to make passing
references to the 'influential sage', and English visitors like
Bertrand Russell and Beatrice Webb found Bryce incessantly
quoted by reform elements in the 90s. C. P. Trevelyan had only
to drop 'the magic name' to gain the attention of the
preoccupied editor of *The Omaha Journal* in 1898.[1]

Having so comprehensively portrayed the workings of the
commonwealth in 1888, Bryce heroically attempted thereafter to
accommodate the vast welter of new information which flooded
in upon him, and integrate a rapidly changing picture into the
body of his text. His chapter on 'Local Extension of Rings and
Bosses', revised in 1910, does precisely this, incorporating the
latest developments provided by a large network of correspondents in Cincinnati, St Louis, Louisville, Minneapolis, St Paul,
San Francisco, Pittsburg, Detroit, Denver, Albany, Buffalo,

---

[1]   Speeches in honour of Bryce delivered by members of the Sulgrave
Institute, Biltmore, 30 Sept 1921. Russell's *Autobiography*, p. 143. Beatrice
Webb's *American Diary*, p. 151. C. P. Trevelyan, *Letters from North America
and the Pacific, 1898*, p. 63.

Rochester, Troy, New York, Philadelphia and smaller New England cities such as Providence, Hartford and Worcester. Further trips to the United States in 1890, 1897 and 1901, and his extensive travel during his ambassadorship from 1907 to 1913 enabled him to collect further personal impressions and extend his range of contacts; so much so that he confessed to Jesse Macy: 'I am beginning to doubt whether at my age I ought to run round so much.'[2] He turned to new men for new insights and current developments — to Charles Beard on primaries and ballots, to Herbert Croly on western progressivism; but naturally he tended to rely on old friends, friends who confirmed rather than questioned his settled opinions. In 1912, for example, C. F. Adams Jr wrote: 'I still recall your injunction, and am bracing myself up accordingly to increase your stock of information as regards things American', but went on to confess: 'I, however, am very much of a back number, and quite out of sympathy with current tendencies.'[3]

Not only were Bryce and Bryce's friends growing old and losing touch, (Beatrice Webb meeting President Eliot considered him a dying species, an eighteenth century relic) but the accelerated rate of change after 1888 was, at times, simply too great to bridge. *The American Commonwealth* was an obituary for the Gilded Age and its Indian summer; the 90s were to witness dramatic changes, and in that decade Godkin suggested Bryce would have to bring out a new edition every six months to keep pace and that the first edition had already become a 'political romance'. The task grew increasingly formidable, and Bryce's sigh to Lowell in 1913 is doubly telling: 'I find it impossible to keep track of your politics, having nothing but the *Nation* to help me'.[4]

Nevertheless a sense of public duty and a desire for private profit compelled Bryce to make continuous corrections and additions; new editions appeared in 1889, 1893 and 1910, with further modifications in 1913, 1914 and 1920. These took three forms: changes in the body of the text, additional footnotes or notes usually added separately to the end of a chapter, or whole

2   *AC*, 1910, II, pp. 124 – 35. Bryce to Macy, 15 Oct 1909, Ms. Bryce USA 22.
3   *AC*, 1910, II, p. 94. Croly to Bryce, 2 March 1917, Ms. Bryce USA 12. C. F.
    Adams Jr. to Bryce, 19 August 1912. Also 27 August 1912, 4 May 1914 and
    14 May 1914, Ms. Bryce USA 3.
4   Godkin to Bryce, 30 June 1895, and 30 Jan 1895, Ms. Bryce USA 5. Bryce to
    Lowell, 4 Dec 1913, Ms. Bryce USA 22.

new chapters on, for example, the Black question and imperialism. Minor changes, often involving only the change of a single word, are profusely scattered throughout the text. In the 1910 edition the chapter on 'Direct Legislation by the People' reflects a changed opinion: 'Reference to the people *may* act as a conservative force', and the Referendum, '*may, therefore, in some States at least*' be bit and bridle rather than spur. His preferred method was to add a separate note, either factual or reflective. 'Remarks on the Growth of Party: Its Perversions and Remedies Applied' of 1910 brilliantly summarises his interpretation of developments after 1893: of a public opinion roused against the exploitative party system, but choosing direct democracy and primaries instead of radical changes in the system of representation, thus enabling the machines to continue controlling the legislative process. The note ends with a typically genial conclusion — the skies, he insists, are brighter in 1910 than 1893 — but the underlying tone is unmistakably disenchanted.[5]

The disenchantment grew. The emergence of strident national, racial and class hatred, of jingoism and the outbreak of world war, did not paralyse his will or action but it did lead to a certain imaginative atrophy and an emotional retreat to the security of pre-1870 certitudes. Having completed his study of New Zealand for *Modern Democracies* in 1921, he spoke to Dicey of a 'sadness which can hardly be uttered'; intended as a paradise for the working man, close examination showed it to be riven by class hatred. He had begun collecting material for this last book in 1905 and privately he admitted that pessimism, a fear of repeating himself, of retailing 'unprofitable platitudes', and not simply the pressure of public work delayed its appearance till 1921. Perplexed, he fell back on the safety of fact in his section on the United States and elsewhere, and avoided the direct statement of opinion, so that even a close friend, Eliot, could point to the lack of an organising opinion, and Harold Laski deplore his 'insatiable appetite for facts and his grotesque inability to weigh them'.[6]

The older he grew the more convinced he became that in essence he had got America 'right' in 1870 with an almost

5   *AC*, I, p. 455, *AC*, 1910, I, p. 475. *AC*, 1910, II, pp. 246 – 7. My italics.
6   Rait, p. 282. Bryce to Dicey, 25 June 1921, Ms. Bryce 4. Bryce to Eliot, 8 August 1919, Ms. Bryce USA 2. Bryce to Holmes, 30 March 1914, Ms. Bryce USA 22. Eliot to Bryce, 13 April 1920 and 3 June 1920, Ms. Bryce USA 1. *Holmes-Laski Letters*, I, p. 563.

instinctual, unerring grasp. Then the faults had stood out most glaringly, their solutions seemed so obvious. The structure of his early thinking was embodied in the structure of the book, and this necessarily exerted a powerful pull against radical reappraisal or radical rewriting.[7] More mundanely, despite his frequently indulged day-dream of retreating into a library, Bryce sought strenuous activity in public life and travel. His travel itinerary in times of fairly primitive transport was daunting, and hardly a year passed without a major expedition being planned and executed. Even during his ambassadorial years he took double leave and made extensive trips to South America and Australia, and on relinquishing his post took the opportunity of returning westward across the Pacific, Japan and the Trans-Siberian railway. All these jaunts had to be fitted in during parliamentary recesses and outside Oxford terms for Bryce did not resign his chair till 1893. *The American Commonwealth* was completed following the defeat of Gladstone's third administration in August 1886. In Gladstone's last government he was appointed to the cabinet post of Chancellor of the Duchy of Lancaster, and was a member of the Committee that drafted the Second home rule bill. Lord Rosebery appointed him President of the Board of Trade and Chairman of the Committee on Secondary Education in 1894, which involved him deeply in educational matters up to the time of Balfour's Education bill of 1902. The 1895 trip to South Africa and the resulting book he published in 1897 involved him in imperial matters in opposition and compelled him to fight hard to hold on to his South Aberdeen constituency when dubbed a pro-Boer. 1905 – 6 found him briefly and uneventfully in Ireland as Chief Secretary when, on Lord Hardinge's advice ('(Bryce) had the quality of liking to make long and rather dull speeches on commonplace subjects which I knew to be a trait that would be popular with the American masses') he was encouraged to retreat to the quieter waters of Washington which meant more travel, more speeches, and a sustained diplomatic effort to ease Anglo-American-Canadian relations. In January 1914 Bryce entered the Lords and with the outbreak of war, and at the age of seventy-six, embarked upon the most hectic phase of his political career, chairing enquiries into atrocities in Belgium and Armenia, working informally for the League ideal and chairing the Second

---

[7]   Bryce to Dicey, 20 Dec 1906, Ms. Bryce 4.

Chamber Conference.[8] Under such sustained pressure, writing, and more particularly revision of *The American Commonwealth*, was sacrificed and took a lower priority beside more immediately useful work.

This inability to thoroughly revise or question the assumptions of 1888 was reinforced by the conscious decision, which he stuck to, of avoiding matters of glaring political controversy. He might broach the wider social and political implications of race and empire, or look back with enlarged perspective to pen an obituary for the mugwump bolt of 1884 as possessing 'a temporary significance which entitled it to the meed of a melodious tear', but only the most minor and oblique references were made to the domestic ferment of populism or insurgent progressivism.[9]

Bryce tended to regard Bryan and the populists as a magnified manifestation of Kearney and the sandlot party he had described in the 80s, as a violent demagogic manifestation of the erratic and irrational western temper. Jesse Macy, one of his few remaining western contacts, tried to impress on him the essential conservatism of the farmer, his genuine sense of grievance and economic vulnerability, but his more numerous eastern correspondents painted a far more threatening picture. Godkin reported in 1895 that the country was on the verge of a general breakdown, Villard spoke of the particular threat posed to the railroads, and Roosevelt, then Commissioner of the New York Police, insisted that the populist campaign of 1896 was not about free silver but free riot. The Great Commoner personified all that the mugwump found most repugnant in America. He was, C. F. Adams Jr said: 'Born a camp-meeting preacher and caucus leader; he seems to be inherently unqualified as an executive.'[10] Bryce, while admitting a certain weakness for Bryan's rustic simplicity, remarked in a letter to Henry White, on his 'being almost unable to *think* in the sense that you and I would use the word. Vague ideas floated through his mind but did not unite to form any system or to crystallise into a definite practical proposition'. The truth is that Bryce was not only

[8]   Lord Hardinge of Penshurst, *Old Diplomacy*, p. 132.
[9]   AC, 1910, II, p. 47.
[10] Macy to Bryce, 13 Dec 1887 and 16 Dec 1891, Ms. Bryce USA 8. Godkin to Bryce, 30 June 1895 and 28 July 1896, Ms. Bryce USA 4. Villard to Bryce, 27 Feb 1891, Ms. Bryce USA 10. Roosevelt to Bryce, 10 Nov 1896, Ms. Bryce USA 9. Adams Jr. to Bryce, 4 May 1914, Ms. Bryce USA 3.

unsympathetic to the movement, but entirely ignorant of its aims: 'I cannot make out the trend of the financial politics of America at present, yet financial questions seem to dominate all others', he admitted to Richard Watson Gilder, and to Roosevelt: 'I have never had time for a study of currency questions at all.'[11]

Bryce should, however, have understood and approved the insurgent progressivism which fully emerged during his ambassadorship, the novel presidential activism of the one time Civil Service Commissioner and the anglophile academic pupil Woodrow Wilson, but behind the discreet commonplaces of his official speeches, his private correspondence with such intimate friends as Adams and Rhodes disclosed substantial misgivings as the New Nationalism lurched towards the more strident utterances of the Bull Moose campaign, and the outbreak of European war led Wilson into vast new areas of federal intervention. Henry White might insist that Roosevelt was a conservative brake on democratic extremism and Roosevelt himself write to reassure Bryce that he had no intention of reviving the Paris commune in America, but he found the president's manic activity — Adams called it a form of insanity — and the radicalisation of his campaign against Taft very disturbing. Roosevelt's extension of national power, his advocacy of female and child labour laws and, most painful of all, the right of recall of judges, constituted 'a disposition to remodel the Constitution upon modern and ultra-democratic lines'.[12] Even during the preoccupations of the war Bryce found time to correspond with Archibald Hopkins of the National Association for Constitutional Government whose aim was to halt the spread of progressive tendencies and the proposed constitutional amendments concerning female suffrage and the direct election of senators. Ironically when all that Bryce had preached and urged for so long had come to pass and the best men, those active reformers who, at times, he had concluded would never be able to redeem the torpor and corruption of the Gilded Age,

---

[11] Bryce to White, 7 July 1915, Ms. Bryce USA 22. Bryce to Gilder, 22 Feb 1895, Century Collection. Bryce to Roosevelt, 10 April 1895, Roosevelt Papers.
[12] White to Roosevelt, 3 March 1912, White Papers. Roosevelt to Bryce, 13 Sept 1910, Ms. Bryce USA 9. Bryce to Rhodes, 27 Feb 1917, Rhodes Papers. Bryce to Wickersham, 18 March 1917, Ms. Bryce USA 21. Bryce to White, 24 July 1914, Ms. Bryce USA 22. Adams Jr to Bryce, 27 August 1912, Ms. Bryce USA 3.

came to control America's destiny, they pressed for a more advanced and more direct democratic participation and a greater degree of centralist intervention rather than for his own mid-Victorian solution of stronger representative government.[13]

Thus for a variety of reasons the formal superstructure of *The American Commonwealth* remained essentially unchanged. Bryce made piecemeal alterations; the California constitution of 1879 was replaced by that of Oklahoma after 1907 in his appendix, but the chapters on 'Why the Best Men Do Not Go Into Politics' and 'Why Great Men are not Chosen President' survived anachronistically into the era of Roosevelt and Wilson, as, for example, did a highly condescending chapter on 'Creative Intellectual Power' which, with an astonishing disregard of creative ferment in America, referred to the United States as an intellectual colony of Great Britain. Eventually in 1920 Brett of Macmillan's New York offices collected a number of academic opinions on a further possible revision of the book; Munro of Harvard, Beard of Columbia, Myers of Princeton and Ogg at Wisconsin were unanimous in agreeing that the book was 'altogether out of focus', that 'its unique position should not be disturbed' because, in the words of Charles Beard, its remaining value lay in its 'philosophic views': 'There is no better way of understanding America of the past generation than by reading the first edition of the work.' *The American Commonwealth* had been consigned to the grave of classic status.[14]

In two areas and two areas only did Bryce attempt to confront the full challenge of change; the first, race, had previously been evaded because of its potential for controversy; the second, imperialism, was a novel experiment unforseen in the 80s. Both issues were treated at some length because he felt both threatened the health of the republic.

The experience gained from his travel and his observation of mixed races coexisting with varying degrees of success in India, South Africa and South America gave Bryce a global comparison

[13] Hopkins to Bryce, 28 May 1916, Ms. Bryce USA 15, who also deplored the 'socialistic leanings' of Wilson's appointments to the Supreme Court. Bryce to Dicey, 15 June 1911, and 22 Jan 1913 — 'Should the existing temper of the public mind continue there is no saying where the general sentiment of discontent and restlessness may carry the people even in the way of amending the Constitution' (Ms. Bryce 4).

[14] *AC*, 1910, I, pp. 719–42. *AC*, 1910, II, pp. 832–44. Brett to Bryce, 8 June 1920, Ms. Bryce USA 25.

in approaching the United States' unique racial problem and made him acutely aware of the profound consequences of improved communication and imperial conquest, as the earth shrank and diverse races were forced into closer contact. It was the British empire's growing sense of destiny, its excessive racial pride and the conqueror's unimaginative philistinism that Bryce first detected on his India journey of 1888 – 9, stirred into activity by the recent passage of Ilbert's Criminal Procedure Amendment Bill of 1884 which enabled all district magistrates and session judges, irrespective of race, to try all subjects of the crown, again irrespective of race. Sir Courtenay Ilbert, an intimate friend and parliamentary colleague of Bryce's had thus made it theoretically possible for an Indian to judge a European, and although Bryce initially supported this relaxation, experience on the sub-continent made him change his mind and conclude that such good intentions had merely exacerbated the situation. He came instead to approve of Dufferin's cautious back-tracking on the issue and this, in turn, reflected his own limitations, his own insularity when confronted with a radically different culture. His Presbyterian soul was outraged by the 'degrading superstitions' of the heathen, his missionary instincts were stirred. Sanskrit he dismissed as almost untranslatable and probably not worth translating; from Rajputana he wrote home expressing the hope that Gladstone and the liberals would not press the Indian National Congress idea — 'these things look very different when one is out here and are not to be solved by European formulae'.[15]

Thus armed with imperial comparisons and a certain amount of imperial prejudice, he was able to emphasise America's uniqueness in possessing an 'unabsorbed and unabsorbable' racial minority only theoretically possessing equal rights. Informal desegregation and disfranchisement had given way to a healthier formal acknowledgement of these social and political facts, and he felt able to broach the matter now that 'a calmer and saner view prevails'. His summary of slavery and reconstruction classically stated the Gilded Age orthodoxy which was developed more fully in the historical works of such friends as C. F. Adams Jr, James Ford Rhodes, Woodrow Wilson, John W. Burgess and William Archibald Dunning: 'Such a Saturnalia of

---

15 Fisher, I, pp. 261, 268, 271, 264, 269, 275. Also Bryce to Godkin, 24 Jan 1889, Godkin Papers.

robbery and jobbery has seldom been seen in any civilised country, and certainly never before under the forms of free self-government.' This oft-quoted sentence was based on the premise that slavery was a species of benign paternalism which had served to protect the child-like Black, which was itself based on the evidence that slaves did not rise in servile insurrection during the war despite Lincoln's emancipation proclamation. Wendell Phillips Garrison, son of the abolitionist and literary editor of the *Nation*, swiftly responded: 'I cannot conceive where you derive the impression that our slavery was not cruel', and argued that fear of white arms and massive white retaliation along with the fact that many Blacks did join the Northern army and cooperate with the conquerors accounted for the absence of insurrection during the war.[16]

Bryce's benign understanding of the 'peculiar institution' stemmed from his racial view of the Black as child-like and dependent, as 'children of nature, whose highest form of pleasure had hitherto been to caper to the strains of a banjo', before misguided Northern philanthropy had insisted on extending full civil rights to them. Abolitionists had been activated by the greatest of human errors — a zealous faith in abstract rights, but in the margin of a letter from Garfield espousing universal suffrage, and stating that there was no middle course between slavery and full citizenship, Bryce dismissed this as being representative of peculiarly American habits of thought, not necessarily true or self-evident to a European. And Bryce could deride this doctrine with increasing confidence as one by one his New England correspondents themselves, Adams and Godkin especially, deserted the Jeffersonian tradition of equal rights as 'pre-scientific', and therefore foolish, impractical and irrelevant. During the darkest days of Black history in the United States, he could confirm that: 'Common sense regained its power, and the doctrine that every

---

[16] Bryce added two chapters to the Black question in 1893 and 'Further Reflections' in 1910. *AC*, 1910, II, pp. 491, 532 – 3, 540, 547, 498. Garrison to Bryce (n.d.), Ms. Bryce Misc. Garrison also criticised Woodrow Wilson's benign Southern description of slavery in his chapter on 'State Rights, 1850 – 1860' in the *Cambridge Modern History* (Garrison to Bryce, 29 June 1903, Ms. Bryce USA 4): 'Now, as then, what the South means by asking to be let alone is that her idea of the relations of the whites and negroes shall everywhere prevail and be accepted without demur. Never has the world seen a more striking whirligig of reaction.'

human being has a natural right to vote, though never formally abandoned, has been silently ignored.'[17]

Bryce offered his most definitive consideration of the race question in 1902 when called upon to deliver the Romanes lecture at Oxford on 'The Relations of the Advanced and Backward Nations of Mankind'. In it he spoke of the four possible consequences of growing world contact and the interdependence of races: the dying out of the weaker, the absorbing of the weaker, the merging of the two, or of the two remaining together yet separate. The last possibility, where the Black man submits and survives, clarified the peculiar American dilemma, reinforced as it was by intense physical repulsion of White by Black and the assumption that miscegenation resulted in a greater loss to the higher race than a gain to the lower.

Private correspondence with friends on the lecture further clarified Bryce's stance. Dicey, while not entirely sane on the matter of Ireland and the Irish, was dedicated to the practical implications of the rule of law and was thus unable to countenance any species of discrimination. Contact at Oxford with Rhodes scholars from the South who refused to dine at Balliol with a Black fellow scholar (Dicey records resignedly that the Northern scholars conceded to the demands of their Southern brethren), the Dreyfus case, and, through his close friendship with Judge Arthur Cohen, details concerning the legal sufferings of the Jews in Russia, all made him painfully aware of the ramifications of racial prejudice and the sickening strategy by which 'despotic power first degrades its victims and then defends its own existence by the plea that its victims are unworthy of freedom or of justice'. Holding belief in equality to be essential to democracy, he observed that the predominant philosophy of the day was anti-democratic as a result of nationalism and Darwinism. Privately he regretted the decline of eighteenth century confidence in human rights, the nineteenth century's 'scientific' obsession with racial differences rather than similarities, and the irrational confusion of national characteristics with race. Publicly, in the pages of the *Nation*, he recognised the lecture to be 'the most important of Mr Bryce's utterances . . . on the most perplexing question of the time', but firmly criticised many of its assumptions and conclusions; that

[17]   *AC*, 1910, II, p. 516. Bryce made this comment in the margin of an article by James Garfield (n.d.), Ms. Bryce Misc. Adams's obsession with the Black question is revealed, in *'Tis Sixty Year Since*, pp. 21 – 2, and *The Solid South*, p. 18. *AC*, 1910, II, p. 503. *Modern Democracies*, II, pp. 51 – 2.

the law, for example, should confirm rather than question or possibly legally forbid social prejudice, and that the solution offered of racial segregation 'fosters that very pride of race and that contempt for men who, on the ground of color, are counted as inferiors, which statesmanship and humanity alike wish to remove'.[18]

Garrison's response was far sharper and more direct. Having already taken issue with Bryce over the practical consequences of his abstract theorising on miscegenation ('the burning of colored men for rape is the logical antipode of the statutes against intermarriage'.), he concluded in his 1893 review of *The American Commonwealth* that the author 'throws the weight of his humane authority into the white scale'. And again in 1902, with American overseas expansion: 'I fear you will comfort both our Imperialists and the lynchers, for the latter have caste for their stronghold, and it seems to me that you justify caste.'[19] This statement, however emotive, was entirely correct and may be gauged by the example of D. H. Chamberlain, the one time New England abolitionist and civil war soldier who settled in the South after the war and became Governor of South Carolina in 1874 where he pursued a policy of radical reconstruction against the conservative Wade Hampton. By 1902, however, his political career was over and after many years in the South he had become a fully fledged white supremacist. Chamberlain's impeccable credentials and his radical change of attitude under the exigencies of practical experience had led Bryce to single him out as a 'trustworthy source' in *The American Commonwealth*, but he was doubtless embarrassed when after the publication of his Romanes Lecture, Chamberlain addressed an open letter to him, published initially in the *Charleston News and Courier* and thereafter in ten major American newspapers, providing copy for a multitude of editorials. In the letter Bryce's 'philosophic' approach to the question of race was praised, as was the whole drift of the lecture which led Chamberlain to conclude that 'our first practical aim should be to undo, as far as possible, all we have heretofore done for the negro since his emancipation; namely, the inspiring in him the hope or dream of sharing with

---

[18]   *Romanes Lecture*, pp. 5 – 46. Dicey to Bryce, 23 Dec 1907, Ms. Bryce 3. *The Legal Sufferings of the Jews*, ed. by Lucien Wolf, Introduction by Dicey, p. ix. Dicey, *NYN*, 16 July 1891, pp. 46 – 7, and 10 July 1902, pp. 26 – 8. Dicey to Bryce, 25 Dec 1901 and 17 May 1912, Ms. Bryce 3.

[19]   Garrison to Bryce, 25 April 1892 and 2 June 1902, Ms. Bryce USA 4. Garrison, *NYN*, 31 Jan 1895, pp. 86 – 8.

the white race here a social or political equality'. This was not Bryce's conclusion, and he must have been extremely vexed at being unfairly embroiled in such a controversial question, but it does amply illustrate Garrison's contention that having adumbrated various racial theories Bryce had exposed himself to, and been exploited by, more extreme racist elements. Through the controversy Chamberlain claimed the superiority of practical experience which corrected 'the crude theorising of distant and uninformed censors'. Garrison replied in the *Boston Herald*: 'That one in the environment of prejudice and murder is more fitted to take a dispassionate view of the situation than those outside the deadening atmosphere is self-evidently absurd.' But it would not have struck Bryce as such; his inveterate dislike of abstract theorising, his profoundly pragmatic instincts and his visits to the South in 1881, 1883 and 1890 — the last during Ben Tillman's vehemently racialist gubernatorial fight in South Carolina — led him to temporise, appreciate the full force of inherited prejudice and accommodate to the social realities which nullified the spirit of the civil war amendments.[20]

If he returned to the question obsessively and enlarged upon it again and again it was because having searched for solutions to the problem he knew that, in the current climate, there were none. Politically matters seemed easier: between the alternatives of federal enforcement of the civil war amendments, or their repeal — particularly the 'dangerous boon' of enfranchisement — he proposed the imposition of educational and property qualifications. But even this presented problems, for along with the three quarters or four fifths disfranchisement of Blacks, would go a considerable number of illiterate and propertyless Whites, along with a proportionate reduction in the South's federal representation. Mississippi's educational qualification of 1891, and the Cape Colony's for its coloured population in the following year, were liberal steps in the right direction; John Stuart Mill had been called upon to legislate for the backward races. But such political complications were as nothing beside the social consequences of an alien and unabsorbable race flourishing in the heart of the White republic. He had visited Booker T. Washington at Tuskegee in November 1908 and lectured at the Hampton Institute in January 1910, and

[20]   Chamberlain to Bryce, 20 Sept 1904, with enclosed material, Ms. Bryce USA 12. Chamberlain, *North American Review*, February 1879, pp. 161 – 73. Garrison in *Boston Herald*, 9 Sept 1904. *AC*, 1910, II, p. 498 n. 2. *Romanes Lecture*, p. 39.

thoroughly approved of the accommodationalism of separate Black self-improvement. He concluded his Romanes lecture on an optimistic note: 'the best hope lies in the slow growth of a better sentiment' among the Whites towards the growing number of educated Blacks, but by his own analysis this conclusion was unrealistic. For while the progress of the Black was dependent on increasing ameliorative contact with the White race, it was precisely in this hopeful area of contact that friction and hatred were most notably engendered. The educated Black was alienated by the corrosive process of social degradation and the White especially distrustful of, and threatened by, the educated Black. In 1910 he briefly noted the novelty of W. E. B. Dubois's *Souls of Black Folk* which offered an alternative of racial pride and racial self-consciousness, and the measurement of Black achievement by Black and not White standards. But Bryce did not consider this seriously any more than he considered racial fusion seriously.[21]

In his Romanes lecture he asserted authoritatively that: 'The aversion to colour reaches its maximum among the Teutons'; the Teutons, but not all Whites, for field study in Latin America revealed the fusion of White, Black and Red and their offspring 'whitened'. There rank or class, not colour, were the basis for social distinctions, while in its strict segregation of races, its insistence on caste, the legal prohibition of miscegenation and its defining of all the offspring of miscegenation as Black, it was the United States that was exceptional. Nevertheless the brief acknowledgement in *The American Commonwealth* of 'illicit intermixture' and the presence of large numbers of mulattoes — he put the figure around three million, that is, a third of the total 'Black' population — contradict Bryce's confident assertions on Teutonic sexual preference. Indeed the entire edifice of his 'scientific' approach and assertion of inexorable natural laws concerning the consequences of miscegenation is built on sand, and reference to the footnotes purporting to buttress the unassailable statements of the text give ample reason for doubt. On page twenty of the lecture, for example: 'Accurate statistics on such a matter are of course unobtainable: I give the impression which I derived on the spot from the best data I could find', or, six pages later, more disarmingly: 'One is surprised . . . to find how little positive evidence there is

[21]   *Romanes Lecture*, pp. 39, 42, 43. *AC*, 1910, II, pp. 529, 530 – 1, 532, 537, 561. Also *Impressions of South Africa*, p. 369.

bearing on (race-mixture) . . . comparatively few data for positive conclusions exist.'[22] Two points require reiterating here concerning the lecture. One is that a writer trained in the rigorous school of scientific methodology and the elucidation and applicablility of scientific laws based a theory of race and race relations on conspicuously non-scientific 'impressions' and subjective prejudice. The other is that a widely read and influential tract, written by a highly respected academic and published under the imprint of a distinguished university, played decisively into the camp of intolerance, prejudice and extremism.

This is both ironic and tragic, for such was not Bryce's intention, and it is a further irony that he only became fully aware of the damaging consequences of his theorising when it was too late to do anything about it. Even in the first edition of *The American Commonwealth*, despite his tendency to deprecate the new immigrant and stereotype him as a rough, corrupt and anarchic 'residuum', he was aware of the use of other races as scapegoats, rather like the cat in the kitchen who is always held responsible for the broken plates and the stolen food: 'New York was not an Eden before the Irish came.' The Latin American trip of 1912 provided ample evidence of fairly harmonious racial mix in Brazil — of Hispanic, Indian and African — and forced him to confront his assumptions, and the assumptions of the English race. 'Instead of being, as we Teutons suppose, the rule in this matter, we are rather the exception.' More profoundly the imperial ethos and the world war fully exposed the implications of racial arrogance, and we find him in the midst of the war questioning the existence of any pure, unmixed race and exploring the links between racial myth, caste superiority and their destructive exploitation, exposing the disastrous manipulation of Darwinism by the advocates of progress through war and of racial survival by the destruction of lower breeds. He could attack these dogmas so forcefully in his last years because, as his correspondence with Adams and Roosevelt shows, he had himself been tempted by

---

[22] *Romanes Lecture*, p. 19 and nn., pp. 20, 26. *South America*, pp. 470 – 2, 567. AC, 1910, II, pp. 549, 555 – 6. *Race Sentiment as a Factor in History*, p. 5. On Bryce's 'racial dilution' theory Dicey wrote: 'The validity of this assumption is disputed by some competent judges', and the consequent 'policy of isolation or separation is at best an experiment that depends for its success on the soundness of a theory that itself rests upon a foundation of dubious strength' (*NYN*, 10 July 1902, p. 27).

the harsh and austere scientific credentials of the genetic sciences, although he had hoped to employ them in a practical policy of racial guardianship rather than destructive extermination.[23]

The issues of race, imperialism and trusteeship were indissolubly linked in Bryce's mind. Europe's last and greatest thrust of territorial expansion brought the conflict of races to the fore, while also serving to justify that world conquest. Goldwin Smith had earlier spoken of the corrupting moral effects of governing subject races, and prophesied the growth of a military spirit in England: an empire required an emperor. Dicey emphasised the impact of Darwinism, and the advocacy of Mahan, Seeley, Dilke and Froude, but saw the imperial impulse stemming primarily from an ideological vacuum at the end of the century following the decline of faith in *laissez faire* dogma and Benthamite reformism. Imperialism became, as it were, a non-democratic species of progress when 'for the moment the progress of democracy is arrested, not by the strength of aristocratic existence, but by the weakness of the democratic impulse'.[24] Bryce drew historical parallels between the Pax Romana and the British empire in India, although Britain's global impact was infinitely greater. 'Europe has annexed the rest of the world, extinguished some races, absorbing others as subjects, and spreading over their native customs and beliefs a layer of European ideas which will sink deeper and deeper till the old native life dies out.' In retrospect, given Britain's brief imperial tenure, this verdict may seem arrogant and premature, but Bryce travelled throughout the empire's vast domain and through India where 'not a dog wags its tail against us among these two hundred and sixty millions of people', and may be forgiven. Both Rome and Britain had triumphed by force of character but the Briton unlike the Roman did not fuse racially with the subject race, and it was a similar fear of Americans having to assimilate large numbers of alien subject races — Spanish, Chinese, Malay and Black — that made him explicitly

23   *AC*, II, pp. 290 – 1. *South America*, pp. 476 – 7, 479 – 83. *Race Sentiment as a Factor in History*, p. 4. *War and Human Progress*, pp. 303 – 14.
24   Goldwin Smith, *Contemporary Review*, April 1884, pp. 524 – 40. *Contemporary Review*, May 1899, p. 622. Dicey, *NYN*, 12 Sept 1901, pp. 203 – 4. Dicey, a brother of Edward and a Unionist, was a staunch imperialist and supported Britain's efforts in the Boer war. In *Law and Public Opinion* he referred to imperialism as 'a form of passionate feeling; it is a political religion, for it is public spirit touched with emotion' (p. 457).

oppose her expansionism in the tropics and sub-tropics. Britain's own species of proconsular absolutism and flexible constitution could adjust, but America's constitutional tradition assumed homogeneity and equality. 'The Declaration of Independence is a plant ill-fitted for transplantation to tropic lands inhabited by backward races.'[25] Many anti-imperialists objected to taking up the white man's burden (Kipling invented the phrase specifically for Americans), and not merely for racial and constitutional reasons: 'who would have thought that our treatment of these races during the last hundred years really argued a deep conscientious concern about them?', enquired Godkin, and Garrison subtly suggested that the adoption of colonial in place of constitutional government served to justify and reinforce Black disfranchisement and segregation in the South. The majority of Bryce's American friends — Eliot, Schurz, Moorfield Storey, William James, Higginson, Gamaliel Bradford, Henry Villard, Godkin — were anti-imperialist, but the issue split the mugwump ranks. This was partly because of the confusions of party strategy. Bryan asserted in 1900 that the nation could not survive half republic and half colony, half free and half vassal, but also held fast to the remnants of his populism. The matter was further complicated because the Eastern elite looked with an ambivalent mixture of pride and envy at Britain's own hugely successful imperial venture.[26] Ernest May has written of the importance of this imperial example to America, and there is much evidence to support it. Godkin, for example, wrote to Mrs Bryce that the Spanish-American war was 'undoubtedly due to your war. You know (the Americans) are very childish, and think, as you have ''a war of civilisation'' they must have one too'. But May fails to appreciate that 'our' imperial adventure in South Africa was faltering, and that while the example of Rosebery's or Salisbury's cabinets might stimulate Americans, the election of

---

25   *History and Jurisprudence*, I, pp. 1, 59, 79. Fisher, I, p. 270. Bryce in *The Century*, Nov 1898, p. 718, and *North American Review*, 1902, Vol. 174, p. 453. *AC*, 1910, II, p. 585. Bryce to Roosevelt, 12 Sept 1898, Roosevelt Papers.

26   Godkin, *NYN*, 17 Nov 1898, p. 366. Villard to Bryce, 3 Sept 1898, Ms. Bryce USA 10. Garrison to Bryce, 23 March 1900, Ms. Bryce USA 4. For the racial undertones of American imperialism and progressivism cf. Christopher Lasch, *Journal of Southern History*, 1958, pp. 319 – 31, and Fred Harrington, *Mississippi Valley Historical Review*, 1935, pp. 221 ff.

Campbell-Bannerman, and of Bryce and Morley in 1905 might hearten the opposite cause.[27]

Most Americans had a high regard for British colonial administration; the issue of acquiring new races might be divisive, but the matter of ruling them tended to unify, either because it served as a species of outdoor relief for the domestically neglected mugwumps, or as an apprenticeship in gung-ho character building. Anti-imperialists of impeccable standing such as Eliot, Schurz and Carnegie found much to admire in Cromer's Egypt and Dufferin's India, and were precursors of those later progressive imperialists like Croly, Beveridge and Roosevelt who saw in American conquest extended fields for experimentation in a new, activist central planning which would, at one stroke, modernise and rationalise, and decisively detach the United States from her retarding traditions of isolation, self-aborption, limited government and states' rights.[28] It is worth remembering Bryce's initially sceptical view of England's civilising mission during his Eygptian and Indian trip of 1887–9; his indictment of her army and civil service, of the conventional, uniform and unimaginative mode of the Anglo-Indians, their obsession with polo and their deliberate offensiveness to natives. He observed an atmosphere of gunpowder throughout India; British rule was more feared than loved. But the real achievement in India was an administration which bestowed on the sub-continent the inestimable gifts of peace, both internal and external, the rule of law and a patrician regard for native welfare, all achieved 'by an efficiently organised civil service, inspired by high traditions, kept apart from British party politics, and standing quite outside the prejudices, jealousies, and superstitions which sway the native mind. Only through despotic methods could that have been

[27] Ernest May, *American Imperialism: A Speculative Essay*, esp. p. 87. Godkin to Mrs Bryce, 18 Nov 1899, Ms. Bryce USA 4. Also Garrison to Bryce, 23 March 1900, Ms. Bryce USA 4. Villard to Bryce, 3 September 1898, Ms. Bryce USA 10, and Higginson to Bryce, who wrote on 30 Jan 1899 that 'England was our school of Jingoes' (Ms. Bryce USA 14).

[28] See Roosevelt to Spring Rice, 2 Dec 1899: 'I believe in the expansion of great nations. India has done an incalculable amount for the English character. If we do our work well in the Philippines and the West Indies, it will do a great deal for our character' (*Letters of Theodore Roosevelt*, ed. by Elting Morison, II, p. 1104). Adams Jr, *The Century Magazine*, May 1906, pp. 103, 108. Godkin to Roosevelt, 5 August 1897, Roosevelt Papers. Schurz, *Atlantic Monthly*, October 1898, p. 433. David Healy, *United States Expansionism*, p. 106.

done for India which the English have done'. He then urged the engagement of enlightened, disinterested servants to rule America's newly aquired possessions, for: 'No country possesses a larger supply of such men than America does, though the public service of the country has heretofore provided comparatively little field for the display of their gifts.' He would still have preferred Americans to concentrate on purifying city government rather than attempting to civilise the savages of Luzon, but, having decided to attempt both, he applied the Indian lessons of a 'healthy despotism' to Cuba and the Philippines: 'No talk of suffrage or any such constitutional privileges for them; but steady government by the firmest, honestest men you can find, and no interference if possible by Congress when the firm and honest men have been found.'[29]

He continued to attack the strident, jingoistic brand of expansionism, and in particular that class of Tories 'which cries out at little mortifications to national pride, that class which assumes that British interests are always to prevail against other interests just as so many Englishmen expect to get the best rooms at a Swiss hotel, the class which takes the whole ocean to be a British possession, and islands appendages of the English crown'. Bryce always insisted that he himself was a moderate imperialist and not a little Englander, distinguishing between an aggressive and a reasonable imperialism 'which recognises that greatness and power bring certain duties with them'.[30] But in this, as in other controversial matters, Bryce's stance could be ambivalent and shifting, and his initial response to the South African question suggests a more full-blooded response than his later, public 'pro-Boer' record would lead one to believe. He made an extensive tour of the colony immediately before the Jameson raid and was a guest of Jameson as well as Rhodes. Like everyone else he was well aware of the imminent possibility of a rising; he spoke in terms of an *opera buffa*; people talked of conspiracy 'but never before was there, except on the stage, so open a conspiracy'. Less certain to ascertain is how much he knew of the actual preparations. Jeffrey Butler in his book on the raid hazards that circumstantial evidence strongly suggests, without proving, Bryce's foreknowledge, but Bryce's fascination with Rhodes, his criticism of Kruger's treatment of

[29] *History and Jurisprudence*, I, p. 14. Bryce, *The Century Magazine*, Nov 1898, pp. 725, 728. Bryce to Roosevelt, 12 Sept 1898, Roosevelt Papers.
[30] Bryce, *NYN*, 5 Feb 1885, p. 116. *The Unity of the Liberal Party*, p. 15. Stephen Koss (ed.), *The Pro-Boers*, pp. 92 – 3.

the Uitlanders, and his alarm at German designs in Delagoa Bay lead Butler to conclude more confidently that Bryce 'had picked up the political attitudes and military assumptions of the plotters, as well as information on the plot itself'. Following the defeat of the raid and Jameson's capture, he wrote a note of sympathy to Rhodes, but by the time his *South Africa* appeared in 1897 he had turned to condemn the raid as unjustified, insist that Britain possessed no legal rights in the Transvaal, and in a new prefatory chapter of 1899 consider the war resulted from Britain's threatening language and her preparations for war. As in Dufferin's India and Ben Tillman's South, when travelling among the ruling class of these regions he took on their shading, their attitudes and apologetics.[31]

Because Bryce regarded the civilising mission of trusteeship as consistent with and indeed dependent upon improved Anglo-American relations the Venezuela boundary dispute came as a grave blow. Godkin wrote him a rambling and deeply disturbing letter which partly reflected the pessimism of Godkin's growing ill health but realistically portrayed America in the grip of a war psychosis: 'A clique of politicians has sprung up, who call for war — any war — as a good thing for character and trade, but by war, they always mean a war with England.' This unexpected news greeted Bryce at Madeira in December 1895 on his way home from South Africa, and indicated how out of touch he was with America's economic situation, the strength of populism and of war fever outside New England. Writing immediately to Roosevelt he expressed astonishment at the ill-will displayed towards England and the absurd claims that she intended, as Senator Lodge remarked, to turn the Caribbean into an English lake. He insisted, on the contrary, that Britain's hands were more than full and considered it bogus for Americans to express sympathy towards a barbaric country simply because it was in the western hemisphere and ostensibly a republic. He also unwittingly outlined the Rooseveltian corollary to the Monroe doctrine: 'If the U.S. are going to assume a protectorate over all Central and South America, and

---

[31] *Impressions of South Africa*, pp. 423, 405, xxxiv. Both Lord Ripon and Sidney Buxton assumed Bryce's foreknowledge, although Bryce had written to Asquith on 9 Jan 1900 denying complicity when an article in the *National Review* directly implicated him. As late as 1913 Bryce insisted that the inner history of the raid remained a guarded secret (Bryce to Dicey, 28 Feb 1913, Ms. Bryce 4). Jeffrey Butler, *The Liberal Party and the Jameson Raid*, pp. 57, 58, 66 – 8, 238.

see that these so-called Republics behave like civilised States, that is another matter. Then other countries will know whom they have to deal with. But the U.S. have not done so — and certainly that is not the Monroe doctrine.' Bryce ended on a personal note: 'But you really must not go to war with us for then how should we be able to come and go and have our talks?' In order that Roosevelt and Bryce might continue talking, and the civilising Anglo-American mission be continued, with all its attendant benefits both for the conqueror and conquered, Bryce so urged the 'special relationship' in the years of the Spanish-American and Boer wars as to become its very embodiment. In a world of combative great powers — Britain, the United States, Russia, France, Germany — Britain and America were unique in speaking the same tongue, in being advanced democracies and, both satiated with the burdens of overseas acquisitions, con-servative rather than revisionist powers.[32] This appeal met a genuine response at complex and varied levels; the desire to advance national and international morality ('This may save Anglo-Saxon principles of law and liberty and nothing else will', Dicey wrote to Bryce); the appeal to 'sympathy of race' and 'community of blood' which implied an overt racial destiny; and in hard terms of power politics an informal world domination aimed particularly against the threat of an emerging Germany and Japan. Thus from a mixture of motives Albert Shaw conceived of American federalism as intended from the first to take an extra-continental imperial form, Roosevelt wished to parcel out the Sudan to Britain and Hawaii to the United States 'in the interests of the white race', and Adams urged that South Africa should enter the English speaking confederation.[33] It is only too easy to show that there was very little special about the 'special relationship', and that all the threadbare rhetoric about 'hands across the seas' cloaked a tougher mutual exploitation and the limitations to cooperation inherent in national self-interest. But the relationship did embody mutual accommoda-tion beneficial to both sides, enabling the United States to con-solidate her western sphere of influence and Britain, the weary titan, to be supported in her isolated maintenance of a far-flung

---

[32] Godkin to Bryce, 9 Jan 1896, Ms. Bryce USA 4. Bryce to Villard, 4 Jan 1896, Ms. Bryce Misc. Bryce, *North American Review*, CLXII, No. 471, pp. 145 – 53, and *Atlantic Monthly*, July 1898, pp. 23 – 8.

[33] Dicey to Bryce, 12 May 1898, Ms. Bryce 2. Albert Shaw, *Contemporary Review*, September 1892, pp. 305 – 18. Roosevelt to Bryce, 10 Sept 1897, Roosevelt Papers. Adams Jr to Bryce, 21 May 1900, Ms. Bryce USA 3.

and unprotected empire. Doubtless Bryce tended to underrate the deep roots of indifference or positive American anglophobia, but the experience of 1895 of his ambassadorship and 1914 onwards made him fairly nicely aware of the relationship's limitations. As Dicey put it: 'Both branches of the English people seem to me to act somewhat better in foreign affairs than do Continental States. But to make up for this both branches of the English people persuade themselves that they pursue in international affairs far more disinterested principle than they in reality act up to.' This, if applied to the special relationship itself, puts it very well, and Bryce's own experience of the relationship at work will briefly help to illustrate Dicey's contention.[34]

Though obliterated by the catastrophe of 1914 the Anglo-American arbitration movement was not entirely nugatory, and Bryce's role in this cause was seminal. As a Gladstonian aware of the beneficial consequences of the *Alabama* arbitration treaty, he hoped the Venezuelan dispute would again bring both nations to their senses and inaugurate a general era of international cooperation. During his ambassadorship he got the long standing Newfoundland fisheries dispute referred to the International Court at the Hague, and clinched a general Anglo-American arbitration treaty in 1911. But this apparent achievement is as much a measure of limitations. Even Roosevelt, an admirer of Britain and Bryce, wished to exclude matters of 'honor and independence' and of 'vital national interests' from any treaty. Not to do so would be 'literally like a man solemnly covenanting that he will arbitrate being slapped in the face'. He also considered the case of Britain and America as unique and was opposed to any general extension of great power arbitration.[35] The arbitration treaty signed by Knox and Bryce was itself emasculated by the Senate which first insisted upon the exclusion of vital issues trenching on the Monroe doctrine, and such domestic matters as immigration laws and state debts, and finally after these crippling reservations, went on to reject the treaty outright. 'Few bodies', Bryce growled, 'are moved by less genuine public spirit, few have less width of view and less susceptibility to high ideas or sense of duty to

34 Dicey to Bryce, 23 March 1911, Ms. Bryce 3.
35 Fisher, II, p. 68. Roosevelt to Bryce, 19 May 1911, 2 June 1911, 10 June 1911, Ms. Bryce USA 9. Carnegie lent financial support to Anglo-American arbitration, offering a 'pile' for the 'holy work' (Carnegie to Bryce, 25 March 1911 and 16 April 1911, Ms. Bryce USA 4).

mankind than has the Senate of the United States.' Secretary of State Knox who, as Bryce observed, had 'cared little, known little, or thought little of foreign politics until he became a minister', was a corporation lawyer who pressed with Taft for a dollar diplomacy in Latin America frequently at odds with Britain's own interests in that area, and, to his disgust, claimed exemption from the Panama tolls, which was in direct contravention of the Hay-Pauncefote treaty of 1900. But Bryce was able to extend his Washington stay just long enough to welcome the new President Wilson and his honourable revision of the tolls.[36]

But Wilson himself became rapidly embroiled in Mexico, and again tested the strengths and weaknesses of the Anglo-American relationship. As during the Venezuelan dispute Bryce attacked the 'outworn shibboleth' of the Monroe doctrine, both publicly in his *South America* which appeared in 1912, and privately to Wilson: 'The Government of Diaz was a pure despotism, and had to be so, for the conditions for honest elections and the peaceable rule of a representative assembly did not exist; any more than they would exist now in your Southern States if they were peopled by negroes, or would exist in Egypt, or in India, if British rule were withdrawn . . . . I can hardly think of any greater misfortune for the United States than to be obliged to set up a Government which it would have to maintain, or to become directly responsible for the administration of any Spanish American country.'[37] This sharp castigation of Wilson's misplaced and meddling idealism was probably coupled with a concern for Britain's own powerful economic interests in Mexico — interests which strong government under Huerta protected. Wilson and Bryan, convinced of an Anglo-Mexican conspiracy, forced Britain to end her support for Huerta and accede to an American intervention which Grey

[36]   Fisher, II, pp. 28 ff. Donald F. Anderson, *William Howard Taft*, p. 8. Bradford Perkins, *The Great Rapprochement*, p. 254. Arthur Link, *The New Freedom*, pp. 304 – 14. G. P. Gooch and Harold Temperley (eds.), *British Documents on the Origins of the War, 1898 – 1914*, VIII, p. 596. These documents capture perfectly Bryce's international legalism at odds with the Senate's and the Foreign Office's political nationalism, and their victory in the face of Bryce's growing disillusionment.

[37]   Bryce to Wilson, 19 Dec 1913, Wilson Papers. Bryce co-operated with Yale's Latin American expert, Hiram Bingham, in undermining America's rigid interpretation of the Monroe doctrine (cf. Bryce to Bingham, 10 April 1912, 4 Oct 1913 and 5 Dec 1913, Bingham Papers, *South America*, pp. vii – viii, 508 – 10).

felt ill-considered. This deferring by Grey to Wilson parallels Salisbury's appeasement of Cleveland over Venezuela, but, while both episodes indicate the tension and friction inevitable between sovereign states, concession was possible because a common interest was seen to exist, a mutual world view based on cooperation rather than rivalry. As the Foreign Secretary Grey recognised, British interests had been preserved in their essentials despite, or perhaps because of, concessions to the United States:

These small Republics will never establish decent government themselves — they must succumb to some greater and better influence and it can only be that of the United States. We cannot compete with that and must obtain the best terms we can as occasion offers for vested British interests and commercial opportunities. The more we can support the U.S. contention for the open door in other parts of the world the stronger our position will be morally in contending at Washington for the open door in Central America.

The tone is that used of a neighbour rather than a close friend, but neighbours have to work together for mutual benefit. Recent historians such as D. C. Watt, Max Beloff and Ronald Hyam have easily disposed of the myth of the 'special relationship' showing that the two sides did not share identical interests and that, in the hard-boiled foreign office language of Sir Eyre Crowe: 'Vague generalities, especially of the high-sounding kind, are no doubt a passport to American favour, but they are of doubtful value.' If Crowe is correct then Bryce's ambassadorship as the archetypal non-career diplomat is rendered worthless. But were all the high sounding generalities of doubtful value? In very practical terms which Crowe would appreciate America twice came to Britain's aid and decisively destroyed German militarism, and even after 1945 when America made it quite plain that she did not intend to deploy her world-wide forces in order to maintain the Churchillian empire the nations shared a common value system — stressed initially with great force both by Bryce and Dicey in their writings of the 80s — which, despite the collapse of the League ideal and the general paralysis of the United Nations, still vitally holds the two powers together though submerged into the more conspicuous and lasting 'free world' identity.[38]

Nothing reveals Bryce's increasing isolation from contemporary political currents more than his strict adhesion to the doctrine of *laissez faire*. The Oxford disciple of Mill's *Political Economy* and of the Manchester school wrote to Dicey in the days of Lloyd George's People's Budget that:

> the most marked contrast between those days and the present seems to lie in the fact that we all assumed individualism as obviously and absolutely right. We were not indifferent to the miseries of the poor, but looked upon them as inevitable and did not feel the restless anxiety to remove them, even in defiance of economic laws, which burns in the breasts of modern youths.

The emphasis here is both on the change in popular opinion and the unchanging laws of economics that public opinion hoped to defy, for he and Dicey remained convinced that in the world of man as in the material world, immutable laws applied, and that the political economists of the mid-nineteenth century had conclusively proved free enterprise to be the natural and optimal dynamic at work in the economic sphere — or as Dicey stated it 'a science containing very definite and certain principles from which were logically deduced conclusions of indisputable and universal truth'.[39] A science which places its trust in a '*hidden* hand' might rather be considered a species of mysticism, and Dicey in his magisterial *Law and Public Opinion* sought to assert rather than prove the economic superiority of non-

---

[38] Gooch and Temperley, VIII, p. 550. Arthur Link, *The New Freedom*, pp. 369 – 77. Max Beloff in *A Century of Conflict*, ed. by Martin Gilbert, pp. 151 – 71; D. C. Watt, *Personalities and Policies*, pp. 19 – 52; Ronald Hyam, *Britain's Imperial Century*, p. 202. Grey quoted in P. A. R. Calvert, 'Britain and the New World, 1905 – 1914' in *British Foreign Policy under Sir Edward Grey*, ed. by F. H. Hinsley, pp. 389 – 90. In Peter Calvert's own words: 'United States' imperialism was not seen as an unpredictable threat, but instead as a predictable stage of development of a power stemming from British origins. Thus benignly regarded, it was accommodated by British governments with a certain sense of paternal pride' (p. 383).

[39] Bryce to Dicey, 14 Nov 1913, Ms. Bryce 4. *Law and Public Opinion*, p. 445. Bryce wrote in his chapter on 'Laissez Faire': 'There are laws of nature governing mankind as well as the material world; and man will thrive better under these laws than under those which he makes for himself through the organisation we call government' (*AC*, II, p. 419).

211

intervention, but because the doctrine was so essential to the tenets of liberal individualism, because economic freedom was deemed a necessary prerequisite for political liberty, to interfere politically to remedy economic ills was considered doubly mischievous. A dogma which was built on the dual foundations of universal political and economic laws had at the same time to keep these two areas separate and distinct. Thus populism was to Bryce 'an effort to apply political remedies to evils, real or supposed, which are economic rather than political, and only a part of which legislation can remove'.[40] The theory presumed an abstract world of atoms and contracts — indeed Dicey referred to the Irish land acts in Maine's terminology of a reversion from contract to status — of an harmonious society of rational individuals pursuing an identical common good — Bryce's Christian commonwealth of 1867 — not of classes pursuing conflicting class interests. Politics became a Gladstonian matter of moral conscience and ardent unifying crusades, be it on behalf of Italy, Ireland or Armenia, not the extirpation of social evils or the lessening of economic disparities. The economics of *laissez faire* naturally engendered political and social quietism.

This was not true of all Bryce's contemporaries. Dicey recalled T. H. Green's absorption in the 'romantic politics' of pauperism at Balliol in the 60s. Lord Acton, who had at first postulated the opposition of liberty to equality, of socialism, which arose from egalitarian principles, as the antithesis of liberalism, later approved a radically obverse formulation which found democracy and socialism compatible: 'When power is declared equal, property should be equal.' Whereas Dicey located the origins of collectivism in Benthamism, Acton found it in the writings of Adam Smith, the father of capitalism, when he formulated the principles of free contract between capital and labour, and labour as the source of wealth. Socialism sprang from the latter principle, but the former too, that bulwark against socialist fantasy as Maine termed it, stimulated the collectivist spirit, for 'free' contract was a delusion, like a duel in which one of the combatants alone provided seconds and ammunition. 'The principle', Acton concluded, 'that authority is a matter of contract, may hold good against kings, but not against the

---

40   *AC*, 1910, II, p. 448. *Law and Public Opinion*, p. 264. Bryce went on to speak of the west 'where the aptitude for politics is so much in advance of economic wisdom' (*AC*, 1910, II, p. 448).

sovereign people, because a contract implies two parties.'[41] However abstract this account might seem, it did have the singular advantage of hazarding a guess at the economic consequences of political change, rather than, like Bryce, insisting on the theoretical separateness of the two spheres.

In the face of the growth of Fabianism, the emergence of trade unions and an independent Labour party, Bryce and other Asquithians like Harcourt and Morley were dismissed in Beatrice Webb's waspish language as 'limps' marooned, 'mere members of a debating society'. Some theoretical baggage simply couldn't be thrown overboard in the trying situation facing the liberals in the early years of the new century. Henry Pelling offers one among many factors contributing to the decline of the liberal party which is especially relevant here: 'As political allegiances became more and more determined by class self-awareness, the Liberal party found it could make no claims on the loyalties of any class.' Both intellectually and in practical terms in his own parliamentary constituency, Bryce felt stranded as the old Gladstonian power base evaporated under the intensity of class politics. Dicey stated unequivocally that collectivism and democracy were incompatible, and that between liberalism and socialism there could be no permanent alliance. Bryce wrote to Seth Low in 1892 that 'should a distinct Labour party obtain a hold in Parliament, the Liberal party would suffer and Home Rule be indefinitely postponed.'[42] The remark is doubly revealing: the I.L.P. offered a threat rather than an alliance, a threat that would divert attention, once for all, from an Irish crusade to a radical domestic programme.

In that same year, in Gladstone's final administration, he attempted, as Chancellor of the Duchy of Lancaster, not only to reverse the Unionist majority on the local bench, but also appoint as many working class liberals as he could to obviate the emergence of a separate Labour interest in the county. He succeeded in appointing thirty-three in all, 13 per cent of his total appointments, but this was no more than a holding

41   Melvin Richter, *The Politics of Conscience: T. H. Green and his Age*, p. 52. G. E. Fasnacht, *Acton's Political Philosophy*, p. 121. *Acton-Drew Letters*, pp. 91-3. *The History of Freedom*, p. 95.
42   Beatrice Webb, *Our Partnership*, p. 145. Henry Pelling, *Popular Politics and Society in Late Victorian Britain*, p. xi, Dicey, *NYN*, 2 April 1903, p. 265, and *Law and Public Opinion*, 1914, ed., p. lxxiii. Bryce to Low, 9 Jan 1892, Low Papers.

operation. Already in that year he had had to fight hard for his own constituency against a novel and rigorous challenge from H. H. Champion, whose socialist publication *The Fiery Cross* pressed for an eight hour day and accused the sitting MP of representing the one-sided interests of employers in Aberdeen. Bryce won, but Champion gained almost 1,000 votes, the highest figure yet recorded in Scotland for a Labour candidate.[43] The 'firm rock of Scottish Liberalism . . . namely the Aberdeen granite' which Gladstone referred to when Bryce was first elected to the constituency in 1885, was beginning to crack. Bryce insisted on a dubious distinction between social reform, which he found acceptable, and Socialist principles, which he did not, but he hoped above all, by timely concessions, to absorb the nascent party into the universal classless church of liberal progressivism, and consequently he differed sharply with Herbert Gladstone's analysis in *The Liberal Party and the Labour Question*, published in 1892, which conceded the Liberal acceptance of a separate Labour party. It was Gladstone who made the electoral pact with MacDonald in 1903 which gave Labour thirty-five uncontested seats and which enabled them to elect twenty-nine MPs in 1906 when only five in their rank were returned against Liberal opposition in the constituencies. In 1910, when Bryce revised *The American Commonwealth*, the number had risen to forty.[44]

In 1870, three years after contributing to the *Essays on Reform*, Bryce transferred his vision of the Christian commonwealth to the United States. The founding fathers had inhabited a social and political world in which: 'There were no questions between classes, no animosities against rank and wealth, for rank and wealth did not exist.' This reading suggests a real ignorance of America's eighteenth century social structure which might have been corrected by a reading of Madison's Tenth *Federalist Paper*, but even in 1888, while forced to concede the growing disparities in wealth and the emergence of class cleavages, he tended to suggest both that genuine party differences did not exist because of the absence of class identification, and insist

---

43 John Shepherd, *Bulletin of the Institute of Historical Research*, Nov 1979, pp. 155 – 69. By such means C. P. Scott of the *Manchester Guardian* and John Morley in Southport hoped to keep the Labour Party 'reasonable' (pp. 158, 161).

44 Fisher, I, p. 200. Bryce to Gladstone, 24 March 1892, Gladstone Papers, Add. Ms. 46019.

that parties strenuously provoked class hatreds artifically for their own ends. If not parties, then trade unions and new immigrants carrying with them the embittered class antago- nisms of Europe fanned and exploited the flames in the form of strikes, unhappy proof that democracy 'does not secure the good behaviour of its worst and newest citizens . . . and it must be prepared . . . to maintain order by the prompt and stern application of physical force.'[45]

The Declaration of Independence may, as Dicey suggested, have been grounded on *laissez faire* principles, stemming both from the 'sentimental' belief in maximum freedom — both economic and political — and the 'rationalist' argument that interference in aggregate did more harm than good, but Bryce's most substantial contribution to an understanding of the American economy was to squarely refute the strongly held belief that the nation in practice was still wedded to that doctrine. The pioneer tables and statistics appended to the chapter on 'Laissez Faire', concerning female and child labour, regulation of railroads, public health etc., revealed instead a greater degree of federal and state intervention in the United States than in Great Britain. More noticeable in later editions were the attempts to regulate trusts; the Oklahoma Constitution of 1907, for example, had thirty-six articles specifically referring to the regulation of companies within that state alone. Bryce could respond humanely to the philanthropic attempt to ameliorate the harsher consequences of classical economic dogma: 'There are benefits which the laws of demand and supply do not procure. Unlimited competition seems to press too hardly on the weak . . .. Unrestricted competition has shown its dark side', but his tone and style betrays a strong academic dislike for those state legislators who attempted to ignore or interfere with those iron economic laws; they were men 'unskilled in economics', 'inept', 'prone to gratify any whim', 'self-interested', 'impatient philanthropists', 'crotchet- mongers', 'intriguers', all of this in one paragraph concerning minor state interventionism which concludes: 'No responsible

---

[45]   *AC*, I, p. 30. *AC*, 1910, II, pp. 309, 620, 648. Bryce held new immigrants chiefly responsible for strike action. Between 1888 and 1910 that percentage of immigrants which he deemed politically ignorant, socially unstable and prone to socialist and anarchist doctrines rose from 50% to 75% (*AC*, 1910, II, p. 912).

statesman is there to oppose them, no warning voice will be raised by a scientific economist.'[46]

The Gilded Age era is associated pre-eminently with that of economic vitality, of large trusts and robber barons, but there is extraordinarily little of this in the pages of *The American Commonwealth*. The reader will find a graphic description of the nervous financial dynamics of Wall Street, a chapter on railroads with material provided by Henry Villard, President of the Northern Pacific, but little on the economic life of the nation, on its businessmen and entrepreneurs apart from their propensity for political corruption, little on the formation and growth of trusts or, apart from a few sparse references to the Interstate Commerce Commission of 1887 and the Sherman Anti-Trust Act of 1890, on the vigorous anti-trust movement of the period. While appreciating that 'the very freedom of association which men sought to secure by law . . . may, under the shelter of law, ripen into a new form of tyranny', little is added to the discussion of corporations by 1910, except brief references to 'anomalous giants' and 'irresponsible management'. This dismissive attitude to such a vast and vital area of American life was the result of his settled conviction that the republic's maladies were political, and specifically party political, not economic. Any insight which insisted on the inextricable connection of the two forces, such as the anonymous Philadelphian correspondent who wrote that the Gas Ring was held together by party managers with the dual support of the reform leaders and manufacturing interests, or Lincoln Steffens who asserted that the financial boss would long outlive the city boss he was behind, was simply not grasped. Again Bryce read but failed to appreciate Herbert Croly's linking together of the political and the economic professional specialist in America, 'Boss' in his *Promise of American Life*.[47] There is little evidence that Bryce visited factories or talked to the urban worker and new immigrant in a period when America became decisively urban the coordinated alliance of the 'Captain of Industry' with the and industrial. There is a brief visit to the Pullman factory on

46   *Law and Public Opinion*, p. 145. AC, II, pp. 418, 421, 424, 420, 422. AC, 1910, I, pp. 719 – 42.
47   AC, II, pp. 89, 532, 526 – 7, 420 – 1. AC, 1910, II, pp. 703 n. 1, 532 n. 1, 537, 526 – 7, 533 – 40, 525. Steffen's assessment was enclosed in a letter from Norman Hapgood to Bryce dated 2 Oct 1909, Ms. Bryce USA 25. Herbert Croly, *The Promise of American Life*, p. 123.

the Northern Pacific jamboree in 1883, and a passing reference to the noise of factory machinery lulling Black workers asleep. Contact with plutocrats was limited to the respectable, philan-thropic variety like Carnegie, Villard, Francis Lee Higginson and C. F. Adams Jr. But as the economic life of the nation loomed ever larger, and the attendant problems of size and control and labour relations preoccupied reformers and legislators, Bryce seemed to turn his gaze further away, to fail to come to grips with the implications, and put even greater faith in the strictly political solution of involving the 'outer circle' to combat the inner professionals; each new edition led to an ever greater emphasis on the proper civic education of the best men as the means of healing the commonwealth. So much so that while the first edition gave about equal space to the universities and to economic topics, by 1910 far more space was given to the former, than the latter (fifty-one to thirty-two pages respectively).

How has the *American Commonwealth* fared, and what critical reception has it received from later analysts of the United States? Even writers as critical as Harold Laski have found much to praise. He acknowledged the book as being the first by a British writer 'in which the greatness of America was acknow-ledged in its due proportions'. Charles Beard was only one among many who identified it as a seminal progressive text, a rousing polemic which, along with Henry George's *Progress and Poverty* (1879) and Henry Demarest Lloyd's *Wealth and Common-wealth* (1894) signalled the abrupt end of Gilded Age com-placency and gave an enormous fillip to reformism in the United States: 'Hitherto most of the books on American government had dealt with the subject in the terms of pious constitutional fictions; but Bryce laid bare the anatomy and morphology of politics-rings, bosses, frauds, machines, intrigue and chicane.' Bryce was rarely criticised on grounds of factual accuracy, comprehensiveness, of a definitive grasp of large areas of American political activity — the party system, local and state government — laid bare for the first time by his boundless curiosity and observation. Rather the criticism concentrated on his assumptions and methods. In reaction to the sweeping *a priori* approach of Tocqueville, Bryce had built up a huge edifice based on the 'resolutely actual', but the complacent rationalism of his approach was seen by many critics as merely provoking a new species of unreality shaped to a preconceived and desired pattern, which ignored the irrational in man and the shaping subjective element in himself. A. L. Lowell's own research on parties led him to the conclusion that man was politically suggestible rather than rational. Justice Holmes also gently drew Bryce's attention to philosophical pragmatism. 'The foundation of reason', he wrote, 'is unreason — the arbitrary fact that we can't help yielding to it — that is what I mean when I say a thing is true . . . my definition of truth is accordingly the system of my limitations.'[48]

More formidably Graham Wallas in his *Human Nature in Politics* singled out Bryce's introduction to Ostrogorski's *Democracy and the Origins of Political Parties* as classically representative of fallacious eighteenth century assumptions of rational human motivation; in particular he alighted on the use of the term 'ideal democracy':

> What does Mr Bryce mean . . .? If it means anything it means the best form of democracy which is consistent with the facts of human nature. But one feels, on reading the whole passage, that Mr Bryce means by those words the kind of democracy which might be possible if human nature were as he himself would like to it be — as he was taught at Oxford to think that it was.

Bryce had declared himself a 'professional optimist'; Wallas insisted that a political scientist had no business to make such assertions, any more than a chemist should be grimly resolved to yield 'optimistic' results in his laboratory. 'One seems', he concluded, 'to be reading a series of conscientious observations of the Copernican heavens by a loyal but saddened believer in Ptolemaic astronomy.' This is not entirely fair. Had he bothered to look elsewhere Wallas would have found substantial evidence of Bryce's political realism, but his introduction was intentionally intended to balance what he took to be Ostrogorski's excessive and unrealistic 'professional pessimism'. Indeed Bryce did, at least until 1914, hold tenaciously to the concept of the rational man in the rational universe, to the beneficent influence of the educative process, the susceptibility of all men to reason and to responsibility, all derived from the exuberance

48 Laski, *The American Democracy*, p. 16. Laski to Bryce, 26 May 1919, Ms. Bryce UB 10. Charles and Mary Beard, *The Rise of American Civilisation*, II, pp. 426 – 7. Lowell to Bryce, 7 Feb 1902, Ms. Bryce USA 8. Holmes to Bryce, 19 April 1914 and 10 Jan 1915, Ms. Bryce Misc.

of liberal Oxford in the mid-nineteenth century. But Bryce presumably, had as much right to reflect upon the ideal as Plato in his *Republic* or More in his *Utopia*, and Bryce's acute awareness of what ought to be, his 'professional optimism', sprang from an equally assured appreciation of that which was. Nevertheless Wallas' critique did rock Bryce's rationalist foundations, his indifference to political psychology, and most tellingly of all, the limitations of the formalistic, scientific approach. R. H. Tawney, in reviewing Bryce's Godkin lecture of 1909, took his cue from Wallas and embalmed it in the following dismissive lines — 'a finely turned gargoyle on the edifice of Victorian paternalistic, moralistic, optimistic, public-minded idealism'.[49]

Even in that area where his approach was more informal and relaxed — the party system — Bryce was accused of holding fast to the fallacy of a united public opinion, of underplaying class divisions which defined parties, and of judging these 'extra legal associations' as an aberration and imposition rather than a necessary function representing various legitimate interests in the political market place. A. L. Lowell's less judgemental, more functional and pragmatic, analysis interpreted the boss as a broker between political power and the public and insisted that the function of the broker was as needful for political life as the entrepreneur in commercial life, as proper and as honourable. It was because America's party system grew spontaneously to meet genuine needs and necessities that Croly argued the futility of attempting to reform or destroy it. Even the patrician and censorious Beatrice Webb appreciated how much more responsive the city boss was to the needs of the people, than were the reformers. 'There is a solid foundation of general capacity and human fellowship in Tammany, however corrupt its ways and bad its traditions. Tammany officials understand and sympathise with the niggardliness of the ratepayer and the anarchic objection to interference characteristic of the American "average sensual man".' The historiography of the Gilded Age between Henry Adams and George Washington Plunkitt of Tammany, and in the New Deal world and after, many

49   *Human Nature in Politics*, pp. 128, 126 – 7. See also Martin J. Wiener, *Between Two Worlds: The Political Thought of Graham Wallas*, p. 66, and Terence H. Qualter, *Graham Wallas and the Great Society*, pp. 84 – 5. Ross Terrill, *R. H. Tawney and His Times*, p. 180.

historians like Carl Becker, Oscar Handlin and Herbert Agar naturally weighed the mugwumps — British and American — in the scales and found them wanting. Agar for example wrote that: 'The purpose — the important and healthy purpose of an American party — is to be exactly what Bryce describes, and by implication deplores.'[50]

Denis Brogan was of this tradition but did not go so far in his criticism; he spoke of Tammany as Robin Hood giving half his spoils to the poor and keeping the rest for himself, while the reformer who would not rob 'gave nothing but counsels borrowed from Samuel Smiles'. Sharing a common liberal Glaswegian background, Bryce and Brogan were temperamentally poles apart; one was a Presbyterian Ulster-Scot, the other a Catholic from Donegal whose own father had earlier emigrated to California, not as a visiting Regius professor, but to seek employment as a tailor. Brogan was convivial and informal, and instinctively grass-roots in a way that Bryce could not have attempted. He was not unaware of the flaws and failings of American politics and politicians, but he approached them in an amused and tolerant fashion which, combined with a highly developed scepticism about Establishments both in Britain and America, made him particularly mistrustful of the patrician pomposity in the late Victorian's tone. The mugwumps approached the problem of municipal reform 'without scepticism of the virtue of themselves and of their class'. Their condescension was combined with an inflexible naivety: 'The guileless Richard Watson Gilder proposed to consolidate a temporary victory over Tammany by starting a weekly which would circulate among the ignorant voters of the East Side and show them how foolish they had been in the past in supporting the machine.' Again the boss flourished despite countless reformist onslaughts because behind the boss was wealth and 'It was much harder . . . to find men of wealth and standing who had nothing to gain from machine rule than was innocently assumed.' Brogan considered it highly indicative that when Bryce turned his attention to California he looked closely at the

50 Lowell, *Public Opinion and Popular Government*, p. 64, Croly, *The Promise of American Life*, pp. 125–6. Beatrice's Webb's *American Diary*, p. 54. Herbert Agar, *The United States*, p. 689. Carl Becker concentrated his attack on Bryce's literal formalism: 'To assume that democracy, and not class rule, exists because it exists formally is much like assuming that Great Britain is not a democracy but a monarchy because it has a king' (*Political Science Quarterly*, Dec 1921, p. 672).

anarchic threat from below — the sandlot party — while Senator Leland Stanford's all-pervasive political machine dedicated to the interests of the Southern Pacific passed almost unnoticed.[51]

Harold Laski was another outsider, a Jew, and a colleague of Brogan's at The London School of Economics, who also relished the relaxed style of the new world, but approached American politics as a socialist and not a latter day liberal. His criticism, particularly of the WASP establishment, with whom he had a number of abrasive encounters beginning with his brief spell as a lecturer at Lowell's Harvard, was all the more trenchant because of it, and his indictment centred on Bryce's ignorance of and intolerance towards the urban working classes, and of their attempts to better themselves whether through the boss system, trade unions or industrial strikes. It was not only that as late as 1910 and just three years before the Pujo Commission Bryce made no mention of the American Federation of Labour or of the labyrinthine political and economic powers exercised by J. P. Morgan, but also that when he did specifically treat of the Homestead strike, the Haymarket riots or the populists, it was couched in language of extreme bias. But, of course, the observer like the observed is in chains, the historian within, not outside, history, and Laski's gloss, like the collection of essays written by an assortment of American academics in 1939, reflected all too faithfully the political preoccupations of the New Deal era. Professor Charles G. Haines, to give but one example, condemned Bryce for lending his authority to further buttress the Supreme Court 'as the determining agency in the development of an acquisitive and exploitative industrial society which has had no parallel in modern society'.[52]

Perhaps the most surprising development in the continuing critical re-evaluation of Bryce comes with the current radical reassessment of the Gilded Age launched by the 'cliometricians'. It can at times be simply dismissive as when Richard Jensen refers to *The American Commonwealth* as 'an outdated classic of middling value', but at other times fresh and

[51] *The American Political System*, pp. 266, 265, 262, 263 n. 1. The first edition appeared in 1933. Also *An Introduction to American Politics*, pp. 26, 130. On Brogan's dislike of the dryness and stiffness of the English see Maurice Cowling, *Religion and Public Doctrine in Modern England*, p. 195.

[52] *The American Presidency: An Interpretation*, pp. 16 – 18. Robert C. Brooks, *Bryce's 'American Commonwealth': Fiftieth Anniversary*, p. 17.

enlightening, as when Paul Kleppner quixotically lumps Bryce and James Ford Rhodes together with Charles Beard and Matthew Josephson in collectively exercising a tyranny over current conceptions of the age — that it was dull and sterile, evasive of the 'real' issues and failed to recognise or control the great social and economic changes that transformed the America of the period. Bryce is especially singled out for his over-concentration on elite politics, for his exclusion of formative mass socio-political subcultures, and for his too narrow definition of party as electoral machine instead of purveyor and unifier of cultural standards and 'aura', (the phrase is Kleppner's and reminiscent of Wallas's on the cultural role of the party's 'image'). But a good deal of this recent writing has also gone some way towards vindicating Bryce's interpretation. Civil Service reform is no longer dismissed as a patrician *idée fixe* or a means of reversing status displacement, but as vital to that process of professionalisation and bureaucratisation which Robert Wiebe takes as a prerequisite for America's progress from a decentralised and rural Jacksonian polity to a modern America. Bryce's overly formalistic approach has been held responsible for the static constitutional and political picture he paints; now it is seen as authentically reflecting the twenty year party deadlock which detailed computerised electoral research has confirmed. Similarly the old criticism put forward, most especially by Carl Becker and Harold Laski, that he ignores class and class divisions, has given way to a re-emphasis on those very sectional and ethnocultural divides which Bryce carefully elaborated on, especially in his section on 'Public Opinion'. Even Kleppner, who more than anyone has destroyed Bryce's settled image of the era as quiescent, concedes the greater pull of cultural over economic and class factors in voting habits and political allegiance in the period.[53]

The first world war

Bryce began a letter to Henry White, the respected American diplomat, on 24 July 1914 discussing their common friend,

[53] Richard Jensen, *The Winning of the Mid-West, 1888–1896*, p. 324. Paul Kleppner, *The Third Electoral System, 1853–1892*, pp. 4–10. Geoffrey Blodgett in Daniel Walker Howe (ed.), *Victorian America*, p. 104. Paul Kleppner, *The Cross of Culture*, pp. 369, 371. Robert Wiebe, *The Search for Order, 1877–1920*, pp. xiii–xiv.

former President Roosevelt. He was interrupted and was unable to take up his pen again till 12 August when he wrote: 'Since this letter was begun, what events, sudden, awful, like a vast black thundercloud suddenly darkening the vault of heaven . . . the bottom has fallen out of our civilisation.' The dream was broken. His strenuous advocacy of general arbitration, his attempts to reduce Anglo-German tension either in his official capacity as Ambassador with Grey, or privately with Americans with strong German connections — Villard and Nicholas Murray Butler — his advice to the Foreign Office as a Balkan expert, and the plans for an Anglo-American conference to celebrate a century of peace ('How pale and bloodless all the organised propaganda for peace appears now', Lowell wrote), all of these efforts were destroyed. In 1916 he was to visit the war zone with John Buchan and C. E. Montague, and witness behind the lines a land silent and bewitched, as if every human had somehow been spirited away. 'Strange to see sweet peaceful landscapes, and warm sunshine over the wheat, with terrific scenes of death so near. Surely the world has gone mad.' At home in the pine forests of the Weald the doors and windows rattled from the guns firing across the channel in Flanders.[54]

He was quite unprepared for the retrogressive barbarism which emerged among what he had called the 'advanced races'. He did not really possess the Christian insight into man's invincible evil which made Acton acutely aware of those 'constant and invariable forces which will resist the truth and the higher purpose . . .. The splendid plausibility of error, the dazzling attractiveness of sin', nor grasp Salisbury's abjuring the 'drab-coloured millennium' of America to face grimmer European realities, or Fitzjames Stephen who rejected the East's cowardly concept of nirvana for the more wholesome and chilling Calvinistic world imagined as a mysterious hall of doom. Bryce was indeed by temperament a professional optimist, and the war not only dented his faith in inevitable progress but set in progress a far reaching disillusionment with the basic tenets of democracy, with the idea of the essential benignity of human nature, and with the liberal presumption that knowledge and understanding would bring wisdom too. In the 90s he spoke of the painful gradualism of progress; 'Passion

[54] Bryce to White, 24 July and 12 August 1914, White Papers, Lowell to Bryce, 25 August 1914, Lowell Papers. Bryce to Rhodes, 2 July 1917, Rhodes Papers. Fisher, II, pp. 149, 191.

and cruelty, and the habits of violence are not to be at once exorcised . . .. Reason is repulsed over and over again from strongholds of prejudice which she might have hoped to carry at the first assault.' In 1920 he was more resigned and even less hopeful — 'there will always be fountains sending forth bitter water'.[55]

He had reports of the psychological effects of shell shock, and turned to that image again and again to suggest the implications, for non-combatants as well as soldiers, of a collective war psychosis. Another recurring image was that of a deadly bacillus let loose on a once healthy population. Bryce recognised the symptoms and knew that he was not immune himself; an old man of seventy-six, he took on an enormous burden of work: a vast correspondence, especially American, labouring for the League idea in the 'Bryce group', Chairman of the Atrocity Commissions and of the Second Chamber Commission. From Paris he wrote to Justice Holmes that: 'The war has destroyed all leisure for most of us, and goes on destroying not less but more by multiplying the calls made upon one's time by demands for things to be written, speeches to be made, applications of all sorts to be dealt with. Besides, it has almost destroyed quiet thinking. The shells seem to be singing over our heads here as they are above the trenches and forcing us to keep our minds fixed on passing events.'[56] Yet despite all this, the war ultimately bore the fruits of his life — long dedication to the Anglo-American cause, when Wilson first entered the war on the side of Britain, then, victorious, attempted a world peace. At first he despaired of ever shaking the United States from her neutral stance, of the hopelessness of the two nations ever understanding one another, and protested in letters to the President, his one-time pupil at John Hopkins, at his taking up a position of moral as well as formal neutrality. But because of his links, especially with Colonel House and Ambassador Page, he could confide in Trevelyan, and suggest that Wilson was more pro-allied than most Britons and Americans perceived. He

55 Acton Papers Add. 8119. Michael Pinto-Duschinsky, *The Political Thought of Lord Salisbury*, p. 89. Leslie Stephen, *James Fitzjames Stephen*, p. 458. Bryce to Dicey, 17 Sept 1893 and 28 Jan 1917, Ms. Bryce 4. Bryce to Eliot, 5 Feb 1920, 19 Nov 1920, Ms. Bryce USA 2. Bryce in *Contemporary Review*, Jan 1891, p. 24.

56 Bryce to Dicey, 12 March 1919, 28 August 1920, Ms. Bryce 4. Bryce to Holmes, 23 Feb 1916, Ms. Bryce Misc. Bryce, *The International Crisis*, p. 2.

remained impatient, continued to overrate American anglophilia and underrate a long tradition of isolationism. Wilson in turn paid compliment to a 'generous friendship', read the letters from Bryce sent on by House, and continued his own policies regardless. The German military decision to unleash unlimited submarine warfare finally brought the United States into the war, but Bryce's influence and contacts, and more particularly his contribution to wartime propaganda as we shall see, were not negligible. House could honestly write of Bryce in his diary: 'I feel he knows America so well that he can understand and advise in the many perplexing questions confronting us.' No one was more aware than Bryce of the incalculable consequences of American intervention in Europe and of the incalculable consequences of America's British origins. The irony is that the alliance was cemented in war, and not in general arbitration as Bryce had hoped.[57]

There is a further irony in that his greatest single wartime contribution was in the field of public propaganda, not private influence. In the latter sphere his achievements were marginal; to facilitate communications and urge limited goals; to ease frictions between the two sides, particularly over the British blockade; to encourage the area of positive cooperation in the future League, and argue forcefully against American bilateral peace negotiations with Germany. He believed absolutely that Germany had caused the war, had lapsed into military barbarism, that the war was a war fought for the preservation of civilisation and the civilised values of the rule of law. Chairing the two Atrocities Commissions was not so much aimed at bringing the United States into the war, as emphasising and re-emphasising the moral distinction between the combatants. Bryce was uniquely qualified. Apart from Morley he was the sole survivor of the Bulgarian atrocities campaign, when he had become a confirmed Turcophobe. He had dedicated his *Transcaucasia and Ararat* to the persecuted Christian minorities of that benighted empire, and urged armed intervention on behalf of the Armenians to Rosebery's indifferent cabinet. His enormous debt to German scholarship, his admiration of their universities, made the invasion of Belgium and the destruction of Louvain all the more painful. Aware of how the dictates of Prussian

[57]   Bryce to Wilson, 22 Dec 1916, Wilson Papers. Bryce to Trevelyan, 22 Jan 1916, Ms. Bryce 19. Charles Seymour (ed.), *The Intimate Papers of Colonel House*, II, pp. 132 – 3, 410. Bryce to Trevelyan, 21 Nov 1917, Ms. Bryce, 19.

nationalism had perverted the writings of German intellectuals like Treitschke, Bernardi and others he was also aware of how the iron could enter the soul in times of war. 'How easily our people are stepping into Prussianism', he wrote to Trevelyan, and two months after the outbreak of war to Lowell: 'Our public is now ready to believe anything reported of German cruelties and it is much to be wished we could have some impartial enquiry to reduce these tales to due proportion.'[58]

The Committee to investigate the atrocities was set up with remarkable speed in September 1914, master-minded from Wellington House by Masterman, and published its report in May 1915, five days after the sinking of the Lusitania. Bryce made it clear from the start that he would not manufacture anti-German propaganda and Fisher, a member of the Committee and Bryce's biographer, wrote that to the Chairman when it appeared 'the report was a matter of unqualified sorrow, signifying the rupture of many kindly associations, and the frustration of many generous hopes . . . it had been an unspeakable grief to find that such things had been done by members of a nation among which he numbered so many warm personal friends.' Thanking him, Charles Masterman mouthed the same sentiments: 'And I wish — as I have no doubt you wish — that you *could* have disproved the evidence or brought in the verdict of "Not Guilty". But as it was *true* — the world must know it — that it may never occur again.' Grief at the findings was doubtless genuine, but an examination of the Committee's work suggests a complexity of motives and at times, under Bryce's chairmanship, departures from the highest standards of legal investigation.[59]

Because he regarded the war as a moral crusade Bryce considered psychological warfare as a quite legitimate means of crushing Germany and imposing unconditional surrender. 'Failure', he wrote in 1915, 'must be stamped upon them, not from revenge, but for the sake of mankind'. Then in 1917: 'War is one of those things that if done at all ought to be done with all

---

58 Peter Stansky quotes Harcourt: 'It is so well known that Bryce has his own idiosyncrasy on the Armenian question' (*Ambitions and Strategies*, p. 211). Bryce to Trevelyan, 9 Feb 1916, Ms. Bryce 19. Bryce to Lowell, 2 Oct 1914, Lowell Papers. Bryce's Presidential Address in the *Proceedings of the British Academy*, 1915–16, p. 12. Bryce thought that the British army were 'abandoning themselves to hatred less than the civilians at home' (Bryce to Dicey, 25 Sept 1916, Ms. Bryce 4).

59 *Report of the Committee on Alleged German Atrocities*, Introduction. Fisher, II, pp. 133–4. Masterman to Bryce, 7 June 1915, Ms. Bryce UB 57.

one's might.' All the members of the Committee — Sir Frederick Pollock, Sir Edward Clarke, Sir Alfred Hopkinson, Fisher, Harold Cox and Sir Kenelm Digby — were entirely aware of the propaganda value of the exercise; it would have been quite impossible not to be. On receiving Attorney General Simons's commission, for example, Lady Bryce sketched her husband's dictated terms of reference on the back of the envelope 'as to the outrages committed', and only as an afterthought added 'alleged to have been' between the two words 'outrages' and 'committed'.

There is evidence throughout of hasty work and heavy pressure for a speedy report. Wellington House, the British propaganda headquarters, had already arranged for the simultaneous publication of 41,000 copies for the American market and interpreters were in the wings ready to translate the report into thirty different languages. In its earliest days Clarke indicated to E. Epinwood Mears, the Commission's Secretary, that 'the value of our report will be in inverse ratio to the time we take in preparing it', and in March 1915 Lord Selborne asked in the Lords when the report was to appear while at the same time reassuring Harold Cox that he had no intention of hustling the commission. Selborne's question occurred as doubts were raised about the veracity of the evidence before the commission, and Pollock had to write stiffening the chairman's resolve. 'I am alarmed at the prospect of a discussion which threatens to be interminable unless you give — as I humbly submit it is the Chairman's business to do — a definite lead . . . within fairly large limits it does not matter so much what it is as that it should be carried through and you should not be persuaded to go back upon it.' Doubts rose from a number of issues; Pollock suspected 'wilful blackening', 'hysterical fiction or delusion' in some of the Belgians' 'monstrous narratives'. Digby thought likewise, and Clarke and Cox questioned the authenticity of some of the 'captured' diaries. Part of the problem, as Fisher freely admitted, was that the diaries indicated in many cases that German soldiers were merely retaliating after being fired on by Belgian civilians. Nevertheless the German diaries were finally used as material evidence because they served to confirm the massive and convergent evidence of the depositions.[60]

60   Bryce to Buxton, 25 June 1915, Ms. Bryce UB 57. Bryce to Bayard Henry quoted in Fisher, II, p. 159. The envelope with Lady Bryce's handwriting is in MS. Bryce UB 57, as is the rest of the material in this footnote. Claud Schuster to Bryce, 12 April 1915 and 11 May 1915. Clarke to Mears, 21 Dec 1914. Cox to Bryce, 9 March 1915. Digby to Bryce, 14 March 1915. Pollock to

Alone, Harold Cox stood out against this complicity, because he alone questioned the acceptance of second hand depositions, anonymous cross examinations and the failure of the commission either to personally cross-examine witnesses or insist on the witnesses signing affadavits. Hence Pollock's stiff letter to Bryce insisting that he break the deadlock and complete the task as swiftly as possible. Cox had proved recalcitrant since the beginning of March, insisting that the committee should examine at least some of the witnesses — he had himself examined forty-five reports and rejected eighteen of them — adding that the lawyers who had collected the depositions, like Harry Atkins and Fitzjames Sawyers, had assumed their own cross-examination was preliminary and not final. Bryce did not reply, and Cox wrote again on 4 March asking that the lawyers at least be interviewed. Receiving Bryce's first draft of the report the following day Cox expressed grave doubts about the entire process of information gathering; he reiterated the point that the depositions were inadequate testimony, that the lawyers who gathered them could not vouch for their veracity, that the German diaries, supposedly deciphered and translated with care, could have been invented or rewritten, that Bryce's statement in the draft report that nothing had been admitted as evidence that an English judge sitting in court would not allow, was 'clearly inaccurate'. Cox added on 9 March that: 'I am greatly afraid that the difference between myself and the rest of our Committee with regard to the calling of witnesses is fundamental, and it would be quite impossible for me to sign the proposed report'; a thorough investigation must take priority over speedy publication.[61]

This impasse drew all the other members together in forcing Cox into line. Pollock argued that Cox was demanding a far greater degree of certitude than any court expected or got, Digby and Fisher urged the 'concurrent evidence' theory as outbalancing any particular contrary evidence or questionable documents, and were willing to overcome Cox's excessive scruples by inserting in the appendix that the committee couldn't vouch for each and every single deposition, in addition

---

Bryce, 6 March 1915, 31 Dec 1914. Fisher to Bryce, 5 March, 7 March and 13 March 1915.

[61]   Cox to Bryce, 1 March, 4 March, 5 March, 7 March, 9 March, 15 March 1915, Ms. Bryce UB 57.

to which Fisher promised to write 'sedative words and hope that we shall bring (Cox) along with us'. Bryce had a long discussion with Cox on 10 March and on the next day he acceded to Bryce's compromise plan of calling a number of lawyers for cross-examination about their methods of procedure and their impressions of the witnesses' reliability, to pursue doubtful depositions more thoroughly, and make it clear in the report that the evidence was based on second hand depositions rather than direct oral evidence given to the Committee. In fact Cox questioned few depositions, and in the final report the matter of indirect evidence was underplayed. The evidence as published was presented as cumulative and confirmatory and constituted a general indictment, any contrary or suspect evidence not withstanding. The 1,200 depositions had forced the Committee to move from doubts to convictions; the killing of civilians, ill-treatment of women and children, looting and burning, and the multiple offences against Belgian soldiers — the wounding or killing of prisoners, the firing on army hospitals, abuses of the white flag and the Red Cross — constituted a system of 'general and deliberate terrorisation', and that 'Murder, lust and pillage prevailed over many parts of Belgium on a scale unparalleled in any war between civilised nations during the last three centuries'. But the indictment was less important than the wider moral implications: 'these disclosures will not have been made in vain if they touch and rouse the conscience of mankind'. A similar moral was drawn in Bryce's introduction to the Armenian Atrocities report of the same year, for they were 'nothing but an echo and an extension of the main story, the central narrative, which must describe the German incursion in Belgium fourteen months ago. That was the determining act, that was the signal to Turk and Kurd . . . we must bear unspeakable crimes in constant memory against the final day of reckoning'.[62]

Arnold Toynbee collected material for the report and many years late explained its propaganda value. The Russian pogroms against their Jewish minorities turned American Jews against Russia and Russia's allies and against Britain's naval blockade, which threatened to influence United States policy in the critical

---

[62] Pollock to Bryce, 6 March 1915. Digby to Bryce, 14 March 1915. Fisher to Bryce, 11 and 13 March 1915. Cox to Bryce, 11 March 1915, Ms. Bryce UB 57. *Report on Alleged Atrocities*, pp. 37 – 8. Bryce reprinted in the *New York Tribune*, 8 Oct 1915.

months of 1915. British counter-propaganda hoped to neutralise Russian atrocities by Turkish atrocities against Armenians and also to condemn the Germans for allowing such atrocities by its allies to occur. It aimed also to win over the Jews of Eastern Europe to the allied cause, which was to be identified with the cause of Zionism. This counter-strategy was not entirely successful, because Armenia was a long way off and the Jewish diaspora far more influential than the Armenian. Nevertheless Toynbee concludes that:'If this political spider's web had been visible to Lord Bryce when he had been asked by H.M.G. to undertake the production of an *Armenian Blue Book*, I believe he would have declined. His integrity was notorious.' Indeed it was, but the dual purpose of saving the remaining Armenians and contributing to allied propaganda was in no sense contradictory to Bryce; on the contrary, they were entirely compatible aims, and he must have been entirely aware both of the propaganda aspect of the exercise and of the kudos and authority his name could bestow on that exercise; this was his war-work.[63]

Without doubt the Germans made deliberate use of terror and intimidation in Belgium and over 1,000 Belgians were executed, many of them non-combatants. Also without doubt, Bryce's reputation gave the report the full imprint of unassailable accuracy and authority. As the *American Press Résumé* of 27 May put it: 'Even in papers hostile to the Allies, there is not the slightest attempt to impugn the correctness of the facts alleged. Lord Bryce's prestige puts scepticism out of the question, and many leading articles begin on this note.' There is also general agreement among the secondary authorites — Harold Lasswell, Kate Haste, Arthur Link and James Morgan Read — that the report was a triumph of war propaganda. Arthur Link, while admitting that the Report created 'an entirely new situation', and had 'a profound and shocking impact' in the United States, suggests its influence has been exaggerated because it preached essentially to the already converted anglophile; that its impact was not profound.[64] But concentrating as he does on the day to day shifting of Anglo-American-German policy-making he may

---

[63]   Toynbee, *Acquaintances*, p. 153, and generally pp. 149 – 60.
[64]   Link, *Woodrow Wilson: The Struggle for Neutrality*, pp. 39 – 41, 42 n. 14. Link, *Woodrow Wilson and the Progressive Era*, pp. 148 n. 7, 147 n. 7. Ernest May, *The World War and American Isolation, 1914 – 1917*, p. 180. Harold Lasswell, *Propaganda Techniques in World War One*, p. 19. Kate Haste, *Keep the Home Fires Burning*, p. 93. James Morgan Read, *Atrocity Propaganda*, pp. 200 – 1.

have underrated the Report which, while perhaps not decisive, was contributory, contributory that is to the American people's and the American President's slow shifting from the grounds of moral neutrality — that the war was no more than a brawl in a bar between two drunks — to moral polarity, when finally in war in 1917 and again in peace in 1919, they joined cause with Britain in casting down Prussian militarism. For when Wilson took the United States into war he took on the moral fervour of a crusader, the moral fervour of a Bryce. One last point: both in the Report and in other writings directed throughout the war at American public opinion, Bryce gave credence to atrocity stories — of Belgian women being forcible deported to Germany, of others being driven off by German bayonets — of which no solid evidence existed or exists. Such stories were strenuously denied by American reporters on the German lines at the time, and all the evidence deposited in the vaults of the Foreign Office library has disappeared. Although George Bernard Shaw dismissed most of the evidence as worthless, he appreciated how far it served the psychological needs of the nation: 'our nerves were so upset that no possible truth could have satisfied our appetite for the atrocity stimulant, and we swallowed the Bryce report in intoxicating draughts'. Fearing so much the infection of war fever, Bryce himself, it seems, was not immune.[65]

The Russian revolution gravely damaged the Allied war effort and unleashed a new species of political madness; the Bolsheviks were men 'intoxicated with new ideas, living in an atmosphere of dreams and vague phrases'. Bryce had travelled through Russia in 1912 and observed on the Tsarevitch's name day at Tomsk prayers offered up to 'Russian Caesarism', and went on to consider the extraordinary fact that from the Baltic to the Pacific, from Tiflis to the Arctic, all Russians were doing likewise. Now, five years later, the Tsar and all his immediate family had been shot at Ekaterinburg, apparently unmourned by those same Russians. He contined to abhor socialism and

[65] 'Murder, lust, and pillage prevailed over many parts of Belgium on a scale unparalleled in any war between civilised nations during the last Three Centuries' (*Report on Alleged Atrocities*, p. 37). *The Last Phase in Belgium*, p. 6. *The War of Democracy*, p. xix. Link, *Woodrow Wilson: The Struggle for Neutrality*, p. 41. Read, *Atrocity Propaganda*, p. 206 n. 96. 'The late Lord Bryce . . . acted as chairman of a committee for the collection of tales from Belgium, and published a collection of horrors and obscenities, vouched for as "told by a Belgian corporal" and the like which had a considerable vogue' (Shaw, *What I Really Wrote About the War*, pp. 120 – 1).

feared the eruption and exploitation of class grievances in time of war, though strangely his work on the League of Nations brought him into close contact with a group of young men many of whom were socialists: J. A. Hobson, Goldsworthy Lowes Dickinson, Graham Wallas and Leonard Woolf. Another young man, Maynard Keynes, reinforced his conviction that the marvellous opportunity for Anglo-American cooperation at the Paris peace conference had miscarried, and future peace was unlikely. In private he encouraged Lowell in his public debate against Senator Lodge's 'reservationalist' stand on the League, and argued that the Monroe doctrine, rather than making America's adherence to the League impossible, actually set an example of non-invervention and guaranteed security against foreign aggression, which the League intended to extend into a collective global principle. Even after Wilson's physical collapse Bryce was still vainly hoping that Harding would bring America into the League.[66]

Some observers noted a growing inflexibility and stiffness in Bryce's intellectual and imaginative responses. As early as 1879 Henry James detected in him a doctrinaire radical who less and less took the 'popular heart' and appeared tainted with priggishness, 'though Bryce less so than some of the others'. Balfour, less kindly, referred to the professor as 'a startling instance of the uselessness of the higher education'. There was a certain discernible vanity, a measuring of private worth by public achievement and public rewards; Bryce and Dicey in their last years busied themselves with trying to guess how much space each might be apportioned when they were finally encased within the definitive pages of the *DNB*. Colonel House observed that, having mentioned A. G. Gardiner's laudatory sketch of Bryce in his *Pillars of Society*, 'Bryce smiled and said he had not read it, and was afraid to do so for fear his head might be turned; at the same time, I noticed he asked me again the title of the book.' Yet the twenty-six year old Arnold Toynbee found Bryce, now seventy-seven, open, responsive, sympathetic and

---

[66]   Bryce to Eliot, 12 July 1917, 8 Feb 1918, Ms. Bryce US 2. *Memories of Travel*, pp. 266 – 7. Bryce to Lowell, 10 March 1919, Lowell to Bryce, 4 April 1919, and Bryce to Lowell, 20 April 1919, 2 Dec 1920, Lowell Papers: Ms. Bryce US 8. Bryce's Introduction to *The League of Nations*, pp. 16 – 18. *International Relations*. Bryce's prefatory note to *Proposals for the Prevention of Future Wars. The International Crisis*. For details of the 'Bryce Group' and its contribution to the League ideal see Keith Robbins, *Historical Journal*, 1967, Vol. 10, No. 2, pp. 255 – 78, and Ions, pp. 266 – 82.

refreshingly unpompous. He had added Bryce's titles and honorary degrees — a daunting thirty-three in all — to the title page of the *Armenian Blue Book*; Bryce struck them all out with one stroke of his pen. It was, Toynbee reflected, 'the simplicity of someone who was incapable of being pompous and who was effective enough, just as he was, to feel neither the need, nor the temptation, to assert himself . . .. The best index of mental activity is curiosity, and Lord Bryce's curiosity never flagged.'[67]

That catches once again the spirit of the youthful Regius professor chatting to train drivers and farmers in the Plains states and day-dreaming of settling in San Francisco. He returned to spend an idyllic last summer on the Maine coast in Eliot's company more than fifty years after his first journey to the United States, and died at Sidmouth in Devon on 22 January 1922. The Washington Naval Conference then in session adjourned its proceedings on hearing the news, and speeches were formally delivered by Charles Evans Hughes and Elihu Root from the American delegation. On sending his condolences to Lady Bryce, Eliot was appalled to hear of James being buried in the Grange cemetery in Edinburgh. 'In this country that word is applied to societies of farmers who are apt to be ignorant and selfish in their policies. It must mean something quite different in Edinburgh, or you would not have put James' body there.' Lady Bryce hastened to clear the matter up; Eliot expressed himself entirely satisfied.[68]

[67] Leon Edel, *Henry James: The Conquest of London*, p. 336. Balfour's remark is noted in Edmund Gosse's *Diary* and is quoted in John Wilson's *Campbell-Bannerman*, pp. 461 – 2. Dicey to Bryce, 17 Sept 1893, Ms. Bryce 2. *The Intimate Papers of Colonel House*, I, p. 390. Toynbee, *Acquaintances*, pp. 155, 157.

[68] Eliot to Lady Bryce, 17 August 1923, 17 Sept 1923, Ms. Bryce USA 1.

Appendix 1

Biographical notes on contributors to the first edition of 'The American Commonwealth'

Information supplied to Bryce specified in brackets

Adams, Herbert Baxter (1850 – 1901). Academic (local government, education). 1876 professor at Johns Hopkins and editor of 'Johns Hopkins studies in Historical and Political Science'. 1844 organised American Historical Association under the auspices of the American Social Science Association.

Allen, William F. (1830 – 89). Educator (black education). Agent for Freedman's Bureau after civil war. 1868 founded Hampton Normal and Industrial Institute for Negroes, Va.

Angell, James B. (1827 – 1905). Academic and diplomat (Michigan state politics). 1871 – 1909 president of the University of Michigan, Ann Arbor. Spoke in inaugural May 1871 of the university as 'the highest positive office of promoting by all proper means the moral and intellectual growth of the citizens'.

Atherton, George Washington (1837 – 1906). Academic (education). Supporter of land grant colleges and federal aid for universities. 1882 – 1906 president of Pennsylvania State College.

Atkinson, Edward (1827 – 1905). Economist (finance and currency). 1878 president of Boston Manufacturers Mutual Fire Insurance Co. and inventor of 'Alladin oven'. 1887 appointed by Cleveland to report on bimetallism in Europe; supporter of free trade and sound money.

234

Baldwin, Simeon (1840 – 1927). Jurist, and governor of Connecticut 1911 – 13, 1913 – 15 (bar, state finance, and granger cases in particular). 1869 professor at Yale Law School. 1878 co-founder of American Bar Association and president 1890. Sat on New Haven Public Parks Commission and the New Haven Common Council. President of American Social Science Association (1897), International Law Association (1899), American Historical Association (1905), Political Science Association (1910). 'His conception of civic duty was Roman' (George Woodbine). Supported castration and whipping of criminals

Bigelow, John (1817 – 1911). Editor, diplomat, author. 1849 – 61 helped edit *New York Evening Post*. 1875 – 77 Secretary of State for New York. President of Board of trustees of New York Public Library, Metropolitan Museum of Art, Tilden Trust.

Bishop, Joseph Bucklin (1847 – 1928). Journalist (New York politics; extensive corrections to 1st ed.). 1870 – 83 editorial writer for *New York Evening Post*. 1920 *Theodore Roosevelt and his Times*.

Bowker, Richard Rogers (1848 – 1933). Editor and publisher (labour and Brooklyn politics). Called 'original mugwump'; 1880 founded Society for Political Education and led young 'scratchers' against Conkling. 1880 – 2 London representative of Harpers; trustee of Brooklyn Public Library and Institute of Arts and Science. 1886 *Civil Service Examinations*. 1889 *Electoral Reform*.

Brace, Charles Loring (1826 – 90). Author. 1851 imprisoned in Hungary for supporting Kossuth. Established Children's Aid Society providing work among immigrants, lodging homes, industrial and night schools. Friend of Mill, Darwin, Morley. 'He came of a pure Puritan New England Stock, the best qualities of which in youth and manhood he always proved himself to possess.'

Bradford, Gamaliel (1831 – 1911). Author and banker (state and municipal government). Met Bryce through J. B. Thayer and William James 1883. Abolitionist, advocate of civil service reform and city charters. 1878 member of Massachusetts Historical Society; 1898 *Popular Government*. Compulsive writer of letters to newspapers.

Brett, George P. (1858 – 1936). Publisher (publishing, copyright). 1869 to America to establish New York agency for Macmillan. 1900 helped establish American Publisher's Association.

Burgess, John William (1844 – 1931). Academic. 1876 – 1912 professor of Political Science and Constitutional Law, Columbia. 1880 established first American faculty of Political Science and edited *Political Science Quarterly*, disseminated by Bryce in Britain.

Canfield, James H. (1847 – 1909). Academic (civil service reform in the west). 1877 gave up bar for professorship at Kansas University; supporter of free trade and political reform, and protectionists failed to get him removed from post. 1886 – 9 secretary of the National Education Association. 1884 *History of Kansas*; 1889 *Local Government in Kansas*.

Carnegie, Andrew (1835 – 1919), Steel magnate and philanthropist. Born in Dunfermline. To US in 1848. Received freedom of fifty-four cities in Britain and Ireland. 1886 *Triumphant Democracy*. 1900 *The Gospel of Wealth*. Admired by Gladstone.

Chase, Thomas (1827 – 1900). Academic. 1875 – 86 president of Haverford College. Wrote to Bryce in 1881 — 'wherever you go our best people will be greatly obliged if you seek them out'.

Clark, Edward P. (1847 – 1903). Journalist (extensive corrections to 1st ed.). 1885 editorial writer for *New York Evening Post*.

Cooley, Thomas (1824 – 98). Jurist (constitutional matters). 1859 professor of Law at University of Michigan, Ann Arbor. 1887 – 91 chairman of the Interstate Commerce Commission. 1885 *Michigan: A History of Government*.

Dunbar, C.F. (1830 – 1900). Economist (state interventionism). 1871 – 1900 professor of Political Economy, Harvard; 1886 – 96 editor of *Quarterly Journal of Economics* the first dedicated wholly to economics in America. 1893 president of American Economic Association. Teacher of A. B. Houghton who provided tables for Bryce's chapter on 'Laissez Faire'.

Eggleston, Edward (1837 – 1902). Author. 1870 – 2 editor on *New York Independent*, president of Atlantic Society.

Eliot, Charles William (1834 – 1926). President of Harvard 1869 – 1909 (wide ranging political correspondence). Cousin of Theodore Lyman Jr, philanthropist and mayor of Boston. Introduced greater choice and depth in undergraduate studies by 'elective system'; encouraged women's education — 1894 Radcliffe established and in 1886 ended compulsory college chapel attendance. Political independent and professional optimist — 'He's the very highest type of a most limited and inspiring pork-chopism' (J. J. Chapman).

Ely, Richard (1854 – 1943). 1881 – 92 professor of Political Economics, Johns Hopkins where he attended Bryce's lectures. 1881 – 92 member of the Baltimore Tax Commission. 1886 – 8 member of Maryland Tax Commission.

Fisher, George Park (1827 – 1909). Academic (American religion and church affairs). 1861 – 1909 professor of Ecclesiastical History, Yale. Member of Century Club, New York.

Forbes, John Murray (1813 – 98). Railroad president (railroad management and politics). President of the Chicago, Burlington and Quincy Railroad Co. Member of the National Executive Committee of the Republican party. Bolter in 1884.

Garrison, Wendell Phillips (1840 – 1907). Journalist (general political commentary and provider of published material). 1865 – 1907 literary editor of *The New York Nation*.

Gilman, Daniel Coit (1881 – 1908). Academic (education). First president of Johns Hopkins 1875 – 1901; member of Commission to draft new charter for Baltimore. 1901 – 7 president of National Civil Service Reform League. Helped establish Sheffield Scientific School, New Haven, Purdue, and University of Illinois at Urbana. 1893 helped found Johns Hopkins Medical School. 1888 *University Problems*. 1899 Introduction to Tocqueville's *Democracy in America*. 1906 *Launching of a University*. A New York divine wrote when T. H. Huxley was invited to lecture at Johns Hopkins — 'It was bad enough to invite Huxley. It was better to have asked God to be present. It would have been absurd to ask them both.'

Gladden, Washington (1838 – 1918). Author, clergyman (politics in Ohio). 1871 – 4 on editorial staff of *Independent* and contributor to *Scribner's Magazine.* 1874 – 82 pastor of Springfield, Mass. 1882 – 1914 pastor, Columbus, Ohio. 1900 – 2 on Columbus City Council. Preacher of social gospel, and to Britain in 1898 to speak on Anglo-American friendship.

Godkin, Edwin Lawrence. (1831 – 1902). Journalist (general political commentary). Born in Ireland, his father had a literary pension for services to the home rule cause from the Gladstonian government. 1853 *History of Hungary and the Magyars* after visit to Kossuth. Settled in America in 1856. 1865 editor of *New York Nation,* and *New York Evening Post* when the two merged in 1882. Often brought to trial for libel by Tammany. Bryce and Dicey secured an Hon. DCL from Oxford for him in 1897. Returned to England to die.

Goodnow, Frank (1859 – 1939). Academic (Tweed ring and municipal government). 1883 – 1914 lecturer then professor at Columbia. 1900 on Commission to redraft Charter of New York City. Co-founder of American Political Science Association and first president 1903. 1893 *Comparative Administrative Law.* 1893 *Municipal Home Rule.* 1897 *Municipal Problems.*

Gurney, E.W. (1829 – 86). Academic (Massachusetts politics). 1869 – 86 professor of History at Harvard. 1868 – 70 Editor of *North American Review* with J. R. Lowell. Contributed to *New York Nation.* Brother-in-law of Henry Adams.

Hart, Albert Bushnell (1854 – 1943). Academic (advice on format of *A.C.*). Instructor in American History, Harvard.

Hay, John (1838 – 1905). Journalist, historian, diplomat (details on Lincoln). Private secretary to Lincoln along with Nicolay. 1878 settled in Washington; close friend of Henry Adams, Henry Cabot Lodge and Cecil Spring-Rice.

Higginson, Thomas Wentworth (1823 – 1911). Author, abolitionist, reformer (female suffrage and Eastern politics). 1880 – 1 sat in Massachusetts Legislature. Took it upon himself to rewrite Emily Dickinson's poems. 'He is the model of a life dedicated with high purpose to duty' (C. W. Eliot).

Hitchcock, Henry (1812 – 1902). Academic and lawyer. 1st dean of St Louis Law School. 1889 – 90 president of the American Bar Association. 1887 *American State Constitutions.*

Holmes, Oliver Wendell Jr (1841 – 1935). Jurist and 'lanky talker' (law in universities and general topics). 1870 – 3 co-editor of *American Law Review*; 1881 *The Common Law* praised by Bryce as 'unique . . . in its mixture of history and metaphysics . . . It really opens up a new and most curious field of enquiry'. 1882 professor at Harvard Law School. 1882 – 99 Associate Justice of the Massachusetts Supreme Court. 1902 – 32 Justice of the Supreme Court. Friend of Mill, Maine, Jowett, James and Leslie Stephen, Dicey, Pollock, Beatrice Webb.

James, William (1842 – 1910). 1872 instructor in Physiology at Harvard. 1880 assistant professor of Philosophy. Friend of Leslie Stephen, Pollock, Sidgwick.

Lea, Henry (1825 – 1909). Historian (Philadelphia politics). 1888 *A History of the Inquisition of the Middle Ages.* 1876 established Municipal Reform Association. President of the Reform Club and member of the committee of 100 in Philadelphia. Contributor to *Cambridge Modern History.*

Low, Seth (1850 – 1916). Educationalist, politician (municipal government). Started in father's tea importing house A. A. Low and Bros. 1880 president of Republican Campaign Club became 'Young Republican Club'. 1881 – 5 mayor of Brooklyn, introducing merit system into municipal service, and reform of public school system — 'I am not a Republican mayor . . . . I am a Mayor of the whole people of Brooklyn.' 1897 unsuccessful 'Citizen's Union' candidate for mayor of New York. 1890 – 1901 president of Columbia moving the campus to Morningside Heights and founding the Low Library. 1902 – 3 mayor of New York. Visited Britain in 1886 and met Bryce through Alfred T. White (q.v.)

Macy, Jesse (1842 – 1919). Academic (mid-west politics and rural populist movements). 1884 – 1912 professor of Political Science at Grinnell; dedicated to 'use every endeavour towards the attainment of a more righteous order in the state and in society'. First to teach civics through study of local government. 1881

Civil Government in Iowa. 1884 *Institutional Beginnings in a Western State.* 1886 *Our Government.*

Moses, Bernard (1846 – 1930). Academic (California politics and Kearneyism). 1876 professor of History at Berkeley, California. 1884 *Politics.* 1889 *The Federal Government in Switzerland.*

Norton, Charles Eliot (1827 – 1908). Patrician, man of letters. 1884 helped edit *North American Review* and in 1865 helped establish *Nation* with financial aid and written contributions. 1874 – 98 professor of the History of Art at Harvard. Cousin of C. W. Eliot. Friend of Browning, Ruskin, Carlyle, A. H. Clough, Leslie Stephen: 'He surely must have done a great deal towards making some of the best men in England and America appreciate one another' (Dicey).

Peabody, Endicott (1857 – 1944). Schoolmaster. Educated Cheltenham and Trinity College, Cambridge, 1884 – 1940 headmaster of Groton College.

Putnam, George Haven (1844 – 1930). Publisher and author (copyright questions). Born in England and stumped for Gladstone. 1866 succeeded to father's publishing business J. P. Putnam and Sons. 1886 established American Publishers Copyright League. Member of City Club and Citizen's Union of New York City, and Bureau of Municipal Research. Established American branch of English-Speaking Union.

Roosevelt, Theodore (1858 – 1919). 26th president of the US (state and municipal government, Civil Service Commission). 1882 – 4 member of New York Legislature. 1884 delegate at Republican National Convention. 1886 ran unsuccessfully for mayor New York against Abram Hewitt and Henry George; 1889 – 95 US Civil Service Commission. 1895 – 7 Police Commissioner of New York. 1897 – 8 Assistant Secretary of the Navy. 1889 *The Winning of the West.* 1886 *Life of Thomas Hart Benton.* 1887 *Life of Gouverneur Morris.*

Schurz, Carl (1829 – 1906). Writer and politician (the independent movement and the Senate). Born in Germany and involved in 1848 revolution. 1852 to America. 1869 – 75 US senator for Missouri. 1872 helped organise independents and presided over Cincinnati Convention. 1879 – 81 Secretary of Interior under

Hayes. 1881 – 4 editor of *New York Evening Post*; again leading independent in 1884; 'he was sincerely devoted to good causes, honest and high minded' (Bryce).

Scudder, Horace (1838 – 1902). Editor and writer. Editor with Riverside Press, later Houghton, Mifflin and Co. 1886 – 1902 editor of 'American Commonwealths' series.

Sedgwick, Arthur G. (1844 – 1915). Author and lawyer (information on Erie Ring). 1872 practised law in Boston and edited *American Law Quarterly* with Holmes. After 1875 on New York Bar. 1872 – 1905 on editorial staff of *New York Evening Post* and *Nation*. 1909 delivered Godkin Lectures. 1912 *The Democratic Mistake*. Brother-in-law of C. E. Norton.

Shaw, Albert (1857 – 1947). Journalist and academic (state intervention and machine politics in mid-west). 1879 graduated from Grinnell; 1884 Ph.D. from Johns Hopkins. 1888 – 9 study in Europe and assisting Bryce with proof reading of *A.C.* 1883 – 8 editor of *Minneapolis Tribune*. 1889 – 90 professor of Political Institutions, Cornell. 1891 established *American Review of Reviews*. 1883 *Local Government in Illinois*. 1888 *Cooperation in the North West*. 1894 *Municipal Government in Great Britain*.

Stanton, Theodore (1835 – 1925). Author and publisher. European agent for *North American Review*, Harpers, Appleton, Holt.

Thayer, James Bradley (1831 – 1902). Lawyer and academic (state constitutions, municipal government and rural New England political life). 1874 – 1902 professor of Law at Harvard. Wrote regularly for *Nation* and *Atlantic Monthly*. Authority on American Constitutional Law — 'not made to be codes of laws, or to embody the opinion of a momentary majority'. Urged tariff reform and granting of corporate franchises.

Villard, Henry (1835 – 1900). Journalist and financier (railroad politics). 1881 president of Northern Pacific Railroad. 1881 purchased *New York Evening Post*. Father of Oswald Garrison Villard (1872 – 1949), editor of *New York Evening Post* (1897 – 1918) and *Nation* (1918 – 32).

White, Alfred T. (1846 – 1921). Pioneering in housing reform. 1878 Committee of Brooklyn Bureau of Charities, Children's Aid

Society. 1893 Commissioner of Public Works, Brooklyn. Political independent.

White, Andrew Dickson (1832 – 1918). Educationalist and diplomat (higher education and general political commentary). Joint founder and first president of Cornell; established its school of History and Political Science and lured Goldwin Smith into a professorship. Opened Cornell to 'persons of every religious denomination, or of no religious denomination'.

Wilson, Thomas Woodrow (1856 – 1924). 28th president of the US (congress). 1879 graduated from Princeton and published 'Cabinet Government in the U.S.' in *International Review*. 1882 – 6 graduate student at Johns Hopkins where he was inspired by Bryce's lectures. 1885 – 8 associate professor, Bryn Mawr. 1880 – 90 professor, Wesleyan. 1890 to Princeton as professor, 1885 *Congressional Government*. 1889 *The State*. 'We have many common friends at Johns Hopkins . . . and know your *Congressional Government* so well and value it so highly that I seem to know you.' (Bryce). Beatrice Webb called him 'a young John Morley'.

Facsimile of table from chapter 91, 'Laissez Faire'

V. RAILROADS.

	United Kingdom	Massachusetts	Pennsylvania	Illinois	New York	Georgia	California	United States
1. Board of Railroad Commissioners	*	*	a	* b	*	*	*	* c
2. Powers of Board.								
α. Judicial		* d						
β. To correct abuses, e.g. extortion, etc.,		* e	* f		g		* h	* i
γ. To regulate charges		* k		* l	m	* n	* o	* p
δ. To inspect accounts	* q		r	* s	s	* t		* w
ε. To decide as to the construction of new roads	y							

Notes.—*a.* No board of railroad commissioners. *b.* The board is given certain powers for the regulation and inspection of public warehouses for grain. *c.* Inter-State Commerce Act of 1887. The board consists of five commissioners, with six years' term, and $7500 salary. The powers of the board apply to routes by rail, or by water and rail, extending from one State to another, or to a foreign country; but not to routes lying wholly within one State. Penalties are prescribed for breach of law, and the board is to see to their enforcement. Persons aggrieved may sue for damages, or complain to the board, which can institute proceedings in the United States courts if, on examination, it finds the complaints sustained. *d.* The board is given power to decide in certain disputes, and in certain matters relative to the construction of railroads. *e.* In case of abuse, the board is to complain to company and, if complaint is not heeded, to request the attorney-general to institute proceedings against such company. Whether or not such suit shall be brought rests with the attorney-general. *f.* The State prohibits discrimination, unequal concessions in rates and drawbacks, and undue discrimination between individuals and companies. *g.* The State prescribes that companies undertaking to transport immigrants must have registered rates of fare, and also that tickets may be sold to immigrants only in places appointed by the committee of immigration. *h.* If rates or fares are lowered for competitive purposes, they cannot again be raised without consent of the govern-

mental authority in which is vested the power to regulate rates and fares. *i.* All charges must be "reasonable and just"; no discrimination is to be allowed between individuals for similar service. *k.* Rates and fares may be fixed by the general court, or by officials appointed by it. Every corporation whose road runs out of Boston must have cheap morning and evening trains at such hours as shall be fixed by the board. The State prescribes the maximum limits for fares on such trains. *l.* The board fixes maximum limits for fares and rates. *m.* The legislature may reduce the fares, rates, or other profits of any railroad built after 1844, provided that these, unless by consent of the railroad company, be not so reduced as to produce, with the said profits, less than 10 per cent on the capital actually invested, nor unless it is ascertained that the company has from all sources a net income of more than 10 per cent. *n.* The maximum rates and fares are fixed by the board; but the board cannot in any way abridge or control the rates and fares charged by companies carrying goods or passengers at less than local charges either beyond, or from beyond within, the boundaries of the State. *o.* The board fixes rates and fares. *p.* It is forbidden to charge more for a shorter distance than a longer distance in the same direction, if the shorter distance is included in the longer, and the other conditions similar. No "pooling of freights" is allowed. *q.* The companies must furnish the Board of Trade with returns of capital, traffic, and working expenses, also with notice of accidents. *r.* The State prescribes a blank form in which companies must fill out their annual report. *s.* The board prescribes a blank form in which companies must fill out their annual report. *t.* All contracts between companies concerning rates of freight and passenger traffic, and all agreements between companies within the State concerning the division of earnings must receive the approval of the board before becoming valid. *u.* All tariffs and agreements must be filed with the board. *w.* Schedules of rates and fares must be printed and posted; and the same may not be reduced without ten days' notice. *y.* This function is partly discharged by the committees of both Houses of Parliament before which railway bills go, and partly by the Board of Trade, the ultimate decision of course resting with Parliament.

Select Bibliography

Bryce

(Bryce's own publications are listed in order of appearance.)

Manuscript collections
Bryce Papers, Bodleian Library, Oxford

Books
The Holy Roman Empire, London, 1876 (first edition, 1864).
The American Commonwealth, London, 1889 (first edition, 1888).
Impressions of South Africa, London, 1899 (first edition, 1897).
Studies in History and Jurisprudence, 2 vols., Oxford, 1901.
Studies in Contemporary Biography, London, 1903.
The Hindrances to Good Citizenship, Yale, 1909.
South America: Observations and Impressions, London, 1912.
University and Historical Addresses, London, 1921.
Modern Democracies, 2 vols., London, 1921.
International Relations, London, 1922.
Memories of Travel, London, 1923.

Articles and pamphlets
'Tests in the English Universities', *North British Review*, March 1865.
'The Worth of Educational Endowments', *Macmillan's*, April 1869.
'The Legal Profession in America', *Macmillan's*, January 1872.
'American Judges', *Macmillan's*, February 1872.
Contributions to the *New York Nation*, 1875 – 1910 (288 contributions). (*The Nation: Index of Titles and Contributors, 1865 – 1917*, ed. by D. C. Haskell, New York, 1951.)
'A Glimpse of the United States', *Cornhill*, October 1882.
'Some Aspects of American Public Life', *Fortnightly Review*, October 1882.

'The Future of the English Universities', *Fortnightly Review*, March 1883.

'An Ideal University', *Contemporary Review*, June 1884.

'England and Ireland: An Introductory Statement' (Committee on Irish Affairs), 1884.

'Do We need a Second Chamber?', *Contemporary Review*, November 1884.

'Prefactory Note', *English Historical Review*, January 1886.

How We became Home Rulers', *Contemporary Review*, May 1887.

'A Word as to the Speakership', *North American Review*, October 1890.

'An Age of Discontent', *Contemporary Review*, January 1891.

'Edward Augustus Freeman', *English Historical Review*, Vol. 7, 1892.

'Political Organisations in the United States and England', *North American Review*, January 1893.

'The Teaching of Civic Duty', *Contemporary Review*, July 1893.

'Legal Studies in the University of Oxford', London, 1896.

'British Feeling on the Venezuelan Question', *North American Review*, CLXII, No. 471, 1896.

'The Mayoralty Election in New York', *Contemporary Review*, Vol. 72, 1897.

'The Essential Unity of Britain and America', *Atlantic Monthly*, July 1898.

'British Experience in the Government of Colonies', *Century Magazine*, December 1898.

'The Relations of the Advanced and the Backward Nations of Mankind', *Romanes Lecture*, Oxford, 1902.

'Some Reflections on the State of Cuba', *North American Review*, Vol. 174, 1902.

'Lord Acton', *North American Review*, May 1904.

'Henry Sidgwick', *Proceedings of the British Academy*, 1903 – 4.

'Lord Acton', *Proceedings of the British Academy*, 1903 – 4.

'American Revisited', *Outlook*, March/April 1905.

'The Study of Popular Governments', *Quarterly Review*, July/October 1905.

'The Teaching of History in Schools', *Historical Association*, February 1907.

'Speech to Pilgrims' Dinner', 23 March 1907.

'Some Difficulties in Colonial Government Encountered by Great Britain', *Annals of the American Academy of Political and Social Science*, July 1907.

'What is Progress?', *Harvard Graduate Magazine*, September 1907.

'The Methods and Conditions of Legislation', *New York State Bar Association*, January 1908.

'The Relations of Political Science to History and to Practice', Address to *The American Political Science Association*, 28 January 1908.

'Speech at Governor's Conference', Washington, DC, May 1908.

'The Government of British Cities', *City Club of New York*, 8 March 1911.

'The Function of a University', *University of Adelaide*, 19 July 1912.

'Presidential Addresses to the British Academy', *Proceedings of the British Academy*, 1913 – 14, 1915 – 16, 1917 – 18.

'Speech to Pilgrims' Dinner', 25 April 1913.

'Speech', *American Academy of Political Science*, April 1913.

'Goldwin Smith', *North American Review*, Vol. 199, 1914.

'Race Sentiment as a Factor in History', *Creighton Lecture*, 22 February 1915.

'The International Crisis', Oxford, 1916.

'War and Human Progress', *Huxley Lecture*, Birmingham, 1916.

'World History', Raleigh Lecture, *Proceedings of the British Academy*, 1919 – 20.

'The Study of American History', Cambridge, 1921.

Introductions or contributions

Conrad, Dr J., *The German Universities for the Last Fifty Years*, Glasgow, 1885.

Bryce, James (ed.), *Handbook of Home Rule*, London, 1887.

Macdonnell, G. P. (ed.), *Two Centuries of Irish History, 1691 – 1870*, London, 1888.

Sigerson, George, *Political Prisoners at Home and Abroad*, London, 1890.

Helmot, H. F., *The World's History*, 2 vols., London, 1901.

Ostrogorski, M., *Democracy and the Organisation of Political Parties*, 2 vols., London, 1902.

Paul, Herbert (ed.), Introduction to Leslie Stephen's *Essays on Free Thinking and Plain Speaking*, London, 1907.

Bassett, A. T., *Life of the Rt. Hon. John E. Ellis*, London, 1914.

—— *Germany's War Mania*, London, 1914.

Toynbee, A. J., *The Armenian Atrocities: The Murder of a Nation*, London, 1915.

—— *The Treatment of Armenians in the Ottoman Empire*, London, 1916.

Bassett, A. T. (ed.), *Gladstone's Speeches*, London, 1916.
—— *The War of Democracy*, New York, 1917.
—— *Proposals for the Prevention of Future Wars*, London, 1917.
—— *The League of Nations*, Oxford, 1919.

Major reviews of 'The American Commonealth'
Acton, Lord, *English Historical Review*, April 1889.
Dicey, A. V., *Edinburgh Review*, April 1889.
Eggleston, Edward, *The Century Magazine*, Vol. 15, 1889.
Freeman, E. A., *Manchester Guardian*, 26 February 1889.
Holst, Herman von, *The Nation*, 24 April 1890.
James, Edmund, *The American Academy of Political and Social Science*, No. 172, 1896.
Phelps, Edward J., *Quarterly Review*, July 1889.
Scudder, Horace, *The Atlantic Monthly*, March 1889.
Smith, Goldwin, *Macmillan's*, February 1889.
Wilson, Woodrow, *Political Science Quarterly*, March 1889.

Material on the life of Bryce
Eliot, C. W., 'James Bryce', *Proceedings of the Massachusetts Historical Society*, Vol. 55, 1921–2.
Fisher, H. A. L., *James Bryce, Viscount Bryce of Dechmont*, 2 vols., London, 1927.
Gardiner, A. G., *Pillars of Society*, London, 1916.
Gooch, G. P., 'Lord Bryce', *Contemporary Review*, Vol. 121, 1922.
Ions, Edmund, *James Bryce and American Democracy*, London, 1968.
Laqueur, Walter, and Mosse, George L., *Historians in Politics* (essay by Keith Robbins), London, 1974.
Lefcowitz, Allan B., and Barbara F., 'James Bryce's First Visit to America', *New England Quarterly*, June 1977.
Lowell, A. L., 'James Bryce', *Proceedings of the Massachusetts Historical Society*, Vol. 55, 1921–2.
McCarthy, Justin, *British Political Portraits*, New York, 1903.
Murray, Gilbert, *A Conversation with Bryce*, Oxford, 1944.
Percy, Eustace, *Some Memories*, London, 1958.
Rhodes, James Ford, 'James Bryce', *Proceedings of the Massachusetts Historical Society*, Vol. 55, 1921–2.
Robbins, Keith, 'Lord Bryce and the First World War', *Historical Journal*, Vol. 10, No. 2, 1967.
Salter, Arthur, *Personalities in Politics*, London, 1947.
Toynbee, Arnold, *Acquaintances*, Oxford, 1967.

Contemporary authors and their works

Manuscript collections

Lord Acton, University Library, Cambridge.
Charles Francis Adams Jr, Massachusetts Historical Society, Boston.
Henry Adams, Massachusetts Historical Society, Boston.
Herbert Baxter Adams, Eisenhower Library, Johns Hopkins.
Simeon Baldwin, Sterling Library, Yale.
A. J. Balfour, British Library.
Hiram Bingham, Sterling Library, Yale.
Joseph Bucklin Bishop, Houghton Library, Harvard.
R. R. Bowker, New York Public Library.
Gamaliel Bradford, Massachusetts Historical Society, Boston.
George P. Brett (*Macmillan's* of New York), New York Public Library.
John William Burgess, Butler Library, Columbia.
Nicholas Murray Butler, Butler Library, Columbia.
Henry Campbell-Bannerman, British Library.
Andrew Carnegie, Library of Congress.
Joseph Hodges Choate, Library of Congress.
William Archibald Dunning, Butler Library, Columbia.
Charels William Eliot, Pusey Library, Harvard.
H. A. L. Fisher, Bodleian Library, Oxford.
James R. Garfield, Library of Congress.
W. P. Garrison, Houghton Library, Harvard.
Richard Watson Gilder ('Century Collection'), New York Public Library.
Daniel Coit Gilman, Eisenhower Library, Johns Hopkins.
Herbert Gladstone, British Library.
W. E. Gladstone, British Library.
E. L. Godkin, Houghton Library, Harvard.
Frank J. Goodnow (Tweed Ring Papers), Eisenhower Library, Johns Hopkins.
Lord Hardinge, Cambridge University Library.
John Hay, Library of Congress.
Thomas Wentworth Higginson, Houghton Library, Harvard.
Oliver Wendell Holmes, Jr, Harvard Law Library.
Edward House, Sterling Library, Yale.
Seth Low, Butler Library, Columbia.
Lowell Institute Papers, Houghton Library, Harvard.
A. L. Lowell, Pusey Library, Harvard.
Henry Sumner Maine, London School of Economics.

John Bassett Moore, Library of Congress.
Bernard Moses, Bancroft Library, Berkeley.
Charles Eliot Norton, Houghton Library, Harvard.
James Ford Rhodes, Massachusetts Historical Society, Boston.
Theodore Roosevelt, Library of Congress.
Theodore Roosevelt, Widener Library, Harvard.
Carl Schurz, Library of Congress.
Edwin Seligman, Butler Library, Columbia.
Albert Shaw, Butler Library, Columbia.
Albert Shaw, New York Public Library.
John St Loe Strachey, House of Lords' Record Office.
WIlliam Howard Taft, Library of Congress.
William Roscoe Thayer, Houghton Library, Harvard.
Henry Villard, Houghton Library, Harvard.
Henry White, Library of Congress.
Woodrow Wilson, Library of Congress.

Journals, letters and biographies

Acton, Lord, 'American Diaries', *Fortnightly Review*, 1 November 1921, 2 January 1922.
Adams, Charles Francis Jr, *Autobiography*, Boston, 1916.
Adams, Henry Brooks, *The Education of Henry Adams*, London, 1928.
Armstrong, William M., *The Gilded Age Letters of E. L. Godkin*, Albany, 1974.
Asquith, H. H., *Memories and Reflections*, 2 vols., London, 1928.
Bahlman, Dudley (ed.), *The Diary of Sir Edward Hamilton, 1880 – 1885*, 2 vols., Oxford, 1972.
Brodrick, Hon. George C., *Memories and Impressions, 1831 – 1900*, London, 1900.
Buckle, J.E., *Letters of Queen Victoria*, Third Series, London, 1931.
Chapman, John Jay, *Memories and Milestones*, New York, 1915.
Drew, Mary, *Acton, Gladstone and Others*, London, 1924.
Edel, Leon, *Life of Henry James*, 5 vols., London, 1953 – 72.
—— (ed.), *The Diary of Alice James*, London, 1965.
Elliot, Hugh, *Letters of John Stuart Mill*, 2 vols., London, 1910.
Figgis, J. N., and Laurence, R. V. (eds.), *Selections from the Correspondence of the First Lord Acton*, London, 1917.
Fisher, H. A. L., *An Unfinished Autobiography*, Oxford, 1940.
Ford, Worthington C. (ed.), *A Cycle of Adams Letters, 1861 – 1865*, 2 vols., Boston and New York, 1920.
Garvin, J. L., *The Life of Joseph Chamberlain*, Vols. 1 and 2, London, 1932 and 1933.

Grant, A. R. C., and Combe, Caroline, *Lord Rosebery's North American Journal, 1873*, London, 1967.

Harrison, Frederic, *Memories and Thoughts*, London, 1906.

—— *Autobiographic Memoirs*, London, 1911.

Haultain, Arnold (ed.), *Goldwin Smith: Reminiscences*, London, 1910.

—— *Goldwin Smith: His Life and Opinions*, London, 1913.

—— *A Selection from Goldwin Smith's Correspondence*, London, 1913.

Henson, H. H. *A Memoir of the Rt. Hon. Sir William Anson*, Oxford, 1920.

Howe, Mark de Wolfe (ed.), *The Pollock-Holmes Letters*, 2 vols., Cambridge, 1942.

—— *The Holmes-Laski Letters*, 2 vols., London, 1953.

James, Henry, *Charles William Eliot*, 2 vols., Boston and New York, 1930.

Knight, William A., *Memoirs of John Nichol*, Glasgow, 1896.

Lecky, Mrs. *A Memoir of the Rt. Hon. William Edward Hartpole Lecky*, London, 1909.

Link, Arthur (ed.), *The Papers of Woodrow Wilson*, Princeton, 1967 – .

McCarthy, Justin, *Portrait of the Sixties*, London, 1903.

Martin, Robert B. (ed.), *The Dust of Combat*, London, 1959.

Maitland, F. W., *The Life and Letters of Leslie Stephen*, London, 1906.

Mineka, F. E., and Lindley, D. N., *The Later Letters of John Stuart Mill, 1849 – 1873*, 4 vols., Toronto, 1973.

Morison, Elting (ed.), *The Letters of Theodore Roosevelt*, 8 vols., Harvard, 1951 – 4.

Morley, John, *Recollections*, London, 1917.

—— *The Life of W. E. Gladstone*, 3 vols., London, 1911.

Neilson, William A., *C. W. Eliot: The Man and his Beliefs*, 2 vols., London, 1926.

Norton, Charles Eliot (ed.), *The Letters of James Russell Lowell*, 2 vols., London, 1894.

Ogden, Rollo (ed.), *The Life and Letters of Edwin Lawrence Godkin*, 2 vols., New York, 1907.

Paul, Herbert, *The Life of J. A. Froude*, London, 1905.

—— (ed.), *The Letters of Lord Acton to Mary, daughter of the Rt. Hon. W. E. Gladstone*, London, 1913.

Pollock, Sir Frederick, *For my Grandson*, London, 1933.

Rait, Robert, *Memorials of Albert Venn Dicey*, London, 1925.

Ramm, Agatha (ed.), *The Political Correspondence of Mr. Gladstone*

and Lord Granville, 1868 – 1876, 2 vols., London, 1952.
—— *The Correspondence of Mr. Gladstone and Lord Granville, 1876 – 1886*, 2 vols., Oxford, 1962.
Rendal, Lord, *The Personal Papers of Lord Rendal*, London, 1931.
Russell, George W. E., *Letters of Matthew Arnold, 1848 – 1888*, 2 vols., London, 1901.
Seymour, Charles (ed.), *The Intimate Papers of Colonel House*, 4 vols., London, 1926.
Shannon, David A. (ed.), *Beatrice's Webb's American Diary, 1898*, Madison, 1963.
Sidgwick, A. S., and E., *Henry Sidgwick: A Memoir*, London, 1906.
Stephen, Leslie (ed.), *Letters of J. R. Green*, London, 1901.
—— *Some Early Impressions*, London, 1924.
Stephens, W. R. W., *The Life and Letters of Edward A. Freeman*, 2 vols., London, 1895.
Trevelyan, Charles Philip, *Letters from North America and the Pacific*, London, 1969.

Books

Acton, Lord, *Essays on Church and State* (ed. by Douglas Woodruff), London, 1952.
—— *The History of Freedom and Other Essays* (ed. by J. N. Figgis and R. V. Laurence), London, 1907.
—— *Historical Essays and Studies* (ed. by J. N. Figgis and R. V. Laurence), London, 1907.
—— *Lectures on the French Revolution* (ed. by J. N. Figgis and R. V. Laurence), London, 1910.
—— *Essays on Freedom and Power* (ed. by Gertrude Himmelfarb), London, 1956.
—— *Lectures on Modern History*, London, 1960.
Adams, Henry, *Democracy*, New York, 1961.
Anson, Sir William, *The Law and Custom of the Constitution*, 3 vols., Oxford, 1922.
Bagehot, Walter, *The English Constitution*, Fontana, London, 1968.
Barrington, Mrs Russell, *The Works and Life of Walter Bagehot*, London, 1915.
Blaine, James G., *Twenty Years of Congress*, 2 vols., Norwich, Connecticut, 1886.
Brodrick, Hon. George G., *Liberal Principles*, London, 1877.
—— *Political Studies*, London, 1879.

Burgon, J. W., *The Disestablishment of Religion in Oxford*, London, 1880.

Dicey, Albert Venn, *England's Case against Home Rule*, London, 1886.

—— *Introduction to the Study of the Law of the Constitution*, London, 1902 and 1923.

—— *Law and Public Opinion in England during the Nineteenth Century*, London, 1963.

Dilke, Sir Charles, *Greater Britain*, London, 1885.

Eliot, C. W., *American Contributions to Civilisation and Other Essays and Addresses*, London, 1897.

Freeman, E. A., *Historical Essays*, London, 1872.

—— *The Growth of the English Constitution*, London, 1873.

—— *Comparative Politics*, London, 1873.

—— *Lectures to American Audiences*, Philadelphia and London, 1882.

—— *Some Impressions of the United States*, London, 1883.

—— *History of Federal Government in Greece and Italy*, London, 1893.

Froude, J. A., *Oceana*, London, 1886.

—— *Short Studies on Great Subjects*, 5 vols., London, 1907.

Godkin, E. L., *Reflections and Comments*, London and New York, 1896.

—— *Problems of Modern Democracy*, New York, 1896.

—— *Unforeseen Tendencies of Democracy*, London, 1903.

Griffin, Sir Lepel Henry, *The Great Republic*, New York, 1884.

Guttsman, W. L. (ed.), *A Plea for Democracy*, London, 1967.

Lecky, W. E. H., *Democracy and Liberty*, 2 vols., New York, 1913.

Lowell, A. L., *The Government of England*, 2 vols., New York, 1912.

Lowell, J.R., *Literary and Political Addresses*, Boston, 1891.

Lucy, Henry W., *East by West: A Journey in the Recess*, London, 1885.

Maine, Sir Henry Sumner, *Popular Government*, London, 1909.

Mill, John Stuart, *Dissertations and Discussions*, Vol. 3, London, 1875.

—— *On Liberty*, Oxford, 1940.

—— *Autobiography*, Oxford, 1940.

—— *Considerations on Representative Government*, New York, 1956.

—— *Essays on Politics and Culture* (ed. by Gertrude Himmelfarb), New York, 1963.

Morley, John, *Critical Miscellanies*, Vol. 3, London, 1886.

—— *Oracles on Man and Government*, London, 1921.
Nichol, John, *The Political Life of Our Time*, 2 vols., London, 1889.
Pattison, Mark, *Memoirs*, London, 1885.
Rhodes, James Ford, *Historical Essays*, New York, 1909.
—— *History of the United States*, Vol. 6, New York, 1928.
—— *History of the United States*, Vol. 9, New York, 1929.
Roosevelt, Theodore, *New York*, London, 1891.
Salisbury, Lord, *Lord Salisbury on Politics* (ed. by Paul Smith), Cambridge, 1972.
Seeley, Sir J. R., *The Expansion of England*, London, 1883.
Sidgwick, Henry, *The Elements of Politics*, London, 1891.
—— *The Development of European Polity*, London, 1903.
—— *Essays and Addresses*, London, 1903.
Smalley, George W., *London Letters and Some Others*, 2 vols., London, 1890.
Smith, Goldwin, *The Foundation of the American Colonies*, Oxford, 1861.
—— *Letter to a Whig Member of the Southern Independence Association*, London, 1864.
—— *The Civil War in America*, London, 1866.
—— *Questions of the Day: Political and Social*, New York, 1893.
—— *My Memory of Gladstone*, London, 1904.
Stephen, James Fitzjames, *Essays by a Barrister*, London, 1862.
—— *Horae Sabbaticae*, 3 vols., London, 1892.
—— *Liberty, Equality, Fraternity* (ed. by R. J. White), Cambridge, 1967.
Stephen, Leslie, *'The Times' and the American War*, London, 1865.
—— *Sketches from Cambridge by a Don*, London and Cambridge, 1865.
—— *The Life of James Fitzjames Stephen*, London, 1895.
—— *Social Rights and Duties*, 2 vols., London, 1896.
Stevas, Norman St John, *The Collected Works of Walter Bagehot*, Vols. 4, 6 and 8, London, 1968–74.
Tocqueville, Alexis de, *Democracy in America* (ed. by Phillips, Bradley), 2 vols., New York, 1945.
—— *Journey to America* (ed. by J. P. Mayer), London, 1959.
Wilson, Woodrow, *Congressional Government*, Boston, 1900.

Articles and pamphlets
Adams, Charles Francis Jr, 'Reflex Light from America', *Century Magazine*, May 1906.
—— *The Solid South*, Boston, 1908.
—— *Tis Sixty Years Since*, New York, 1913.

Anson, Sir William, 'The Government of Ireland Bill and the Sovereignty of Parliament', *Law Quarterly Review*, October 1886.

—— 'Objections of an Oxford Liberal to Home Rule', *National Review*, March – August 1887.

Arnold, Matthew, 'A Word about America', *Nineteenth Century*, May 1882.

—— 'A Word More about America', *Nineteenth Century*, February 1885.

—— 'Civilisation in the United States', *Nineteenth Century*, April 1888.

Bagehot, Walter, 'The American Constitution at the Present Crisis', *National Review*, October 1861.

Brodrick, Hon. George G., 'The Universities and the Nation', *Contemporary Review*, June 1875.

Chamberlain, D. H., 'Reconstruction and the Negro', *North American Review*, February 1879.

Chamberlain, Joseph, 'A New Political Organisation', *Fortnightly Review*, July 1877.

—— 'The Caucus', *Fortnightly Review*, November 1878.

Dicey, Albert Venn, Contributions to the *New York Nation*.

—— 'Judicial Policy', *Macmillan's Magazine*, April 1874.

—— 'How is the Law to be Enforced in Ireland?', *Fortnightly Review*, November 1881.

—— 'Home Rule from an English Point of View', *Contemporary Review*, July 1881.

—— 'Federal Government', *Law Quarterly Review*, January 1885.

—— 'New Jacobinism and Old Morality', *Contemporary Review*, April 1888.

—— 'Ought the Referendum to be Introduced into England?', *Contemporary Review*, April 1890.

—— 'The Defence of the Union', *Contemporary Review*, March 1892.

—— 'Alexis de Tocqueville', *National Review*, Vol. 21, 1893.

—— 'The Referendum', *National Review*, March 1894.

—— 'A Common Citizenship for the English Race', *Contemporary Review*, April 1897.

—— 'The Teaching of English Law at Harvard', *Contemporary Review*, November 1899.

Dicey, Edward, Contributions to the *New York Nation*.

—— 'Common Sense and Venezuela', *Nineteenth Century*, January 1896.

—— 'The New American Imperialism', *Nineteenth Century*, September 1898.

Eliot, G. W., 'English and American Universities Compared', *North American Review*, March – April 1878.

—— 'Charles Francis Adams Jr', *Proceedings of the Massachusetts Historical Society*, April 1915.

Freeman, E. A., 'Reform of the House of Lords', *Contemporary Review*, October 1884.

—— 'Disestablishment and disendowment: What Are They?', reprinted from *The Pall Mall Gazette*, London, 1907.

Garrison, Wendell Phillips, Contributions to the *New York Nation*.

Gladstone, W. E., 'England's Mission', *Nineteenth Century*, September 1878.

—— 'Kin beyond Sea', *North American Review*, September – October 1878.

—— 'An Olive Branch from America', *Nineteenth Century*, November 1887.

—— 'Universitus Hominum', *North American Review*, December 1887.

—— 'Mr Carnegie's "Gospel of Wealth" ', *Nineteenth Century*, November 1890.

Godkin, E. L., Contributions to the *New York Nation*.

—— 'An American View of Ireland', *Nineteenth Century*, August 1882.

—— 'An American Opinion on the Irish Question', *Nineteenth Century*, August 1887.

Green, J. R., 'Review of "Essays on Reform" ', *Saturday Review*, 6 April 1867.

Lowe, Robert, 'Reform Essays', *Quarterly Review*, July 1867.

Maine, Sir Henry Sumner, 'Mr. Godkin on Popular Government', *Nineteenth Century*, March 1886.

—— Contributions to *The Saturday Review*.

Morley, John, 'Young England and the Political Future', *Fortnightly Review*, April 1867.

—— 'The Government of Ireland: A Reply', *Nineteenth Century*, January 1887.

Norton, Charles Eliot, 'Tocqueville', *Atlantic Monthly*, November 1861.

Pollock, Frederick, 'A Fresh Puzzle of Home Rule', *National Review*, Vol. 21, 1893.

Rhodes, James Ford, 'Some Recent Impressions of England', *Proceedings of The Massachusetts Historical Society*, 1900.

Salisbury, Lord, 'Democracy on Trial', *Quarterly Review*, July 1861.
—— 'The Confererate Struggle and Recognition', *Quarterly Review*, October 1862.
—— 'The United States as an Example', *Quarterly Review*, January 1865.
—— Contributions to *The Saturday Review*.
Schurz, Carl, 'Manifest Destiny', *Harpers Monthly*, October 1893.
—— 'The Anglo-American Friendship', *Atlantic Monthly*, October 1898.
Shaw, Albert, 'An American View, of Home Rule and Federation', *Contemporary Review*, September 1892.
—— 'Mr. Bryce's New Chapters on Current American Questions', *Review of Reviews*, Vol. 11, 1895.
Sidgwick, Henry, 'Alexis de Tocqueville', *Macmillan's Magazine*, November 1861.
Smith, Goldwin, 'Has England an Interest in the Disruption of the Union?', *Macmillan's*, May 1864.
—— 'England and America', *Atlantic Monthly*, December 1864.
—— 'The Danger of War with America', *Macmillan's*, April 1865.
—— 'The Death of President Lincoln', *Macmillan's*, June 1765.
—— 'The Case of the "Alabama" ', *Macmillan's*, December 1865.
—— *America and England and their Present Relations*, London, 1869.
—— 'A Word More about the Presidential Election', *Macmillan's*, March 1877.
—— 'The Decline of Party Government', *Macmillan's*, August 1877.
—— 'The South since the Civil War', *Contemporary Review*, November 1883.
—— 'The Expansion of England', *Contemporary Review*, April 1884.
—— 'The Conflict with the House of Lords', *Contemporary Review*, Vol. 46, 1884.
—— 'The Organisation of Democracy', *Contemporary Review*, March 1885.
—— 'England Revisited', *Macmillan's*, October 1886.
—— *The Schism in the Anglo-Saxon Race*, New York, 1887.,
—— 'If Christ came to Chicago', *Contemporary Review*, September 1894.

—— 'The Manchester School', *Contemporary Review*, March 1895.
—— 'Reform the House of Lords', *Contemporary Review*, April 1897.
—— 'Imperialism in the United States', *Contemporary Review*, May 1899.
—— 'England and the War of Secession', *Atlantic Monthly*, Vol. 89, 1902.
—— *The Early Days of Cornell*, Ithaca, 1904.
—— 'Froude', *Atlantic Monthly*, Man, 1906.
Spencer, Herbert, 'On the United States', *Pall Mall Gazette*, 31 October 1882.
Stephen, James Fitzjames, Contributions to *The Saturday Review*.
—— 'The Dissolution of the Union', *Cornhill*, August 1861.
—— 'Liberalism', *Cornhill*, Vol. 5, 1862.
—— 'Parliamentary Government', *Contemporary Review*, December 1873 and January 1874.
Stephen, Leslie, 'Reform', *Macmillan's*, April 1867.
—— 'The Political Stiuation in England', *North American Review*, October 1868.
—— 'Our Rulers: Public Opinion', *Cornhill*, March 1870.
—— 'Thoughts of an Outsider: International Prejudices', *Cornhill*, July 1876.
—— Contributions to the *New York Nation*.

The Nation: Index of Titles and Contributors, 1865 – 1917, ed. by D. C. Haskell, New York, 1951.
The Saturday Review, 1855 – 1868: Representative Educated Opinion in Victorian England, ed. by M. M. Bevington, New York, 1941.

Secondary Sources

Books

Adams, E. D., *Great Britain and the American Civil War*, London, 1925.
Alexander, Edward, *Matthew Arnold and John Stuart Mill*, London, 1965.
Allen, H. C., *Britain and the United States*, London, 1954.
Annan, Nöel, *Leslie Stephen*, London, 1951.
Armstrong, William M., *E. L. Godkin: A Biography*, Albany, 1978.

Barker, Ernest, *Political Thought in England from Herbert Spencer to the Present Day*, London, 1927.

Beer, Samuel, *Modern British Politics*, London, 1965.

Bellot, H. Hale, *American History and American Historians*, London, 1952.

Beloff, Max, *The Great Powers*, London, 1959.

Bentley, Michael, *The Liberal Mind, 1914–1929*, Cambridge, 1977.

Blodgett, Geoffrey, *The Gentle Reformers: Massachusetts Democrats in the Cleveland Era*, Harvard, 1966.

Blum, John Morton, *The Republican Roosevelt*, Harvard, 1954.

Bradgon, Henry, *Woodrow Wilson, The Academic Years*, Harvard, 1967.

Briggs, Asa, *Victorian People*, London, 1954.

Brinton, Crane, *English Political Thought in the Nineteenth Century*, New York, 1962.

Brogan, Denis William, *The American Political System*, London, 1944.

—— *An Introduction to American Politics*, London, 1954.

Brooks, Robert c. (ed.), *Bryce's 'American Commonwealth': Fiftieth Anniversary*, New York, 1939.

Butler, Jeffrey, *The Liberal Party and the Jameson Raid*, Oxford, 1968.

Callow, Alexander B., *The Tweed Ring*, New York, 1966.

Clarke, Peter, *Liberals and Social Democrats*, Cambridge, 1978.

Collini, Stephan *et al.*, *That Noble Science of Politics*, Cambridge, 1983.

Cowling, Maurice, *1867: Disraeli, Gladstone and Evolution*, Cambridge, 1967.

—— *Religion and Public Doctrine in Modern Britain*, Cambridge, 1981.

Cosgrove, Richard, *The Rule of Law: A. V. Dicey, Victorian Jurist*, Chapel Hill, 1980.

Crick, Bernard, *The American Science of Politics*, London, 1959.

Croly, Herbert, *The Promise of American Life*, New York, 1909.

Crook, David Paul, *American Democracy in English Politics, 1815–1850*, Oxford, 1965.

Duberman, Martin, *Charles Francis Adams, 1807–1886*, Boston, 1961.

—— *James Russell Lowell*, Boston, 1968.

Dunn, W. H., *James Anthony Froude*, 2 vols., Oxford, 1963.

Faber, Richard, *The Vision and the Need: Late Victorian Imperialist Aims*, London, 1966.

Fasnacht, G. E., *Acton's Political Philosophy*, London, 1952.

Feaver, George, *From Status to Contract: A Biography of Sir Henry Sumner Maine, 1822 – 1888*, London, 1969.
Garraty, John, *The New Commonwealth, 1877 – 1900*, New York, 1968.
Gatell, F. O., Goodman, P., and Weinstein, A. (eds.), *Readings in American Political History*, New York, 1972.
Gilbert, Martin (ed.), *A Century of Conflict, 1850 – 1950* (essay by Max Beloff), London, 1966.
Gordon, George S., *Anglo-American Literary Relations*, London, 1942.
Graybar, Lloyd Jr, *Albert Shaw of the 'Review of Reviews'*, Kentucky, 1974.
Green, Martin, *A Mirror for Anglo-Saxons*, London, 1961.
—— *The Problem of Boston*, London, 1966.
Green, V. H. H., *Religion at Oxford and Cambridge*, London, 1964.
Grimes, A. P., *The Political Liberalism of the 'New York Nation'*, Chapel Hill, 1953.
Grosskurth, Phyllis, *John Addington Symonds*, London, 1964.
Guest, A. G. (ed.), *Oxford Essays in Jurisprudence*, 1st Series, Oxford, 1961.
Hacker, Louis (ed.), *Introduction to 'The American Commonwealth'*, 2 vols., New York, 1959.
Hamer, D. A., *John Morley*, Oxford, 1967.
—— *Liberal Politics in the Age of Gladstone and Rosebery*, Oxford, 1972.
Hammack, David C., *Power and Society: Greater New York at the Turn of the Century*, New York, 1982.
Hammond, J. L., *Gladstone and the Irish Question*, London, 1964.
Hanbury, H. G., *The Vinerian Chair and Legal Education*, Oxford, 1958.
Hanham, H. J., *The Reformed Electoral System in Britain, 1832 – 1914*, London, 1968.
—— *Nineteenth Century Constitution*, Cambridge, 1969.
—— *Elections and Party Management: Politics in,the Time of Disraeli and Gladstone*, London, 1969.
Harvie, Christopher, *The Lights of Liberalism: University Liberals and the Challenge of Democracy, 1860 – 1886*, London, 1976.
Himmelfarb, Gertrude, *Lord Acton: A Study in Conscience and Politics*, Chicago, 1952.
—— *Victorian Minds*, London, 1968.
Hinsley, F. H. (ed.), *British Foreign Policy under Sir Edward Grey*, Cambridge, 1977.
Hofstadter, Richard, *The Progressive Historians*, New York, 1959.

The Age of Reform: From Bryan to FDR, London, 1962.
—— *Anti-Intellectualism in American Life*, New York, 1963.
—— *Social Darwinism in American Thought*, New York, 1965.
Holdsworth, W. S., *The Historians of Anglo-American Law*, New York, 1928.
Hoogenboom, Ari, *Outlawing the Spoils: A History of the Civil Service Reform Movement, 1865 – 1883*, Urbana, 1968.
Howe, Daniel (ed.), *Victorian America*, Philadelphia, 1976.
Howe, Mark de Wolfe, *Justice Oliver Wendell Holmes: The Shaping Years*, Harvard, 1957.
—— *Justice Oliver Wendell Holmes: The Proving Years*, Harvard, 1963.
Hyam, Ronald, *Britain's Imperial Century, 1815 – 1914*, London, 1976.
Jennings, Sir Ivor, *Party Politics*, 3 vols., Cambridge, 1961.
Jensen, Richard, *The Winning of the Mid-West: Social and Political Conflict, 1888 – 1896*, Chicago, 1971.
Jones, Howard Mumford, *The Age of Energy, 1865 – 1915*, New York, 1971.
Jordan, D., and Pratt, E. J., *Europe and the American Civil War*, Boston, 1931.
Keir, David Lindsay, *The Constitutional History of Modern Britain, 1845 – 1937*, London, 1943.
Keller, Morton, *Affairs of State: Public Life in Late Nineteenth Century America*, Harvard, 1977.
Kelley, Robert, *The Transatlantic Persuasion*, New York, 1969.
Keuhnemann, Eugen, *C. W. Eliot*, London, 1909.
Kirkland, Edward C., *Dream and Thought in the Business Community, 1860 – 1900*, Cornell, 1956.
—— *The Patrician at Bay: Charles Francis Adams Jr., 1835 – 1915*, Harvard, 1965.
Kleppner, Paul, *The Cross of Culture: A Social Analysis of Mid-Western Politics, 1850 – 1900*, New York, 1970.
—— *The Third Electoral System, 1853 – 1892: Parties, Votes and Political Cultures*, Chapel Hill, 1979.
Kochan, Lionel, *Acton on History*, London, 1954.
Kurland, Gerald, *Seth Low: The Reformer in an Urban and Industrial Age*, New York, 1971.
Laski, Harold, *The American Democracy*, London, 1949.
—— *The American Presidency*, London, 1962.
Lawson, F. H., *The Oxford Law School, 1850 – 1965*, Oxford, 1968.
Lillibridge, C. D., *Beacon of Freedom: The Impact of American Democracy upon Great Britain 1830 – 1870*, Philadelphia, 1954.

Link, Arthur, *Woodrow Wilson and the Progressive Era*, New York, 1954.
—— *Woodrow Wilson: The New Freedom*, Princeton, 1956.
—— *Woodrow Wilson: The Road to the White House*, Princeton, 1968.
Lippincott, Benjamin E., *Victorian Critics of Democracy*, New York, 1964.
Lively, Jack, *The Social and Political Thought of Alexis de Tocqueville*, Oxford, 1962.
Lynd, Helen, *England in the 1880s: Towards a Social Basis for Freedom*, Oxford, 1945.
McFarland, Gerald, *Mugwumps, Morals and Politics, 1884 – 1920*, Amherst, 1975.
McKenzie, Robert, *British Political Parties*, London, 1963.
Mansergh, Nicholas, *The Irish Question, 1840 – 1921*, London, 1965.
Marcus, Robert D., *G.O.P. Political Structure in the Gilded Age, 1880 – 1896*, New York, 1971.
Mathew, David, *Lord Acton and His Times*, London, 1968.
May, Ernest, *American Imperialism: A Speculative Essay*, New York, 1968.
Morgan, H. Wayne (ed.), *The Gilded Age*, Syracuse, 1970.
—— *Unity and Culture: The United States, 1877 – 1900*, Baltimore, 1973.
Mumford, Lewis, *The Golden Age*, New York, 1926.
Ogg, David, *H. A. L. Fisher*, London, 1947.
Packe, Michael St John, *The Life of John Stuart Mill*, London, 1954.
Parrington, Vernon L., *Main Currents in American Thought*, Vol. 3, New York, 1930.
Pelling, Henry, *America and the British Left*, London, 1956.
—— *Popular Politics and Society in Late Victorian Britain*, London, 1979.
Perkins, Bradford, *The Great Rapprochement*, London, 1969.
Persons, Stow, *The Decline of American Gentility*, Columbia, 1973.
Pinto-Duschinsky, M., *The Political Thought of Lord Salisbury*, London, 1967.
Qualter, Terence, *Graham Wallas and the Great Society*, London, 1980.
Richter, Melvin, *The Politics of Conscience: T. H. Green and His Age*, London, 1964.
Rothman, David J., *Politics and Power: The United States Senate, 1869 – 1901*, Harvard, 1966.

Samuels, Ernest, *The Young Henry Adams*, London, 1948.
—— *Henry Adams: The Major Phase*, Harvard, 1964.
Schleifer, James T., *The Making of Tocqueville's Democracy in America*, Chapel Hill, 1980.
Shannon, R. T., *Gladstone and the Bulgarian Agitation, 1876*, London, 1963.
Solomon, Barbara, *Ancestors and Immigrants: A Changing New England Tradition*, New York, 1956.
Sparrow, John, *Mark Pattison and the Idea of a University*, Cambridge, 1967.
Spender, Stephen, *Love-Hate Relations: A Study of Anglo-American Sensibilities*, London, 1974.
Sproat, John G., *The Best Men: Liberal Reformers in the Gilded Age*, London, 1968.
Stansky, Peter, *Ambitions and Strategies*, Oxford, 1964.
Strouse, Jean, *Alice James: A Biography*, Boston, 1980.
Strout, Cushing, *The American Image of the Old World*, New York, 1963.
—— *The Veracious Imagination: Essays on American History, Literature and Biography*, Middletown, 1981.
Thornton, A. P., *The Imperial Idea and its Enemies*, London, 1966.
Tomsich, John, *The Genteel Endeavour: American Culture and Politics in the Gilded Age*, Stanford, 1971.
Vincent, John, *The Formation of the British Liberal Party, 1857–1868*, Pelican, 1972.
—— and Cooke, A. B., *The Governing Passion: Cabinet Government and Party Politics in Great Britain, 1885–1886*, Brighton, 1974.
Wallas, Graham, *Human Nature in Politics*, London, 1910.
Watson, George, *The English Ideology*, London, 1973.
Watt, D. C., *Personalities and Policies*, London, 1965.
White, Leonard, D., *The Republican Era: A Study in Administrative History, 1869–1901*, New York, 1965.
Wiebe, Robert, *The Search for Order, 1877–1920*, London, 1967.
Wiener, Martin J., *Between Two Worlds: The Political Thought of Graham Wallas*, Oxford, 1971.
Wilson, Edmund, *Eight Essays*, New York, 1954.
—— *The Triple Thinkers*, Penguin, 1962.
Wilson, John, *A Life of Sir Henry Campbell-Bannerman*, London, 1973.
Wormell, Deborah, *Sir John Seeley and the Uses of History*, Cambridge, 1980.
Young, G. M., *Today and Yesterday*, London, 1948.

Journal articles

Baum, Dale, ' "Noisy but not Numerous": The Revolt of the Massachusetts Mugwumps', *Historian*, February 1979.

Becker, Carl, 'Lord Bryce on Modern Democracy', *Political Science Quarterly*, December 1921.

Beloff, Max, 'Is there an Anglo-American Political Tradition?', *History*, February – June 1951.

Blodgett, Geoffrey, 'The Mind of the Boston Mugwump', *Mississippi Valley Historical Review*, March 1962.

—— 'The Mugwump Reputation: 1870 to the Present', *Journal of American History*, March 1980.

Brogan, Hugh, 'Alexis de Tocqueville and the Liberal Movement', *Historical Journal*, June 1971.

—— 'Alexis de Tocqueville: The Making of a Historian', *Journal of Contemporary History*, July – October 1972.

—— 'America and Walter Bagehot', *Journal of American Studies*, Vol. II, No. 3, 1977.

—— 'Tocqueville and the American Presidency', *Journal of American Studies*, December 1981.

Brown, Everett A., 'The Contribution of Thomas M. Cooley to Bryce's "American Commonwealth" ', *Michigan Law Review*, January 1933.

Burns, J. H., 'John Stuart Mill and Democracy, 1829 – 1861', *Political Studies*, June – October 1957.

Collyer, C., 'Gladstone and the American Civil War', *Proceedings of Leeds Philosophical and Literary Society*, Vol. 6.

Cosgrove, Richard A., 'A. V. Dicey at the Harvard Law School: A Study in the Anglo-American Legal Community', *Harvard Library Bulletin*, July 1978.

—— 'The Relevance of Irish History: The Gladstone-Dicey Debate about Home Rule, 1886 – 1887', *Eire-Ireland*, Vol. XIII, No. 4.

Crawford, Martin, 'British Travellers and the Anglo-American Relationship in the 1850s', *Journal of American Studies*, August 1978.

Crook. D. P., 'Portents of War: English Opinion on Secession', *Journal of American Studies*, February 1971.

Dunne, Tom, '*La Trahison des Clercs*: British Intellectuals and the first home-rule crisis', *Irish Historical Studies*, November 1982.

Dusinberre, William, 'Henry Adams in England', *Journal of American Studies*, August 1977.

Feaver, George, 'The Political Attitudes of Sir Henry Sumner Maine', *Journal of Politics*, Vol. 27, 1965.

Filler, Louis, 'The Early Godkin: Towards the Evaluation of a Significant Victorian', *The Historian*, Autumn 1954.

Ford, Trowbridge, H., 'Dicey as a Political Journalist', *Political Studies*, June 1970.

Hamer, D. A., 'The Irish Question and Liberal Politics', *Historical Journal*, Vol. 12, No. 3, 1969.

Harrington, Fred, 'The Anti-Imperialist Movement in the United States', *Mississippi Valley Historical Review*, Vol. 22., 1935.

Harvie, Christopher, 'Ideology and Home Rule: James Bryce, A. V. Dicey and Ireland, 1880 – 1887', *English Historical Review*, XCI, 1976.

Hawkins, Hugh, 'C. W. Eliot: Reform and Religious Faith in America, 1869 – 1909', *Journal of American History*, September 1964.

Herrick, Francis, 'The Second Reform Movement in Britain, 1850 – 1865', *Journal of the History of Ideas*, April 1948.

—— 'Gladstone and the Concept of the English Speaking Peoples', *Journal of British Studies*, November 1972.

Himmelfarb, Gertrude, 'The American Revolution and the Political Theory of Lord Acton, *Journal of Modern History*, December 1949.

Hobhouse, L. T., 'Review of "Modern Democracies" ', *The Sociological Review*, July 1921.

Hurst, Gerald B., 'Review of "Modern Democracies" ', *English Historical Review*, Vol. 37, 1922.

Kochan, Lionel, 'Acton on History', *Cambridge Journal*, September 1952.

Lawson, F. H., 'Dicey Revisited', *Political Studies*, Vol. 7, June/October 1959.

Mitchell, Lee Clark, ' "But This was History": Henry Adams' Education in London Diplomacy', *New England Quarterly*, September 1979.

Oman, Sir Charles, 'Review of "Modern Democracies" ', *Quarterly Review*, July 1921.

Pilling, N., 'The Conservatism of Sir Henry Sumner Maine', *Political Studies*, March 1970.

Reuter, William, 'The Anatomy of Political Anglophobia in the United States, 1865 – 1900', *Mid-American*, April – July 1979.

Roach, John, 'Liberalism and the Victorian Intelligentsia', *Cambridge Historical Journal*, Vol. 13, 1957.

Shepherd, John, 'James Bryce and the Recruitment of Working Class Magistrates in Lancashire, 1892 – 1894', *Bulletin of the*

Institute of Historical Research, November 1979.

Smith, Brian, 'Maine's Concept of Progress', *Journal of the History of Ideas*, Vol. 24, 1963.

Smith, F. B., ' "Democracy" in the Second Reform Debates', *Historical Studies*, October 1964.

Tulloch, Hugh, 'Changing British Attitudes towards the United States in the 1880s', *Historical Journal*, December 1977.

—— 'A. V. Dicey and the Irish Question, 1870 – 1922', *The Irish Jurist*, Summer 1980.

Vincent, John, 'Gladstone and Ireland', *Proceedings of the British Academy*, 1977.

Theses

Calhoun, Richard B., 'The Dethronement of Boss Tweed' (Columbia MA, 1967).

Horwitz, Morton, 'The Problem of Tyranny of the Majority in American Thought' (Harvard PhD, 1964).

Lasch, R. C., 'The Strenuous Life: Roosevelt, Beveridge and Lodge' (Bowdoin Prize, Harvard, 1954).

McFarland, Gerald W., 'The New York Mugwumps of 1884' (Columbia MA, 1960).

—— 'Politics, Morals and Mugwump Reformers' (Columbia PhD, 1965).

McLachlan, J. S., 'The Genteel Reformers, 1865 – 1884' (Columbia MA, 1958).

Rassekh, N., 'Lord Bryce and "The American Commonwealth" ' (Stanford PhD, 1962).

Roach, John, 'Sir James Fitzjames Stephen' (Cambridge PhD, 1953).

Weinberg, Michael A., 'The Liberal Image of America in France and England, 1789 – 1890' (Harvard PhD, 1960).

Reference works

Dicionary of American Biography.
Dictionary of National Biography.
Hansard.
Who Was Who in America.

Index

Croly, Herbert, 10, 173, 189, 216, 219
Curtis, George, 93, 168, 185

Darwinism, 40, 49, 62 – 3, 197, 201, 202
Dicey, Albert Venn, 2, 3, 88, 96, 97, 232; *and*: American civil war, 21, 25n; *AC*, 60, 99; 'Americomania', 7, 101 – 17, 113 – 28; British constitution, 108; Bryce, 17 – 18, 152 – 3; civil service reform, 175 – 6; Darwinism, 49, 197, 202, *Essays on Reform*, 30 – 1; France, 48; Gladstone, 70, 130; historical method, 49 – 53; Irish question, 78, 128 – 34; *laissez faire*, 211 – 12; 215; Maine, 117n; party government, 148, 157; public opinion, 104, 117, 126; race, 125 – 6, 201n; reconstruction, 130 – 1; referendum, 7, 121 – 4; 'rule of law', 75 – 6, 106 – 7, 124 – 8; supreme court, 126; Switzerland, 103 – 4
Dicey, Edward, 21, 26
Dilke, Sir Charles, 2, 202
Dubois, W. E. B., 200

Eliot, C. W., 2, 9, 86, 95, 135, 185, 233; *and*: Adams, C. F. Jr, 182; Adams, Henry, 186; Bryce, 58; Chapman, John Jay, 186; Harvard, 183; Webb, Beatrice, 189
Ely, Richard, 184 – 5
Emerson, R. W., 45, 47, 52
Essays on Reform, 27 – 33

federalism, *see* Bryce, Dicey, Maine on 'Americomania'
Federalist papers, 52, 214
Fisher, H. A. L., 1, 153n, 226 – 9
Forbes, John Murray, 84, 171
France, 48, 65, 101, 124
Freeman, E. A., 4, 5, 38 – 44; *and*: Bryce, 98; 'historical method', 40 – 5; race, 40 – 5, 126; Roosevelt, 43; Goldwin Smith, 38; Switzerland, 48; United States, 41 – 3, 56

Fronde, J. A., 2, 78, 132, 202

Garrison, W. P., 82, 87, 93, 96, 196, 198 – 9
George, Henry, 62, 86 – 7, 217
Gilder, Richard Watson, 97, 193, 220
Gladstone, Herbert, 69, 76, 214
Gladstone, William Ewart, 2, 7, 9, 155, 171; *and*: Acton, 74 – 5, 149; *Alabama* claims, 69 – 72; American constitution, 113; American revolution, 49; Bryce, 68 – 79; Burke, 129 – 30; Dicey, 71, 130; Godkin, 72; Irish question, 73 – 9, 111, 129 – 33; Newcastle speech, 69, 130; United States, 69 – 73; Woodrow Wilson, 173
Godkin, Edwin Lawrence, 2, 6, 38, 93, 120, 135; 181; *and*: *Alabama* claims, 70; *AC*, 94 – 9, 189; Bryce, 82 – 3; Chamberlain, 157; Ely, 184 – 5; Gladstone, 72n; imperialism, 203; Irish question, 128 – 31; James, William, 96n; Maine, 116; Parrington, 179; populists, 192; reconstruction, 130 – 1, 196; Rhodes, 96n; Roosevelt, 94 – 8; Venezuelan dispute, 206
Goodnow, Frank, 91 – 4
Green, J. R., 27
Green, T. H., 16, 20, 212
Grey, Sir Edward, 210
Griffin, Sir Lepel, 56n, 80n

Hall, Oakey, 91 – 4, 156
Harvard Law School, 125
Hay, John, 83
Higginson, Thomas Wentworth, 58, 70, 83, 171
historical method, 4 – 5, 40 – 53
Hofstadter, Richard, 2, 179 – 80, 181
Holmes, Oliver Wendell Jr, 70, 84, 125, 134, 183, 217 – 18, 224
House, Col. Edward, 225, 232
Howe, Frederic, 10

Ilbert, Sir Courtney, 195
Independents, *see* Bryce
India, 195, 202, 202 – 5

Interstate Commerce Commission, 82, 216
Ions, Edmund, 1
Irish question, 6 – 7, 68 – 79. *See also* Bryce, Dicey, Gladstone, Godkin, Maine
Ivins, William Mills, 90

Jacksonianism, 85, 127, 161, 167, 173
James, Henry, 60n, 135, 188, 232
James, William, 67, 96n
Jeffersonianism, 52, 62, 85, 127, 140, 161, 162, 167, 173, 196

Kearney, Denis, 86 – 7, 91, 192
Kingsley, Charles, 56
Ku Klux Klan, 130, 144 – 5

Laski, Harold, 3, 67, 154n, 190, 217, 221, 222
Lea, Henry, 84
Lecky, W. E. H., 64, 78, 128, 186
Lincoln, Abraham, 83 – 4
Low, Seth, 10, 135, 171, 187, 213
Lowe, Robert, 27 – 8
Lowell, Abbott Lawrence, 155, 158, 184, 189, 217, 219, 223, 226, 232
Lowell, James Russell, 59, 100

Macy, Jesse, 86, 192
Marcus, Robert, 170
Maine, Sir Henry Sumner, *and*: Acton, 114, 117; 'Americomania', 7, 101, 113, 114 – 17; Bryce, 116 – 17; Dicey, 117n; France, 48n; Godkin, 116; historical method, 50 – 1; Irish question, 78, 112; *laissez faire*, 118 – 19, 212; Morley, 116; party government, 148, 154, 156 – 7; referendum, 121; Leslie Stephen, 117; United States, 22, 142
Marshall, John, 52, 118
Mill, John Stuart, 2; *and*: American civil war, 21, 24 – 5; historical method, 50, 52; parliamentary government, 107, 154; party government, 181; Reform bill (1867), 26 – 7; scientific method, 15, 61; supreme court, 101

Morley, John, 7, 19, 27, 30, 61, 76, 116, 128, 132
mugwumps, *see* Bryce

Newcastle programme, 156, 158
New Deal, 1, 219, 221
Newman, John Henry, 14 – 15, 16, 61
Norton, Charles Eliot, 97, 181

Ostrogorski, Moiséi, 157 – 8, 218

Parnell, Charles Stewart, 111, 136, 155
Parrington, Vernon L., 179
party government, 8 – 9, 147 – 60, 160 – 7, 173 – 4, 190
Pattison, Mark, 14, 61
Plunkitt, George Washington, 90, 175, 219
Pollock, Sir Frederick, 227 – 9
populism, 180, 192 – 3, 212, 221
presidency, 105, 155, 160, 164, 166, 168, 171, 173 – 4, 187
progressivism, 10, 193 – 4, 217, 219

reconstruction, 130 – 1, 195 – 6
referendum, 7, 121 – 4, 190
Reform bills: (1867), 25 – 33, 108; (1885), 75, 110 – 11
Rhodes, James Ford, 96n, 193, 222
Roosevelt, Theodore, 2, 6, 10, 100, 135, 186, 193; *and*: AC, 80, 81, 180n, 94 – 9; arbitration, 268; Freeman, 43; Godkin, 94 – 8; populists, 192; Venezuelan dispute, 207
Rosebery, Lord, 55, 151, 156, 225
'rule of law', 3, 8, 75 – 6, 106 – 7, 124 – 8

Schutz, Carl, 120, 168
scientific method, 61 – 7
Seeley, Sir John, 129, 131, 202
Shaw, Albert, 86, 131, 135, 185n, 207
Sidgwick, Henry, *and*: AC, 10, 115; Bryce, 76; development, 12; Maine, 115; party government, 148; United States, 104
Smith, Goldwin, 4, 5, 17, 18; *and*: *Alabama* claim, 36, 70; American civil war, 20, 21; Bryce, 37 – 8;

NOTTINGHAM
270
UNIVERSITY LIBRARY